THE HAUNTING OF THE MEXICAN BORDER

THE HAUNTING OF THE MEXICAN BORDER

A Woman's Journey

KATHRYN FERGUSON

UNIVERSITY OF NEW MEXICO PRESS ✦ ALBUQUERQUE

© 2015 by the University of New Mexico Press
All rights reserved. Published 2015
Printed in the United States of America
20 19 18 17 16 15   1 2 3 4 5 6

Library of Congress Cataloging-in-Publication Data
Ferguson, Kathryn.
  The haunting of the Mexican border : a woman's journey / Kathryn Ferguson.
      pages cm
  ISBN 978-0-8263-4058-0 (pbk. : alk. paper) —
  ISBN 978-0-8263-4081-8 (electronic)
  1. Ferguson, Kathryn—Travel—Mexican-American Border Region.
  2. Mexican-American Border Region—Description and travel.
  3. Mexican-American Border Region—Social life and customs. I. Title.
  F787.F45 2015
  972'.1—dc23

                         2014049533

Frontispiece photograph by Tim Fuller
Cover photograph courtesy of Sandy Huffaker Jr.
Designed by Felicia Cedillos
Composed in Adobe Jenson Pro 11/14
Display fonts are Asphaltum WF and Univers LT

For those who must leave home and travel to another land.

For Ed McCullough, the Pathfinder.

CONTENTS

This is a work of nonfiction. Some names and details have been changed in consideration of privacy.

TO BEGIN . . .

I AM NOT a migratory bird. I have always had a place. It is located west of the tall saguaro, south of the dry river, beyond the certainty.

Before I knew that place intimately, I thought it was easy to get there.

For the earliest road trip, I just threw a few things in the back and inserted the key. The ignition turned over the first time. Good omen. All thinking was behind. Now it was the doing. Did I remember my cash, my map? What if there's trouble? The hour-long drive south was full of doubt. But when I crossed the border, the smell of burning mesquite carried away the worry. We know where we belong.

Beginning in the mid-1980s and for fifteen years thereafter, I made documentaries in Mexico. I researched, hiked trails, talked with strangers, and filmed in the rugged Sierra Madre in the state of Chihuahua. Then I returned home to Tucson to produce, organize, and edit. Swinging between my country and the neighbor to the south was as vibrant as chile on the tongue, and as scary as freedom. For years I traveled in Mexico, sometimes with a film crew or a friend or just an idea.

Most of the time I had few problems. But in the '90s, changes began to occur in Mexico and the United States that affected my day-to-day life, and I began to be watchful. I became aware that as I made my journey south, people from Mexico made their journeys north. Our paths converged, and I learned that the line on which these journeys pivot is deadly.

Mexico treated me well with an occasional run-of-the-mill jolt of fear thrown in. Fear is a funny thing. When you think of fear, you think about the five-foot-long Black Iguana with alligator eyes, ridges of teeth, and spiked backbone. It looks terrifying. As it charges you with world-record speed, you panic. But upon observation, you see that it prefers to dine on flowers and fruit. Such is the nature of fear. It is only your imagination, up until the day you are eaten.

In my own country, I came to know the *wake-up-in-the-middle-of-the-night-something-is-wrong* fear. The *I-haven't-heard-from-him-for-eight-hours* fear. The *what-am-I-going-to-do-if-I-have-to-leave-my-country-forever* fear. The *what-is-this*-click-click-*on-the-phone* fear.

There is the kind of fear when you are startled; it takes your breath away. There is the stab-in-the-stomach sudden fear. There is the growing fear, the slow-cooking Crock-Pot kind of fear (there is also the crackpot kind but I'll get back to that), when you listen in the dark to an out-of-the-ordinary rustle—was it really a rustle or just something in your head? When you wait for the sound to repeat and you slow down the run-away-train breathing. When you walk from the dark hallway to the dark kitchen to stand near the door where you heard it, hoping not to hear it again.

Fear is when you drive around the little dirt roads in the cemetery and can't find your parents' graves. You know they were buried here a few months ago but the graves are not here. Fear is when you sit on the ground by the big memorial moose statue with antlers and know that the graves have gone missing and so has your family. Fear is when you are twenty-two years old and you know that there will be no more times together.

After my parents die, words like *edgeless*, *limitless*, and *formless* wake me in the middle of the night, and I realize I am free to do whatever I want. So I decide to start moving around. At first, it feels like an unnamed flailing dance that urban street kids do that no one pays any attention to. But then the freedom dance formalizes into a rock-solid new cathartic social art form like hip-hop or becomes a national competition like krumping, and then you just keep dancing hard until it morphs into some other rock-solid thing, like hope.

I Sierra Madre Trails
Hunting

CHAPTER I

GUNS AND GERSHWIN

FIRST COMES THE wind. The breeze brushes lightly against your cheek. You are convinced of your safety until sharp grains of sand rise up, dust devils surround you, and the sky grows dark as lightning clicks from cloud to cloud until it suddenly shoots to the ground at 140,000 miles per hour like a disturbed rattlesnake and the sliced air snaps back together in a burst of thunder and the wind blows fierce, lifting all in its path, and roars to the edge of the earth.

If luck is with you, there will be a rock to brace against. And wind will jerk your head as fear bites into your heart and you cannot take your eye off the spectacle as rain pelts your skin, fills your pockets and shoes with water, and pours over your body as if you are cattle of the field.

August, my birth month. The season of chubascos, storms with elephant-gray and tangerine clouds. When wet dust is heavy and smells the way a rock tastes.

It is the time of petrichor, a liquid that flows in the veins of gods. A profound description for a profound experience: to smell rain on the desert. The smell of creosote. It is my birth plant. If I could bottle it as perfume, I would, but not everyone agrees. Some call it *maloliente*, Spanish for "stinky."

My name of choice was Spurs (my father was the only family member who agreed to call me this) and my gun of choice was Wyatt Earp's Buntline Special, which arrived in the mail in a cardboard box. I had to glue the plastic parts together and bind them with rubber bands until they dried. I wore an Annie Oakley hat but at heart was Calamity Jane.

One day I was hit by a grand dream that I could ride two galloping horses at once, standing up with one foot on the back of each horse, straddling the rushing air beneath. To this end, I put two sawhorses side by side, jumped up on the narrow spines, and practiced each day, whipping my steeds into a mad race to nowhere.

When I was a little older, I tossed away the sawhorses as I discovered *Rhapsody in Blue*. I wanted to leap and fall when I heard Gershwin's music. I heard it with my insides. After school, when my parents were at work, I would close the curtains in the living room, push the furniture into the proper positions, and turn on the music. I was ready to dance.

I sat quietly. My eyes shut. Slowly my arms started to rise, my head dropped. There was nothing but music. When the moment arrived, I wrapped my arms around me, coiled like a serpent.

The saxophone screamed; I jumped up on the edge of the couch and leaped from sofa to chair, then ran around the small room like a gopher, jumping and tumbling until the final note of *Rhapsody in Blue*. When it ended, I lay on the floor panting. Then I moved the furniture back into position, opened the curtains, and continued my day. I never told my parents.

Then I discovered "Mal Hombre," "Bad Man," sung by Lydia Mendoza, *La Alondra de la Frontera*, the Lark of the Border. Only I thought her voice was more like the call of the Elegant Trogon bird deep in the Sierra Madre, a Morse code tapping out haunting minor chords. And that was that. I started wearing crimson flowers in my hair. I discovered men and tequila all in the same day. That's enough to make you run around like a gopher, too. I never told my parents.

Lydia's mom taught her family to play guitar, violin, and percussion. They were well-respected *muy famosos* musicians. They made records. They traveled extensively but could not enter places with signs that said, "No Dogs or Mexicans Allowed."

They entertained, but when the cupboard was empty, they lived as migrant laborers. I remember when I was young, men would arrive at our house to help build a wall or a ramada. My father liked to build things but didn't know how. So he would hire them, and then work side by side with them to learn.

They taught me words in Spanish, and I sat with them to eat a chicken lunch that my mother had prepared. They removed their vaquero hats to sit at the table. Their black hair was crushed flat against heads, bent and dipped like the inside of a hat, matted with sweat. They wrapped chicken into tortillas with hard, dark fingers as they told me about their children who were my age, who lived on the other side of the border.

When my dad hung gourds from the ramada, the men showed me how to paint them orange and yellow and tie them together with skinny leather ropes. When the work was finished, they went home to Mexico. A few months later, they returned to do more work. It seemed normal, this coming and going.

Like the famous Lydia, these men were migrant workers from Mexico who came and went, but now the problem is they can't anymore.

They come to work in the United States. If they return to Mexico to be with family, there is no way to reenter this country without crossing a gauntlet of death. So they swim or walk. Their bodies are found in water and dirt.

I didn't understand about the bodies when I was young. There weren't too many. In fact, there weren't that many people living at the border. But in recent years, people from the south have moved by thousands to live on the line.

What used to be an empty nuisance of a border forgotten and far from the center of government in both Washington, D.C., and Mexico City is now jammed with hungry people. Now there are many bodies and I still don't understand.

When I was a child in Tucson, it was a slow time with family trips to Nogales, Sonora, Mexico, an hour south of Tucson, to buy coffee beans.

It was a slow time of changing seasons in the desert with rain falling on parched earth like clockwork beginning every Dia de San Juan, storms arriving each afternoon with water pouring through the Santa Cruz River in August. Today the Santa Cruz is dry as a snake's rattle.

It was a slow time when the border was open on Cinco de Mayo and a parade crossed the border from Nogales, Sonora, to Nogales, Arizona, and no one had to show papers.

It was a slow time of Thanksgiving with turkey and tamales, and Christmas singing "Noche de Paz" and "Jingle Bells."

It was a slow time in Arizona when people from south of the border drove to Tucson to work and then returned home to live, a time when the U.S.-Mexico line was a wire lying on the ground and we crossed the border like birds.

CHAPTER 2

JOB

I CAN DO this. There are some jobs I just can't make myself do. An eight to five is deadly; I need to fill more than my stomach. I can't work in the mines, can't work at Walmart, and can't be a Border Patrol agent. For those jobs, you'd have to wear a hairnet or some ridiculous rectangular uniform, or be there for hours on end, like being in a cage. That would be impossible.

But I can do this. I can sell art posters. I love the *real* painting where you touch the ridge of paint on canvas and slide fingers over the glossy surface made of linseed oil and crushed pigment ground on glass with patience, like grinding flour into a buttery paste of color that smuggles you across borders of the spirit and shoots light into caverns of the heart.

But posters will do in a pinch. He hands me an application. I lean on the counter to fill it out. I really want this job. I turn the application over and write extra lines on the back. I want him to know how much I love posters. And postcards. I have to get this job. There. Done. I hand him the application.

The proprietor of the shop begins to read it over. There are no other people in the shop. I walk around looking at the walls crowded with posters. In front of me is Goya's *El tres de mayo* with the Spaniard, standing in blood of his dead compadres, shouting at Napoleon's soldiers who are set to execute him, bayonets jabbing the air.

And over there is Ferris's *Writing the Declaration of Independence*, with the white men and their quills. On the other wall is the red *Man in Armour (Alexander the Great)* in his copper helmet, pearl earring, and grimly set lips by Rembrandt. All a bit dramatic for midday. I think this shop needs to lighten up a little.

Oh, finally, I see movie posters. The *Blow-Up* poster with Veruschka's body making its serpentine path across the floor. *Blade Runner* with the curl of smoke. The yellow *Chinatown* poster with Jack Nicholson's profile. The blue *Edward Scissorhands* with Johnny Depp and the snow-covered scissors. I could like it here.

The shop owner says sorry, I can't hire you. I'm shocked. But I would be perfect here I say. You won't be here more than two weeks, he says. But I love posters, I plead, I love art. You're overqualified; I need someone who will be here day after day. You'll be gone in a month. Besides we don't pay anything, he says. I know how much you pay, it's fine. No, you need to get a real job.

A real job. I try not to cry all the way back to my studio. I walk into the dance room and lie down on the oak floor. I search the ceiling for answers. I'm desperate. I can't pay the bills. I'm two months away from being a bag lady.

And I'm losing my business. For years I have been dancing and teaching at my small studio in Tucson and performing in other countries. The international jobs dried up. Tastes change. The world isn't so interested in the arts any more. It's the era of Wall Street, corporate greed, insider trading, and ruthlessness. Oh, I forget, it's always that era. Anyway, my dance life is slipping away. I attend a week-long dance workshop in New York and temporarily injure my back so I teach dance sitting down. I can barely move and my students don't like having a teacher who commands from a stool, so they slip away, too.

OK. Stop whining. I lie on the floor. There is no one to help me. I have to fix this myself. What can I do? What am I capable of doing? Not much, at first glance. This is hard. And lonely. Whatever happened to childhood, when the only problem was to comprehend what was meant by "now" and "later"? Everything just "was," and everything in it was equal. Now everything has an edge and boundary and deadline and consequence.

OK, if I add up all the pieces, what does that make? I get off the floor and grab a piece of paper. I sit at a desk. I write down everything I am capable of doing. Teach. Dance. Move. Blank paper. I don't know what else to write. I should have taken that class How to Write a Resume. I twist the pen over my fingers. Roll it on the desk. I feel knots in my stomach. This is serious. How am I going to make money?

I change gears and write not what I can *do*, but what I *like*. Color. Movement. Music. Romanian violins. Minor chords. Rattles. Shadows. People.

Foreigners. Cactus. Animals. Vast empty spaces. Rocks. Moonlight. Words. Stories. Twists and turns.

The list gets long. I look at it. If you pour it all into a bag and shake, it's chaos. Is that what I am? But if you lay out the pieces of paper and move them around and put the shadows next to the violin, you hear a minor chord, you put moonlight in the window, a stranger walks in, well, you have a story, don't you? Add a little dimension and you have a movie. I'll make a movie.

How is that done? I spend hours at the cinema. I read film critiques. I watch bad movies, good movies, read about filmmakers, editing, writing scripts. I read a million subtitles, rewatch scenes. Yes, this job I want to do. Who do I know that makes movies and will hire me to help and learn at the same time?

A friend tells me to go to the PBS TV station and talk to Franz. When I arrive, Franz tells me to enroll in a couple of media classes and come back each day and hang around. I say what does that mean exactly, "hang around"? He says whenever I have time, just come sit in the studio.

I go to the studio at 3 p.m. each day when they begin to package a nightly news magazine that airs at 6 p.m. I just sit on a stool day after day. I feel a little weird on my stool but no one regards me strangely. People rush around rolling out huge studio cameras, adjust lights, go upstairs to the director's booth and set audio, correct script on the teleprompter, and put makeup on the anchor and guests.

At last, Franz comes over to me on my perch and says come in the office, let's sign papers. Suddenly, I have a part-time job for $4.80 per hour working for Arizona Illustrated. Less than minimum wage but worth every minute of my time. Best job ever.

As a member of the production crew, I do many jobs. One of my least favorite is to diaper lights. On the set is a desk and chairs where the anchor sits with guests. All persons have their own overhead light. I climb a ladder to the ceiling, or use a cherry picker, depending on the height of the lights in the two-story cavern, and adjust barn doors on the Lowel lights to focus light on the set. Sometimes I climb to change a burned-out bulb. I also change filters, and then hang them onto the barn doors with clothespins.

It is exacting work and I have a fear of heights. "Just don't look down" is the rule. As a newbie, you are timed on how quickly you can climb the ladder, change the bulb, and return to the floor. Sometimes a light burns out during an interview, and a crew member has 120 seconds to grab the cherry picker, climb, and change the bulb while there is a short break in the live news show. While a preview of PBS coming attractions runs, you only have time to gulp before the on-air interview returns.

Because it is a nightly news magazine, we have political guests. Lights are softened to make them look less aggressive. One afternoon as I uncoil massive camera cables on the floor, the guest of the day, U.S. senator from Arizona John McCain, walks over to his chair on set, points at me, and shouts, "Hey, girl, get up there and fix that light NOW. I need more light on my left." Hey. Girl.

What I love is the crew and I love using the cameras. Mostly I'm a grunt but little by little I get to do more jobs until finally I move to the "booth," where I am assistant director. And from the beginning, I'm champing at the bit to make a film. One day I'm lying frozen on the floor in fear of my future, next day swinging from a cherry picker.

I plan a movie. And the adopted Mexico of my childhood will be the star.

Map of Mexican states by Kathryn Ferguson.

CHAPTER 3

INTO MEXICO

SMOKE. MEXICO'S WELCOMING mat. Delicious carne asada smoke, or pine-in-the-wood-burning-stove smoke, or burning tires smoke. I like it all. It's the first thing we notice when we enter Mexico. Step on over. Fill your lungs with it.

Then move on south to the origin of the smoke. Inside the house, pine logs burn in stoves; step out to the yard where fire burns in pits. Dogs sit around, men stand around, women work around, carrying raw meat to cook over flames and pots of water to boil beans. Hair and fingers smell like smoke.

Go south to city streets lined with carretas, carts with smoking onions on the grill. Go south to the forests. Go south to where charcoal is buried in rocks, the coal of prehistoric fires that began from volcanoes. South to canyons and stone walls that glisten like burning copper, one hundred million years old. The Barranca del Cobre. Copper Canyon.

Uh-oh, there's the pain again. My thighs are fire; my calves are knots. I don't think I can take another step. This is definitely not the flat border between the U.S. and Mexico anymore. I look up. The trail rises to the clouds.

Doesn't anyone ever walk downhill around here? A friend and I venture out for a morning walk. Wrong choice of words. Not a walk, a march. I'm a dancer and I never thought that it would be taxing to walk up a hill.

Outside of Divisadero, Chihuahua, there's a hotel with oil lamps like my grandmother had on her farm. This is before electricity arrives in the small pueblos of the canyon. We leave the hotel to climb a trail winding through pine trees. There is no easing onto this trail. The first step should be a clue. I have to lift my foot and stretch my hamstring in a vertical lunge just to get onto the trail.

Fortunately, I am distracted from pain by the beauty. Pine trees smell fresh, and boulders balance on top of each other as if a sleeping earth had recently rolled over and stretched, knocking pieces of itself willy-nilly. There are great gulfs between mountains, and once I reach the top, I see grand canyons in the distance. It never occurs to me that I will come to know parts of those canyons intimately.

As we walk, a few Rarámuri pass us on the trail. Rarámuri, the beautiful sound rolls off the tongue. In the seventeenth century, when the Spanish conquistadores arrived in the Sierra, they called the indigenous people Tarahumara, a derivative of what the people call themselves, Rarámuri.

A yellow dog joins us, keeping a polite tree's distance between us. She doesn't look directly at us, the way you don't look at someone you have known for a long time. She trots along as if we had always done so.

After climbing and climbing, it's a relief to slip over to the downward side of a hill. We end up at a cave cut into the dusty, white wall of the mountainside. A couple of Rarámuri kids sit in the dirt playing with sticks, and an elderly woman stirs a pot. Inside the open cave are bedding, a stool, and a couple of goats. Outside, clothes dry on a rope.

Although we startle them, I have a feeling this particular cave is a tourist destination because they tell us how hungry they are, and how their ancestors have always lived in caves and so on. Later in my life, when I have Rarámuri friends, they never talk about being poor and never ask for money, except when it is a setup for tourists.

My friend and I finally reach Divisadero, a railroad stop with a view into the yawning Copper Canyon. But just before we would fall off the edge into a deep canyon, a world of pale smoke hangs like gauze over the rim where Rarámuri vendors perch, selling baskets, dolls, and pots, with tight fires charring food that tastes as good as it smells.

Divisadero overlooks a junction of the Urique, Tararecua, and Copper Canyons in the Mexican state of Chihuahua. Copper Canyon is one of six canyons loosely called the Barranca del Cobre. If I curled up into a ball and rolled down the drainages of the canyons, I would eventually float west into the Gulf of California.

When I was in kindergarten, I learned three things. I learned how to tie my shoelaces and what kind of food to give caterpillars. And I learned about mountains. My teacher gave us pieces of colored paper. She told us to go outside and look at the Catalinas, one of four mountain ranges surrounding Tucson. Then we were to make mountains that looked like what we saw. We weren't allowed to use scissors. It annoyed me that we couldn't use scissors. I was unaccustomed to improvisation. I was taught to be perfect, polite, and cut straight lines. Thank god that changed.

The teacher told us to tear paper so it looked like a random silhouette of mountains.

So I chose blue, green, orange, purple, and red paper. I ripped the tops of each page into sharp angles, then into jagged curves. I glued wads of crushed paper on top of paper, all mismatched, all colors. This is how the Copper Canyon looks.

"Pass this to the person behind you," Professor Ed McCullough says to his class at the University of Arizona. He hands a roll of toilet paper to a college student in the first row of the classroom.

"This roll represents the age of the earth, about five billion years old. Unroll it and pass it along. Don't tear the roll."

Students pass it from one person to the next, until a ribbon of white travels through the room.

"There are five hundred sheets in each roll. Each sheet represents ten million years. The last sheet represents the last ten million years, which goes back before the last glaciation." He continues to explain that if you take the last single square of toilet paper, divide it into hundredths, the last pencil mark, or last one-hundredth of that sheet of toilet paper, represents time since the beginning of agriculture ten thousand years ago when the hunters and gatherers decided to stay in one place.

Once, Ed told me that an individual life-span doesn't even show up on the geologic timetable, it is so insignificant. *No somos nada*, Spanish for "we are nothing." I bemoaned that fact. Ed said that "insignificant" and "nothing" are two different things.

The Barranca del Cobre is not an easy place. It is deep. It is a journey from snow-covered pines to a warm land of mango trees. A descent in rapid time, like falling. You plunge from snow to the subtropics way too quickly for any sane person.

On the "top" of Batopilas Canyon is the small village of Kirare. Driving out of Kirare on a one-lane road, you turn a corner for a sudden jaw-dropping view of where the earth fell from the sky.

It is a dizzying panorama of a canyon that lured treasure hunters and miners to drop to the bottom, build mines with Indian slaves, and pack silver ore back to the top by burro train. Leaving the village of Samachique, it takes forty-five minutes to drive a heart-stopping switchback dirt road that drops seven thousand feet to a one-lane railroad-tie bridge that crosses the Río Batopilas. After the bridge, for another six miles the hairpin road hugs cliffs all the way to the river's edge town of Batopilas.

In 1632, adelantados, advance guards for the Spaniards, also came around this corner, immobilized by the terrifying drop from the plateau edge. As they came to their senses, they saw raw silver shine in the river. That was the end; it was all over for the pristine canyon. Since then, the Rarámuri have shared their land with conquering Spaniards, engineers, miners, drug cartels, and, most invasive of all, tourists from around the world.

Yellow Dog trots with us when a truck pulls over. The driver tells us to jump into the bed of the truck. As I step up onto the bumper, Yellow Dog barks and jumps. Suddenly she leaps up and bites my calf as I swing my leg into the truck. Then, decidedly upset, she attacks the rear tire of the truck. Maybe she just doesn't want us to leave. My leg doesn't hurt but it bleeds.

We ride to Divisadero, enter a hotel that perches on the edge of the magnificent canyon, and have margaritas. I keep thinking about the bleeding. I like my new canine friend but wonder about her health. I had a friend whose husband, a U.S. citizen, died from rabies. He lived on a ranch in Sonora, and one of his Labradors bit him when they were playing.

At first, the rancher didn't think much about it. A while later, he got to feeling poorly, went to the doctor, and found out he had rabies. Although his Lab had gotten the rabies vaccine, it turned out the dog became ill. They had to kill the beloved dog and take the head to a lab in Hermosillo to test the brain.

Sure enough, it tested positive. The rancher died of rabies after being bitten. I think of this as I drink my margarita and look out over the beautiful canyon with big white cumulous clouds suspended above.

After the long hike and margaritas, my friend and I return to the hotel and ask the owner if she knows the dog. We explain what happened. To my surprise, she says yes she knows the owner, then gets upset and says they should shoot all the dogs around there, says she doesn't want any trouble. So she takes us to the owner's house.

Yellow Dog sits in front of the log cabin and jumps up to greet us, wagging her tail. The hotel owner wants the dog owner to shoot the dog. The distressed man pleads that Yellow Dog has vaccination papers, shows them to us, and everyone is satisfied.

But back at the hotel, my friend, after I tell him the story about the rancher, thinks that maybe I should see a doctor. We don't know how long it takes after you are bitten before rabies sets in. A day, a week, a month? Or is it immediately and am I already dead?

We go to the train station at Divisadero to buy a ticket for the nearest city, but the local we want to take is a few hours late. Standing on the tracks is a train called the Sierra Madre Express, a tour train operated by a company out of Tucson. It is a 1940s vintage Pullman with sleeper cars, etched-glass panels, a dining car, and an upstairs level with a two-story glass dome so you can see up to the sky. Kind of makes you think you are in an Italian cathedral with an illusionistic ceiling painting, only when you look up, the clouds are real.

My friend tells the engineer about the dog bite and that we are headed for a doctor, and the engineer says to climb on board. So we ride under the glass dome all the way out of the canyons. Since acquiring money has never been my forte, this is as luxurious for me as a ride to Egypt on the Orient Express. I am so happy on this ride that a month later, I apply for a job on the train. I get the job. But by the time I am to begin shouting "All aboard," the Sierra Madre Express goes out of business.

I eventually get to a doctor in Tucson, have three rabies shots (it used to be twenty in the abdomen), pay $600, and am set for life. The physician, head of the Infectious Disease Unit of the University Medical Center, tells me that he had treated the rancher who acquired rabies. He remembers him because there are so few cases of death by rabies in the United States.

The physician explains that when the rancher came into the office, he had gotten extremely agitated because a minuscule amount of water dripped one drop at a time from the faucet in the room. The rancher had twitched, jerked his body, and panicked. He couldn't bear the sound of the drips. He couldn't look at water. He was parched from thirst. To drink, he had to hold a glass behind his neck and drink through a straw so he wouldn't see the water. He backed his way into showers.

A year later in Tucson, with my rabies scare long gone, I yearn for another trip. A trip just for knowing. My private world of investigation. So I drive again to the edge of the Sierra but continue south down the highway to the beautiful state of Michoacán.

Near a small town outside of Morelia, I drive slowly because of the *topes*, speed bumps. I pass a woman who walks along the road. She glances back over her shoulder to look at something, and that look is still in my mind.

She wears a yellow scarf suspended on the back of her head; long hair with dark curls rolls over her shoulder, half covering gold earrings. Dark eyes glare. She looks as if she just had an argument and thought of one more thing to say. She quickly turns to say it, a slight frown on her face. But there is no one behind her. She turns forward and stomps alone along the road. She wears a striped blouse, a long wide skirt of polka dots that rustles with each step. Bracelets ring her wrist. She is out of place. I have never seen anyone like her in Mexico before.

It is the first time I realize that Romani people, Gypsies, live in Mexico. I later learn that the Hungaros, as they are called in Mexico, came from Hungary to Mexico, exported by the Austrians to help the French fight the war in Mexico. Or they came from Argentina. Or came over with Columbus. Or they were fleeing what the Rarámuri flee, and the slaves in the south of the United States fled, and countless others flee. Persecution. The green poison of empire fans wide.

A friend from Sonora told me that as a child, he would walk to a tent two hundred yards from his house. The tent sat on a large empty lot. In front of the tent was a cine truck. Inside the tent were mismatched chairs lined up facing a wall of stretched white fabric. Behind the chairs was a film projector. Hungaro families traveled the roads of Mexico setting up impromptu movie theaters.

Something about the dog bite and rabies grounds me. Something about misplaced Hungarians fleeing to Mexico grounds me. It is this Mexico that I am hooked on, not bright, bubbly Mexican restaurants in the United States, not Tucson streets named Placita Plata or Calle de Pantera, not calendars with kitschy señoritas in low-cut dresses, not the American view of a two-toned Mexico that is either beer and beaches or cartels and poverty.

I am hooked on the place. The dust, smoke, music, the people rich and poor, the *quinceañeras*, the carved santos, the *ni modo*—"whatever"—attitude that is the answer to all unavoidable situations, the hard work, the fun, the desert, the colonial architecture, the knowledge of the *abuelitas*, the confident hip, young, and savvy middle class, the *vatos* and vaqueros, the huge families of *tías* and *sobrinos* and all their fights and kisses, the laws and the lawlessness. Which brings us to the land of "we-make-our-own-laws," the wild Sierra Madre. It is a big place. I am small. It is old. I am young. I have a lot to learn.

And rolling around the back of my mind is that somewhere in my trips to Mexico, I will stumble onto exactly what movie I am looking for.

CHAPTER 4

MOVIES

"YOU MUST RUSH over and see this, Kathryn." He pronounces the first syllable of my name like the caw of a crow. Kawthryn.

"Which one is that?"

"The first film of *The Decalogue*."

Giulio Scalinger, a cordial, witty man who plays it close to the vest, an Italian with a British accent, left Europe for adventure in the States and settled in Tucson to open a movie theater.

A Sea of Cortez teal-blue wall is the first thing you see when you enter. As you step in, you glance down at the floor and see a circle of copper-colored tiles creating the Man in the Maze labyrinth.

It is a petroglyph pattern of Arizona's Tohono O'odham people, with concentric circles and lines leading to a small spot in the center of the maze. They say that the little man at the center of the maze is an individual who travels labyrinthine twists of life to finally arrive at the outer edge, where life as he knows it is over, and he begins something new.

With nonchalance, you step into the maze as you enter the Screening Room, a movie theater in amiable downtown Tucson. If you become a regular, you find yourself on a journey of flickering images that can alter your life. With film fare ricocheting from Sam Shepard's haunting medicine show of a film, *Silent Tongue*, to Japanese vampire movies, you experience the gamut of life without ever leaving your comfy movie-house seat. And there's popcorn to boot.

It has become my home away from home. Giulio and his wife, Claudia Jespersen, opened the theater, an artful place designed with deep knowledge and love of film.

"I'll be the first person in line at the box office," I tell him as I hang up the phone. Where else can you see films by the brilliant Polish director Krzysztof Kieślowski?

In the early 1990s, Giulio's Arizona International Film Festival was established, Bill Clinton was inaugurated as president, and the power of the media was on a roll. With footage of an American soldier's corpse being dragged through the streets of Mogadishu, our involvement with Somalia ended. In the Persian Gulf War, both the U.S. government and Saddam Hussein used the media to influence world opinion.

Newspapers and television covered the life of Cesar Chavez, who died in 1993. The North American Free Trade Agreement (NAFTA) was signed into law. As NAFTA sneaks through the back door of my life, my future is profoundly affected by a legal proclamation that barely caught my attention when it was enacted.

The stars must have aligned for many people because the best films since the brilliant decade of the '70s were produced in 1993. An electric time for filmmaking and filmgoing, the world ignited with creative cinema.

Released that year was Robert Altman's *Short Cuts*. And then there is Wim Wenders, the German filmmaker whose films crowd my life. His 1993 *Faraway So Close* is a sequel to my almost-all-time-favorite movie, *Der Himmel über Berlin*, or, *Wings of Desire*.

Later I will see Wenders's film, *Paris, Texas*, written by Sam Shepard. Watching these films in a dark movie theater, I will experience in advance what I will later come to see on a desert trail—that we are all the myth of America. The playwright Shepard's American dream of abundance is a fragile thing lined with longing, alienation, and rage, things that we here in this country know, and foreigners who adopt our country come to know.

In *Wings of Desire*, an angel becomes human as he passes though the Berlin Wall. He is on the east side of the Berlin Wall, a very real no-man's-land of landmines, and walks through it as an angel, finding himself on the "free" side as a human, bleeding from a cut.

In the future, I will stand on both sides of my country's wall. I will watch as people from other cultures approach the barrier. They will not walk through a solid wall like angels but will climb the wall as humans, headed for an America of dreams lined with blood.

But now, in my comfortable movie seat, I ricochet from culture to culture and fall in love with Nuevo Cine Mexicano, New Mexican Cinema. Works like Alfonso Arau's 1993 *Como agua para chocolate* (*Like Water for Chocolate*) and Alejandro González Iñárritu's *Amores perros* again bring Mexican films to international attention.

Although Giulio has sophisticated taste in cinema, he believes in the fresh, independent vision of the common person. He wants an international grassroots festival that presents "community" cinema in its most original form, as opposed to Hollywood's Extreme Filmmaking sport.

So he creates the Arizona International Film Festival. It fits Tucson like grooves in a saguaro. It's as rough and ready as Tucson's history, and as diverse, screening films as varied as the multicultural people who live there. It is not your glossy, cookie-cutter film festival.

Behind the scenes, in the dark cavern of the theater, wizards Giulio and Claudia watch thousands of films, magically culling one gem after another, stirring in sensibilities, sounds, and images created by international artists, and presto! The most honest U.S. film festival rises again each April. To an informed Tucson audience, they present grand and humble films, and invite humble and not-so-humble filmmakers to talk about how each film was created. In a two-week festival, you can see 137 films from thirty-one countries.

I see a documentary by Mel See with grainy night scenes of a Rarámuri Easter ceremony, shot on an Arriflex 35 millimeter camera. Mel is a geologist by trade, a filmmaker by passion. A bearded Ernest Hemingway type, he once showed me his Arri, whipping it around like a pistol, apologetic that it shot frames instead of bullets.

In the downtime, weeks before the film festival begins, Mel and Giulio talk by the ticket counter when I enter the theater. The three of us while away the afternoon with tall tales of geological faults of the Sierra Madre, El Cordobés (the Spanish bullfighter whom Mel filmed), and worn-out treasure maps. I mention that I am interested in the Rarámuri people in the Barranca del Cobre, and the next thing I know, I'm riding down the road in an old Bronco with Mel on our way to the Sierra Madre.

We cross the Mexican border and drive toward Hermosillo, then head east on a dirt road. It is a winding, narrow mountain pass, difficult to maneuver with oncoming traffic. We have to lean the vehicle up onto the side of the mountain to let a car pass.

We stay the night in Creel. It is a mountain town with a couple of main streets, restaurants, tourist shops, a small church, and motorcycle-riding

German tourists head-to-toe in black leather. The next day, after looking over worn topo maps, we leave Creel.

Ours is a trip of improvisation. It is subject to weather, miscalculations, mechanical breakdowns, our own ignorance, and spell-inducing owls. Although I have no idea where we are going, I figure Mel knows the way. He traveled in the Sierra years before.

According to the map, we are in the Sierra Madre on the Continental Divide. According to the map, we are nowhere. The lines on the map end. Mel's maps are old. Our road is a warp of holes and boulders. It is so quiet that it seems no one is around, that we are in an empty wilderness. But I keep butting up against my own Anglo urban limitations and north-of-the-border ignorance.

What I think is an impossible road in an empty wilderness I come to learn is, in fact, a highly traveled road in a highly populated area. Occasional Rarámuri buses with low gears, pickup trucks, women with packed burros, and lone goats travel the road. Although we don't see anyone for an hour at a time, out of sight down intersecting trails, there are ranchos and families doing their daily thing. But the road is rough. It takes five hours to go fifty miles.

Around sunset, after many roads turn into trails that turn into solitude, we find flat land at the bottom of a valley. An older man walks with a boy. The man wears the red headband of the Rarámuri; the boy wears no shoes. I lean out the window to ask if there is land nearby where we can throw down sleeping bags. As fast as a hawk spies prey, the man assesses, diagnoses, turns inside out, approves, and devours us. We are his. Ventura Pacheco León. We are his to play with, and he is my new friend for life.

Ventura says come with me and opens the door of the Bronco. He puts his son in the backseat and climbs in after him. He says we can camp outside his house.

Bumping down a hill on a dirt road, we see a small valley with log houses, each a half mile apart. Surrounding the valley are magnificent thirty-foot-tall rock columns. In the 1930s, Antonin Artaud, the French avant-garde playwright, lived in the area with the Rarámuri. He wrote a book about his experiences called *The Peyote Dance*.

He attempted to enter the cosmos through natural surroundings of volcanic rock, which he was certain were towering phalluses. I look at these rock columns and think Artaud must have been smoking powerful *mota* to come up with that vision. The columns reach toward clouds floating between spirals. Stunted corn plants struggle in caliche fields near the road.

Ventura directs us to the first house. Smoke rises from a pipe in the roof of the house, which is built of logs. We pull up in front of the cabin. Skinny dogs and chickens ignore us, instead wandering around in an eternal search for food, peering under stones, retrieving objects that surely cannot pass through the digestive system. I briefly wonder what the life-span is here. Upon hearing a vehicle, kids run out to look; a woman stands in the shadow of the door.

Seeing strangers, the kids stop, younger ones hiding behind the oldest girl. Ventura gets out of the car, opens his arms, grins, and says something in Rarámuri, and the three-year-old in a dirty white lace dress with long black hair throws up her arms imitating Ventura and runs toward him as fast as her unaccomplished legs allow. They run toward each other as if it had been years, but it was only in the wee hours of that morning that Ventura had left the house to cut firewood.

Ventura tells us to proceed as he walks into the house. We look around for a place to set up camp. It is getting cold and we want to be situated before the sun is down. As we work, Ventura returns and says come inside; his wife has beans on the fire. We carry a box of canned food, cups, utensils, and oranges into the house.

Inside are a hard-swept dirt floor, a wood-burning stove made from an oil drum with a door cut into it that guards a roaring fire, a table with a small oil lamp, one chair, a long bench, a small window covered with plastic, and a door leading into another room.

On the stove sits a pot of beans. Ventura's tiny wife pushes thick black hair from her eyes as she pats masa into tortillas. With the smell of tortillas over fire, I am suddenly ravenous.

Meanwhile, Ventura snoops through our canned goods. He pulls out a can with the same lust in his eyes that I have for the tortillas. "Comida china?" he asks as he turns the can of chop suey in his hands. "¡Me encanta comida china!" I love Chinese food, he says. When he worked for the Mexican electric company cutting telephone poles in a faraway city, he used to eat Chinese food. He explains that he likes the food of the whites, whites being the Mexicans and Chinese.

So it is a happy trade. We eat fresh beans and they eat canned chop suey. During the meal, he asks where I learned to speak Spanish. I say in school and on the streets. He says they should fire the teachers and clean up the streets because my Spanish is so bad. In his deep, slow, preacher's voice, he says he can teach me Spanish if I hang around long enough.

He grins. From his wide mouth shine oyster-white teeth. In the firelight, his white hair looks orange, set against a square bronze face. He seems accustomed to laughing. As he lifts his chin to speak, he seems accustomed to telling people what to do. He nudges his commands and I find myself wanting to jump at his wishes.

Drums in the night. *Doom tak tak tak doom tak tak tak.* All night. Deep inside, wherever that is, I am content and excited at once. There is no place I would rather be. Drums and the smell of smoke. What more could you ask for? In the cold night, in a warm sleeping bag, I alternately doze and awaken to drums.

At first light, I hear, "¿Catalina, dónde estás?" Ventura calls me. I throw on my warm clothes and make my way to the wood-burning barrel where Ventura's wife has just stoked the fire with pine. I heat water for coffee. His wife chooses one of two coffee cups from a wooden plank that serves as a shelf fastened to the log wall. I realize that they eat and drink in shifts because there are not enough dishes for the family to all eat at once.

I walk outside Ventura's house with a cup of hot instant coffee, stand in the crisp air, stir the coffee with my finger, and take a look at the morning. Mist covers most of the valley.

But even in paradise there are quirks. All my life, my family and I would cross into Nogales, Sonora, to buy delicious Mexican coffee beans. Whether it is cheaper to make, or faster to fix, or just a matter of changing taste buds, passionate, from-the-gut Mexican brewed coffee went the way of analog to digital. I have to make do with instant.

Running across the valley, past where I stand, are eleven Rarámuri in red headbands and red sashes that cover white cloth girdles around the hips. Instead of headbands, some men stick turkey feathers into torn fabric tied around the head. Coin-size white spots are painted over their entire bodies. The leader hits a big round drum; they all turn in circle, do a three-step dance, and continue running.

This repeats all the way to the Catholic church. No one speaks. They

Rarámuri tambor player at a Semana Santa ceremony.
Photo by Bill Yahraus.

know what to do. They have been doing it for five hundred years, since the Spaniards arrived and ordered the Rarámuri to get on their knees and pray, or die.

Unable to capitulate, the Rarámuri mixed it up and danced instead. When they were commanded to think about Judas and Jesus, they went a step further and made life-size stuffed dolls of Judas's wife and dog, which they now carry on their shoulders as they dance. Yesterday, they drank *tesgüino*, a fermented corn beer, painted their faces white, stuffed a cowboy shirt and Levis with straw, and built Judas, a straw doll as tall as a human.

The family dons its best clothes. Ventura wears a black-and-white-striped sweater that Parisian Apache dancers wear, his white hair combed back from his dark skin and tucked under a blue ball cap. His son wears a dark sweater with Levis, and wife and daughters wear traditional flower-print skirts and blouses. Not a flower grows in the drought-stricken valley, only on fabric. Today they wear sandals. We all walk a half mile down and up the hills, past Artaud's phalluses, to the church for Semana Santa (Holy Week) activities.

A solo burro nearby. Over there, a chicken house on stilts because coyotes don't climb poles. We sit on a boulder to watch the procession. Hungry dogs dart between dancers' legs, traveling their own stations of the cross. Dancers shuffle and duck, crying a "whoop" redolent with defiance. The conquistadores brought pale skin and eyes to the mix, in exchange for blood. They gave words and took life. But the whoop goes on.

I ask why Ventura doesn't participate. He says he had been traditional, a part of the Catholic Church, and had been governor of the Choguita rancho for four years, but one day he realized that a wooden image has eyes but cannot see, has ears but cannot hear, has a mouth but cannot speak, so he became an Evangelist.

I am not sure I understand. I am curious. It isn't language. It is never just language. It's not words. It is the gesture. The shift of weight. The tilt of the head. Understanding is in the exhale. No matter how many years you are there, you are always merely a visitor to another culture. I remind myself to stop trying to make sense. The objective is to do no harm. We bury the moon by calling it a reflection of the sun like we bury others by seeing them as a reflection of ourselves.

After a few hours, we walk the dirt trail looking for the *conasupo*, a kiosk where local Mexicans sell government-subsidized food. Ventura mentions that he needs protein to keep the diabetes demon at bay. At the conasupo, we stack up on eggs, canned tuna, ground chiles, flour, masa, *queso*, coffee, CDs with corridos, ballads about *narcotraficantes*, and all the junk food we could possibly want in the form of chile-drenched Takis and month-old Oreo cookies.

I notice Ventura's stiff gait. I ask him about his diabetes. He says it comes and goes. He says, "They say I will die a curious death," and chuckles. He says when he is gone, he will have a traditional end. "They will wrap me in woven cloth like a piece of cheese." More chuckles.

As I walk down the trail, the first vehicle I have seen passes on a nearby road. It is a Volkswagen van with three men in the front seat. They wave. As the van passes, I see the lean face of a man in a baseball cap peering out the back window. He looks like a gringo. In two months, I will learn that his name is Santiago Barnaby.

On the return trip to Tucson, I feel I want to make a film about Ventura and his culture. But mostly about him. In any culture, he would be a special person. For some reason, I feel connected to him. He makes me laugh in the same way my father did. I laugh late at the punch line, realizing that he intended it that way.

But how much has been done about the Rarámuri? Tons. Books, movies, dissertations, music, poetry, postcards, comic books. Everything and in every language. So I sit at my desk feeling small, like a lizard under a hawk's shadow. If I make a feature-length film I'm going to be chewed up and spit out. I don't know what I am doing.

But it is clear I need to be in the Sierra again. It's like pulling petals: loves me, loves me not, make a movie, make it not.

I teach dance classes, work for minimum wage on the crew at KUAT-TV PBS in Tucson, and will have to beg for grant money. Not exactly a member of the Fortune 500. Frankly, I'm scared. How will I get money (I don't even know how to write a grant proposal), how will I travel, but most of all, what if I fail? I know what bad movies are. BAD.

I have no idea how to make a feature film. But I do know how not to make one. No clichés, no plodding Ken Burns predictability, not linear, not cloying, no Anglo narrator with a cropped white beard talking about "the other." I understand a couple of things from my job at the PBS station. I have made shorts, used cameras, and can white-balance with the best of them.

The biggest thing, though, is what if Ventura wants no part of it? We think the Rarámuri are illiterate, they think we are insane. We think they are heathens, they think we have no inner being. We call them shy, they call us naïve. We think they are poor, they think we don't have the capacity to find food in the Sierra. The first thing is to see what Ventura thinks. So I need to return to his house to ask if he's game.

CHAPTER 5

MEXICAN NAVY

I HAVE TO confess. I slept with the Mexican Navy. About thirty of them. I was with my friend Sandra Lanham. Mea culpa.

Before making a final decision to do a film about Ventura, I sit with my coffee under a mesquite tree in my backyard tossing a few more ideas around in my mind. I want to make a film in Mexico but am still not sure what about or where. Although I like Ventura and like being in the Sierra, Rarámuri life is a subject covered often in the media.

I believe Ventura to be an interesting man but I need to know him much better to have real insight. The film will require spending a lot of time in Mexico. And I want to know that there is an audience for it. That is the first thing asked by all funders—who is your audience?

And the subject matter of the film needs to be interesting to me, too, since I will probably work on it for a couple of years. And it will be in three languages. How do I deal with that? I can handle the English and Spanish but the Rarámuri? Where will I get Rarámuri translated into English? Maybe this is a bad idea all round. I am comfortable on this old wooden chair under the mesquite tree. Maybe I just belong here in the shade with the lizards.

Sandy has another suggestion for a movie. She knows a woman in Maruata, Michoacán, Mexico, who has an experimental iguana farm at the edge of town. The lady raises them so the women in town can sell the rascals for food and send the rest of the iguana population into the trees to repopulate, as they are an endangered species. This gives the village women a steady income; at the same time, it prevents the men from killing every iguana in sight for beer money. If the iguana farm is successful, the town will tend to a population of fat, happy iguanas, and random iguana killings would be considered personal theft, an unacceptable activity in a small pueblo.

From a bird's-eye view, Maruata is a village that lies on the Pacific coast of Michoacán, a sea turtle nesting beach, fifteen miles south of Titzpan. On one side of Maruata, sharp cliffs slip down to the sea; on the other, mountains rise above. The seven hundred inhabitants speak Nahuatl and Spanish.

Purportedly, there are men in the mountains who come down to steal girls from the pueblo. (Sandy wonders if she is the right age to be stolen.) And an occasional jaguar shows itself at the edge of Maruata. All in all, it sounds like a good movie to me.

A crackerjack pilot, Sandy says, "Let's fly down to Maruata and check it out. We'll be there in two days and can sleep on the beach." I jump at the invitation. On a perfect April morning, we take off.

Elbows in the eyes, shoulders bumping, my knees knock the control yoke in the cockpit. "Watch out!" Sandy shouts to me through the headsets. As we sit almost shoulder to shoulder and talk to each other through mouthpieces, I feel like I am seven years old talking to a best friend through orange juice cans and a string.

"Don't let the wind take the door!" she calls into the headset. I grab my door against a big gust, then buckle up, straps across my chest and waist. I am ratcheted into the seat like *La momia azteca*, the Aztec mummy, bound for burial, straps over the shoulders, upright like a board. I suddenly realize that the only thing that will be between me and the earth 6,500 feet below is a tiny piece of tin into which I'll be strapped as it hurtles through space.

"Clear, *libre!*" she calls out to any poor soul who might be silly enough to be standing nearby and walk into a rotating prop that will turn him into mincemeat. When all is clear, she starts the engine.

Inside, it is quite cozy, and loud. I try to make myself small as Sandy does her takeoff dance from the pilot's seat, checking off her list, and pulling the yoke to check its fluidity. But it seems that in moments we move down the runway and lift off.

Years earlier, Sandy created the nonprofit Environmental Flying Service. She flies Mexican researchers who have wildlife and environmental projects in Mexico. In the United States, we have fleets of airplanes that do natural-resource flights, but Mexico has very little help for scientists.

Mexican researchers can't afford to fly, and how do you count sea turtle nests on a three-thousand-mile coastline if you have to walk from nest to nest? Instead, you call Sandy and fly low and slow, at eighty-five knots and two hundred feet above the water.

Sandy's 1956 single-engine straight-tail Cessna 182 has only the required basics, no navigation radio, no directional gyro (DG)—only a wet compass, the kind a boy scout would carry. The way we fly is dead reckoning, basically the same as Charles Lindbergh. There are no instrument lights, so you can't see in the dark. Sandy has been known to fly with a flashlight in her mouth at night in order to see the panel. So I grab the map, look down at the ground, and we follow the Mexican coastline. On the return trip, we will follow the Río Fuerte inland.

I pull out the cylindrical vent by the front window and twist it so we can get fresh air. The only air inside the plane comes from outside the plane. If it is ninety-five degrees outside, it is hotter inside. If it is cold outside, it is cold inside.

Sandy often flies in serious drug country. Occasionally there are bandits who hide at the end of dirt runways, wait for a pilot with a small plane to load up and start the engine for takeoff, then jump out of the bushes and run up to steal the plane. To ward off these bandits, Sandy paints the rudder pedals pink and adds red toenail polish. No self-respecting thief is going to steal a plane with pink paint. So far it has worked.

Once we pass through the gauntlet of takeoff, we enter Serenity. Floating high above our fellow man's problems. This must be what it is like to be an angel. Boundless. The sea, an eternal turquoise mirror, hangs from our toes. All we see is water and the horizon. No wonder they thought the earth was flat.

Every four hours it is necessary to land to gas up the plane. But in Mexico, you land wherever there is an airport that sells fuel. It's not like the United States where there is an airport every fifteen minutes. And because of drug wars, the Mexican government closes small airports and instead funnels planes to larger airports where the army inspects them.

On the return trip, we will gas up in Puerto Vallarta and Los Mochis. In every city, Sandy jokes with airport personnel and is always treated with great respect from the men even though, as a female pilot, she is an anomaly.

The first night we sleep in the relaxed, almost abandoned coastal town of San Blas, Nayarit. We are bitten by a few *jejenes* (sand gnats), have a beer at an outdoor cantina, walk around the town to take in the sights, and see a suspiciously huge private estate with corner watchtowers perched on tall, whitewashed walls.

We fly the next morning to subtropical Maruata. Since cliffs hide the landing strip, we comb the coast with our eyes. We don't see the town or the strip. We search walls of rock. They look an awful lot alike. Finally Sandy points, indicating that she found the correct ones. We fly beyond, and then Sandy turns the plane for an approach to the empty strip.

Looking down from the air, there is deep stillness. No people or animals. Sandy glides onto the short dirt runway like a smear of molasses on warm bread.

The landing strip divides the town that lies at the ocean's edge. But something is not normal. Sandy says that usually people, dogs, or goats walk back and forth across these small strips, going about their daily business, never looking up to the sky since it is so rare that anyone lands there. Once as she was landing near a small town, a boy, oblivious to the sky, dropped a grocery bag as he ran across the strip. She was afraid that he would run back to retrieve it in front of her landing plane . . . and he did. She had enough air speed to yank back the yoke, make the plane hop over the boy, and land on the other side.

But today we land in the emptiness of a Sergio Leone dreamscape. White noon light erases the shadow's edge.

Palms stand in clumps like taxidermied giraffes. In midday light, jagged cliffs look as formless as beach sand. Everything has a yellow pall. No curious being stands by a thornberry tree to watch an unknown plane drop out of the sky. It is very quiet. I feel that something bad could happen.

We land unannounced, of course. But in our favor, we have no government logos on the plane. The only people who would land on a small dirt strip like this would be Mexican Social Security, or invading drug thugs arriving to do their special brand of "business." We step out of the plane carrying no AK-47s, so whoever may be watching can scratch that one off his list. Still, no one comes to greet us. We might as well be from Mars. This is probably the first and last time that two women land on this strip.

It's the lure of the lizard. I'm telling you, it is powerful. We knowingly fly during drug wars, land on a strip in an area of drugs, poachers, and bandits, and only want to see lizards.

In order to cut through the eeriness, we grab a few belongings, lock up the plane, and walk in search of normalcy, like for a beer or something. Finally, we see a lone figure under a *palapa*, sweeping around a table.

We walk to the palapa to sit and drink a *tamarindo* while looking out at the sea, and we ask about the Iguana Woman. "Allá está," says the sweeper, never looking directly at us. She's over there. He offers no other information.

We head across the beach to a cluster of small buildings of wood slats and palm fronds, flanked by coconut and banana trees. Behind, mountains rise up to meet the sky.

On the ground are wooden quadrangles enclosed by chicken-wire fence. Inside, green iguanas move slowly. My heart stops. It is love at first sight. What could be more exciting than a huge green lizard? Whenever I see a big lizard, I want to whoop and holler like Warren Oates when he robs trains in *The Wild Bunch*.

My primary memory of early childhood is shoeboxes full of horny toads that I corralled from the desert surrounding our house. I scientifically observed, talked to, and adored them.

I loved petting the head. You had to pet in the correct direction or it didn't feel right and the horny toad didn't like it. I made houses in shoeboxes and carpeted the boxes with grasses and dirt and served dinners of live ants. That is their favorite food.

One day, I saw blood come out of the eye of a horny toad. I ran to my father to ask if the little lizard was sick. He said that the horny toad was shooting blood to frighten off a predator.

I asked, what is a predator? When he explained that it was an enemy of the horny toad that wanted to do it harm, I was appalled. I was the enemy? My beloved lizard was shooting blood at me because he was afraid of me? He didn't like me? I was horrified.

I immediately let all the horny toads out of the shoeboxes and was sad for days. No more horny toad suburbs. Let them be wild. Let horny toads run free. Let horny toads run amok. But if they really did, there would be news articles about savage horny toads. Well, maybe not mainstream news articles, but at least you would see paragraphs in scientific journals or tabloids the way you occasionally read articles about caged elephants that escape and go crazy.

It's understandable. My own species runs amok. Not just in cages, but in the finest parts of the finest cities where decisions are made about power, enforcement, and domination. The amokness of animals is tempered by nature. Man's amokness knows no boundaries.

So when I see the many green iguanas in front of me, I am fascinated. They stand, exhibiting their motionless, cryptic behavior. I watch.

In my yard at home, I sit with stocky black-collared lizards. The longer I sit, the closer they come. I want them to sit in my lap. Yes, I know they are not dogs. But I want to crawl with them and be in lizard time. I try several things. I make eye contact, I don't make eye contact. I move, I don't move. I talk in a low voice, I don't make a sound. I lie on the ground. I get back in the chair. I hold out my arm to see if they will walk up my hand.

Unfortunately, iguanas share the world with humans so they appear on menus as *sopa de garrobos*, or charbroiled tail of iguana. On the roadsides, they are seen hanging, not quite dead, from the hand of the hunter who displays them for sale. No, I'm not a vegetarian, but I do live on the border of either slit a warm soft throat for lunch, or eat a turnip. Only when I have to do my own slitting does it become a problem.

Walking toward us is a thin, dark-haired woman. We have made no contact with her to tell her we are coming. Cell phones are not yet invented. But she greets us in an elegant manner, happy to answer questions about her project. She guides us around the quadrangles, and we watch iguanas watch us.

I visualize how it would look through a lens. Trees stand tall as light filters through the leaves. Tilt the camera down to a close-up of the enclosures. Get on your belly and aim the camera directly at the iguana's face. Watch eyelids drop over narrow eyes to quickly lift in a delayed blink, lazily belying the superman x-ray vision with which it sees shapes, shadows, and edible beings as it navigates crowded forests, thornberry trees, and humans.

This is all good material for a documentary. But is it realistic to fly back and forth deep into Mexico to shoot a film with a miniscule budget that wouldn't even cover the cost of flights? I guess I would have to live here.

Sandy and I return to the palapa and order a couple of beers. The sun lowers to the line of the sea. Clouds are on the horizon. We have another beer and decide to find a place to lay the sleeping bags for the night before the clouds roll in and the sun goes down.

Near a sand dune, we find the perfect spot. We look out to the setting sun, feel a cool breeze, watch the buttermilk clouds over the sea, and know what heaven is.

In the dark, however, the beach is different. It has its own nocturnal sense. Imagine. It is 2 a.m., a cobalt-blue and shadow-black world. The moon gives just enough light to turn the most innocent shadow sinister.

Imagine. A sixty-foot rock cliff looms out of cold black water like a humpback whale. There is a cave with a passage through a rock arch that you could kayak through. But it is 2 a.m. and no one is kayaking.

Imagine that in the distance a visitor arrives. You look twice because you don't want to believe you saw him. It is a lone figure silhouetted against the cliff. Water laps at his feet. He carries something in his hand. He moves with stealth. He sees you. He waits. For you. You step forward. He disappears into the shadow of the cliff.

We are in the land of *hueveros*, or egg poachers. Seasonally, hundreds of sea turtles come up on the beach in the dark to lay eggs. If it is not a biologist you encounter near the turtles in the middle of the night, it is probably a poacher. And they are serious about their job. Recently, a biologist was murdered on the beach.

But Sandy and I aren't thinking about this. We set up our simple camp. We smooth the sand, lay out sleeping bags, and arrange a coffeepot and cups for morning.

Two men walk down the beach. We all look at each other. They keep going.

Sandy and I settle in for the evening, but before the light is completely gone, four more men approach. They don't continue down the beach; they walk toward us. Sandy doesn't want to be caught in her *chonis* so she struggles quickly to slam her legs into her Levis, then jumps out of the sleeping bag.

The lean men, in their twenties, wear mollusk-colored pants and shirts, and have black hair cropped short. They walk directly toward us and say hello. By then, we are standing and reply to their comments. We wish they would go away.

"¿Hola. Cómo están?" a man asks. How are you?

"Bien."

"¿Qué andan haciendo aquí?" What are you doing here?

"We are watching the sunset. It's beautiful, no?"

"Sí, muy linda." He smiles large. "Where do you come from?"

"Tucson."

"Is it far?"

"Yes."

I glance at Sandy. Her long, straight black hair blows in the rising wind, her crisp, white cotton shirt is an iridescent apricot from the sunset, and her dark, careful eyes keep watch.

I really am not in the mood for company. The beers have made me sleepy.

"Look, the rain is coming." In the distance a storm sits, so far away it can't be heard.

But it seems that the rain is indeed arriving. The wind picks up.

"Are there a lot of storms here?"

"In this season, every afternoon."

That is worrisome.

"Whose airplane is that?"

"Mine."

"Is the plane broken"?

"No, it works," says Sandy.

"Well, we are from the Mexican Navy; let us know if you need help."

We say no thanks; we're fine. Halting conversation drags on as we turn toward our belongings.

The winds picks up. We glance over at the plane. It rocks. I wonder if it can be lifted off the ground. With a worried look, Sandy assures me it can. In mere minutes, pink clouds far on the horizon become blue clouds over our heads. Sweat turns to goose bumps. It's hard to believe that a storm can move in so fast. I look at one of the men. Single drops of water land on his hair.

In the distance, the faint line of horizon is no longer there. What is coming is black on black, and all shadows have been sucked inside.

Weather is the largest thing I know. It's bigger than buffalo, bigger than dinosaurs, bigger than the Pleistocene, bigger than prediction, bigger than order. I feel the vastness and fastness. The change of light. Sand shifts under my feet, cold water smacks my face. It starts to rain. The sailors again offer help. *Tak tak tak*, raindrops torpedo the plane. We say no thanks as we run to the rocking plane. They run with us.

Sandy opens the cockpit door, grabs ropes. We attach the ropes to tie-down rings under the wings and tail of the plane. We look around for something to tie down the other ends of the ropes. We barely notice when the men leave. We need to secure the ropes with boulders or posts but there is nothing near us. This is a sandy beach.

The light is gone and we have to turn on big camping flashlights. We have no choice but to sleep sitting up in the cockpit, knowing that the plane might lift with us in it.

As we work, we hear something. We look around. Through the palm trees, eight men run toward us, led by a short, stocky middle-aged man.

He stands up very straight, chin high, and says, "Soy el capitán de la base naval estacionada aquí en Maruata." I am captain of the naval base in Maruata. Let us help you. You can trust us. We are the navy.

Running out of options, Sandy and I look at each other, shrug, and say, "Claro que sí, por favor ayúdanos." Of course, please help us.

The men carry ropes over their shoulders, shovels, and burlap bags. They jump into action as the *capitán* calls orders. An assembly line forms: two men tie more ropes to the plane, others dig sand and fill burlap sacks, and others wrap ropes around the heavy stuffed bags.

Rain increases. Water pours off their faces. As the men work in the dark, the capitán says something about coming to the camp. He invites us to join them for the night, out of the rain. Although he is elegant and gracious and seems tuned into our fears, and definitely has control over his men, there is some mystery as to exactly where he wants us to go and what he invites us to do. If only our Spanish were better.

In the pitch black, I glance over to where I think the ocean is. I hear waves bang against the shore. I feel small. I see quick flashes of light. Thunder booms. The night wild surrounds us.

The storm queen gallops over the floorless ocean. She devours the moon and they say she brings fifty-two years of rain to the land. Atlacamani is her name—*alborotada y tempestuosa*. The agitated, tempestuous Aztec goddess of oceanic storms. In her rowdy mood, she flings out hurricanes helter-skelter. Her black hair explodes into sapphire clouds while bolts of lightning pin it to the sky. She hurls toward us. Dark rain slams. The idea of the navy camp starts to look good. The capitán leads into the trees. We follow.

We are pelted with rain but soon arrive at an open space with tents and trailers. The capitán whispers something to a sailor, who trots away to deliver the message. Then the capitán escorts us to a long trailer.

Inside are thirty bunks with a man in almost every bunk. No lights are on, so we move by flashlight. He shouts to the men, "We have guests for the night. No one is to move, leave the bunks, or make any noise during the night."

No one says a word. The capitán bids us good night; his assistant takes us to two lower bunks across from each other. We sit on the bunks in our soaking clothes, remove our shoes, and get under the covers to a stupendous crack and snap. Each bunk is made of hard wood, with a wafer-thin mattress encased in hard plastic and covered by a rough sheet. This allows no secret or subtle movement. With every inhale and exhale, our beds snap, the crackle of even the tiniest movement amplified by utter silence in the trailer.

When I lay my head on the plastic pillow, it sounds like ice breaking on a lake. In a startling cacophony of crinkles and rustles, Sandy lies down on her bunk and I hear her try to smother her laughs as if we are in church. I soon fall asleep. Hours later, I am awakened when a sailor enters the trailer, whispers, "Where are the women?" "Here, so don't talk," whispers a compadre. The sailor goes to the far end of the trailer.

Just before dawn, I feel someone pushing my shoulder. It's Sandy, shoes on, ready to leave. I get up and silently follow her out. We tiptoe through camp, passing men asleep on cots under tarps.

We get to the beach overjoyed to see that the plane is still there in good condition, tied down to the sandbags. We do our morning chores and sip coffee as the sun comes up. The capitán appears with an assistant.

"Did you sleep well?"

"Perfectly, capitán," we chime. "Thanks for everything."

"The weather is better," he says, surveying the sky.

It's a great day, we agree.

"When do you leave?" he asks.

"After our coffee. Do you want some?" He declines.

"If you don't want coffee, would you like to take a ride in the plane?" asks Sandy. "We would like to thank you."

"Great, but let's do it soon because my boss arrives today and I don't want him to see me flying around."

"OK, vámonos!"

He and Sandy get in the plane and fly away.

When they return, he thanks Sandy for the ride and says he will wait for the day when we return.

We don't return. But twenty years into the future, Sandy still flies. Today she is flying over the Sea of Cortez as the scientist next to her counts three hundred small boats fishing in an area that permits only seven boats to fish.

It looks like the Milky Way of the sea, she comments. Hundreds of small white boats like stars on the water. The Mexican boats fish for jellyfish, which will be sold to China because the Chinese are certain that jellyfish make them virile. She sighs and shrugs at the thought of a country full of men gulping down jellyfish, then tilts the wings for a closer look at the water.

Wooden carving. Photo by Paige Hilman.

CHAPTER 6

TRAILS

I'M ON THE road back to Rancho La Choguita to make a "movie deal" with Ventura. I feel like a grown-up.

I have decided to make the documentary with him and not the Iguana Woman. As much as I like the idea of the Iguana Woman and her work, logistically I don't think I can find enough money to cover living and filming expenses. I also think it will be more difficult to get investors interested in a documentary about lizards. So I continue to work at the PBS station and teach dance.

I plan to return to talk with Ventura. I need to know if this private person from another culture wants to have his life probed and exhibited to strangers. I wouldn't.

Pinned on my refrigerator is a card that says, "Security is mostly a superstition. It does not exist in nature, nor do the children of men as a whole experience it. Avoiding danger is not safer in the long run than outright exposure. Life is either a daring adventure, or nothing."

Whenever I get nervous about what I am about to do, I go to my refrigerator and read this quotation from Helen Keller and am reminded that fear is in the mind of the beholder.

Next to that is a card advertising *Bullets for Breakfast*, a movie by Holly Fisher about a writer of pulp Westerns who never shot a bullet in his life. He just wrote about fictional cowboys, with pretend courage. That is really more my speed for the days when Helen Keller's bravery exceeds my reach.

And next to the movie card is another quotation: "The universe is inherently benevolent since it has no vested interest in cruelty," a cheerful thought by cartoonist Jonathan Morris.

Armed with aphorisms, I sail along in my red Nissan pickup, packed to the gills, and I am truly ecstatic to be on the move. I cross the border at Agua Prieta and travel Mexico's Highway 2, which parallels the U.S. border. It's weird to be driving alongside another country, my own. Because the landscape doesn't change from one country to the next. There is just this little piece of barbed wire running through the middle of the land that subtly tells you of the gigantic trouble you will incur if you step over it, thus crossing an international border without papers.

But that would happen only if someone sees you. If you start hopping back and forth across the wire like "skip rope" and no one sees you, are you "illegal"? Like if a tree falls in the forest . . .

If I thought Nature gave a damn, I would think she made this landscape just for the enjoyment of the humans and animals who live here. I see hectares of flat ranchland, skinny horizons, nonstop sky, and occasional birds. When I look beyond, I see dark mountains hiding obscure canyons. A couple of hours east of Agua Prieta is a road that goes to Pan Duro, a friend's ranch in the Sierra at the bottom of a box canyon where we will eventually film a stampede.

As I drive through a small mountain pass, I see ahead that there is a pull-out for vehicles with a view of the entire valley below. I'm hungry and want to stop driving for a few minutes. I pull into a parking area. As I park, I look over at a huge semitrailer just in time to see thirty people standing shoulder to shoulder inside the semi. They look at me.

A man outside the truck sees me and quickly trots alongside the trailer, pulling the sliding door across the faces that watch me, shutting the people inside with a loud clank. Painted on the outside of the semi's door are the words *Frutas y Verduras*, fruits and vegetables. I look over the valley, eat some cheese, and wonder about this truckload of faces. It feels weird that I sit here in this fresh breeze eating while they are in there sweating. And they are standing, not sitting. Unknown to me at the time, I will come to know well these people who travel in semis through Mexico.

Continuing into Chihuahua through Nuevo Casas Grandes and San Buenaventura, I start to climb through the Santa Catalina hills up to a higher elevation. I like that a mountain pass has my name. Catalina. Kathryn. I always wanted to change my name to something like Soledad, or Violet Splurge, but now I'll just keep it.

Before the Mexican government builds the toll road straight to Ciudad

Chihuahua, my trip is an extra two hours, but the hours are worth it. I get to pass through pueblos like Ignacio Zaragoza and Gómez Farías. They are small towns with a slow lifestyle like the Mexican towns I remember from childhood. Being off the beaten track, they don't see many tourists, so few of these towns have a hotel. I always keep an eye out for somewhere to stay overnight in case of emergencies.

In early-morning Zaragoza, the topes slow me down to a lazy speed, dogs walk the plaza, and women sweep the sidewalk. I stop for a soda, and smell bread from the *panadería*. In another small town, I stop at a roadside taquería for hot birria. These become regular haunts for me on my trips to the Sierra. I like to eat at the same places so I can get to know proprietors and hear local gossip.

After eleven hours of driving, I arrive in Creel. The first few years on the road, I carry gasoline tanks because Pemex stations are so few. But then the Mexican government starts building roads and Pemex stations like there's no tomorrow.

In Creel, I find a hotel at the end of a street. I like the proprietor, a quiet, watchful man, and he explains how to use the propane heat in the room without blowing up the place.

After visiting the few tourist spots in town, I walk around the back streets. I like to keep a low profile, so later I eat dinner and return to my hotel, happy that now I can spend time with *The Forests of the Night*, one of the all-time great books about the Sierra Madre, by J. P. S. Brown. If you pick up the book and read the first paragraph, your life is on hold until you reach the last word.

At the moment, I am at a part where the mestizo and a big wild cat stalk each other, and I'm scared. I listen for the sounds of jaguars in the hall outside my room but, alas, hear nothing.

The next day, I leave my truck with the hotel owner. I don't have low gears, no four-wheel drive, and don't think I can navigate the road to Choguita.

I get on a bus filled with Rarámuri. Not knowing what to do, I try to do what they do. I throw my backpack through the back doors of the small bus, climb in, and sit on the backpack. A man motions for me to move to a bus seat instead.

Later, I hear some quiet laughter and look behind me to see a couple of Rarámuri flipping up and down the straps of my backpack, turning the pack upside down. They seem to get a real kick out of it. Although it is an old thing, it is not the same as their bundles wrapped in white cotton that they carry on their back or around their waist.

As I ride I think, what if Ventura isn't home, do I have enough food and water to hold me over a few days until the erratically scheduled bus goes back to Creel? The bus leaves Creel on Tuesdays, goes to Norogachic, a mestizo and Rarámuri pueblo where the bus driver lives, then comes back to Creel on Fridays unless the driver drinks too much lechuguilla—then the bus returns whenever.

If Ventura is not home, I'll be stuck outside his house alone and will just have to figure it all out when I get there. Should I sleep outside his front door, or find a nice spot in the forest under a pine? This is not the era of e-mail or texts—this area does not even have electricity. So he has no idea I am arriving.

The bus stops occasionally to let people on and off. Twice we stop so the Mexican driver, moustache on his lip, pistol on his belt, can have a cigarette. Men go to the left side of the bus, women to the right. The women go into the pine trees and squat with their long skirts. I adjust my Levis as discreetly as possible and am envious of their convenient skirts.

Eventually we are at the rise of the hill, and I see smoke from Ventura's stovepipe. ¡Padrísimo! Someone's home. We drop down into the valley, and I get off the bus on the dirt road. I don't have to walk far to get to the house.

The four-legged doorbells run toward me barking, next the kids come running, and then Ventura comes out of the house. He wears a traditional red headband but, upon seeing me, takes it off and dons a blue cachucha. With a big smile, he walks out with the family to greet me. He says it is a surprise to see me but, for some reason, he doesn't seem all that surprised.

Walking into the house for coffee with the family feels like an everyday occurrence. We catch up on what's been happening. They give me a small clay olla, I give them photos of Max the Airedale and Tucson. Ventura comments on how he would like to go to Tucson, that he would like to leave his boring rancho life. It's true. There is a lot of downtime for the citizenry of poverty.

Ventura and I hit the trail and take a long walk through the community. The trails are wide and well used. He introduces me to various people but warns me against talking to them too much. He says they will try to take advantage of me.

"Near the rocks over there, see that house?" He points out a single-room log house. "Don't go there. It is the home of a bruja. Ella tiene dos caras," he explains about her two faces, first distorting his face into a grimace, then tilting his head and smiling sweetly.

I just watch. He's more entertaining than a TV program.

"She will invite you in for coffee, then when you leave she will find a hair that dropped from your head, and weave it into a dark rag. She will make a spell."

"Has she ever put a spell on you?"

"Oh yes, one day after coffee with her, I went home and soon got a headache. It ached for days. Then, everywhere I went, I saw a shadow. But it was a shadow standing by itself. It wasn't a shadow of anything, just its own self. It followed me everywhere."

"How did you get rid of it?"

"I had to go to a brujo for a spell big enough to cover hers. So be careful if anyone invites you for coffee."

Not certain about reality here in the Sierra, I chalk it up to what, in our culture, we might call jealousy. Maybe they don't share their gringa friends. Or maybe I'd better wear chile inside my blouse, just in case. Spells don't like chile.

Later we take a burro and walk an hour into the pine trees to gather wood he cut at dawn. He picks up the ax and asks me to chop a little wood. It must be the highlight of his day, watching a gringa chop wood, like watching Lucille Ball bake bread.

He has two little houses built next to his main house. Inside one is a large open room with clothing on the dirt floor. He points out that the piles of clothes are taller than he is. He says that people always want to give the Rarámuri used clothes, but "we don't need old clothes, we need money." He has a black London Fog raincoat.

After dinner, he shows me a room inside the family house where I can sleep. It is a big empty room with one bed made of old springs and a thin mattress. The room is built of logs and has one window covered with plastic and a well-swept dirt floor. He says he and his family can sleep in the middle room on a wooden platform. They give me the master suite where they normally sleep.

I return to the jaguar book, read for a while with a flashlight, set the book and light on the floor, and fall asleep. Wham! I am hit on the head and wake up with a jolt. My forehead hurts immediately.

I don't move. I'm scared and listen for someone in the room. I hear my heart. I can't see anything it is so dark. I hear something. Making no noise I reach for the flashlight on the floor, ready to hit someone with it. I whisper, "Ventura?" No answer. I wait. A small sound. I turn on the flashlight just in time to see a dark rock sail by my face. I swing the flashlight beam around the room. No one. I do it again. No one.

The room is tiny and there is no one in it. I swing the light up to the ceiling just in time to see a forty-foot rat run across the rafter above my head. As he runs, another chunk clunks to the bed, just missing my head. The logs in the room are chinked with dried mud, which must have fallen from the ceiling onto the beams. In his scramble, the rat knocks clods of rock-hard mud off the beam. Relieved that there are no murderers or jaguars in the room, I put my coat over my head and go back to sleep.

In the morning, I stand outside the house with my coffee and watch the morning light spread over the valley. The mist rises to reveal a few goats and pigs rooting around. In the distance, I see some Rarámuri walking to the hills to find firewood to cut. They have to walk further every year because the trees are disappearing.

They have lived in this area for hundreds of years and cut thousands upon thousands of trees. In most areas, they don't reforest. In addition, lumber mills are a welcome business, since there are few ways to earn a living. Ventura shows me a big orange log-cutting machine with which he wants to create a lumber business for Choguita. Only a plan, so far.

Immediate hunger overrides the ideal of reforestation and the love of landscape. Although in a perfect world, a new tree would be planted for every tree that is cut, the reality of no food on the table takes precedence over conservation.

The only work available in the area besides tending a few animals and subsistence plots of vegetables is making ollas to sell to tourists, selling canned goods and cookies from small *abarrotes* run by mestizos, and being paid to put a spell on an enemy. And of course, growing and selling marijuana. All the abuelitas do it. They grow plants down in the canyon and sell the harvest out of their kitchens.

Everyone is hungry. As much as I think Ventura and I have a developing friendship, I am aware that I am also a business deal to him.

He mentions that he might go north to the United States to look for work. I cringe. It is a dangerous trip to cross the desert into the U.S. People die there, I tell him. It is unforgiving and hot. Ventura doesn't know hot. He lives in pines, not mesquite. I tell him not to go to the U.S. We talk a little of getting a visitor's visa for him. But getting a visa is as treacherous as navigating the trails of the Barranca del Cobre.

I walk over to the outhouse. It is a tilting cartoon building, constructed of mismatched lumber. It has a door that hangs crooked, and it has what you don't get from cartoons—odor. I go inside and shut the door for whatever privacy I can glean.

There is a solid raised box to sit on, but where the feet rest is a board that floats. It floats in indescribable muck. I am startled by a noise and glance behind me to see a chicken pecking and diving under an opening in the wall to join me in the outhouse, swimming in the surrounding liquid as it looks for food. I leave as quickly as possible.

In front of Ventura's house is another log house that he rents to a family of Evangelists from Arizona. They say they have come to the valley to save the lives of children who die from drinking bad water. They promise they will dig new wells and install new pumps so that the water is clean.

The only cost is your soul. You must become an Evangelist. Ventura was governor of Choguita when the Evangelists arrived. He and the community agreed to build a church up on the hill a polite distance away from the Catholic church, where Semana Santa, Holy Week, takes place.

When the church got rolling, the minister asked for donations at each sermon. To be a member of the church, each Rarámuri has to give money. That is like asking a crow to give bananas. Oh, by the way, the Evangelists pay rent for Ventura's house in beans and old clothes. No cash. Ventura casually mentions this.

After my experience in the outhouse, I look around for other options. Next to the Evangelists' house is a shiny new outhouse. The boards are fresh with the still-new scent of pine. I think, wow, this is great, how generous. They are sprucing up Ventura's property.

I walk over to use it. There is a padlock on the door so I can't go inside. Silly me. I still don't get it. I ask one of the Evangelists for a key. They say point-blank, "You can't use it. It is for our family only." Ventura's family can't use it. No pesky poor people or strangers allowed.

In all fairness to the Evangelists, they do some good. I become ill and can't get out of my sleeping bag without vomiting. It continues for three days. Ventura says he will take me up the hill to a clinic run by the Evangelists.

The family that rents his house says I can't use the clinic. It is only for Indians. I'm not sure why they dislike me so much. Everyone in the canyons seems to have a sense of proprietorship over something. Perhaps these people think they own Ventura and feel that I interfere with that ownership.

It takes us twenty minutes to walk a quarter of a mile to the clinic, first on a trail, then a dirt road. Because I keep vomiting, and Ventura's diabetes bothers him, we have to sit down often. When we finally arrive at the clinic, it is well equipped, and the medic is kind. He searches my tongue and throat, looks at samples of this and that under a microscope, gives me some big white pills, and in a few days I am on the move again.

Days later, Ventura and I sit on a log in front of his house. In an unusually direct manner, he asks, "What are you doing here? Why did you return?" I say, "I like you and your family. I want to know more about you and think your story would make a good movie."

He doesn't say anything. I go on. I say, "I think people in other parts of the world would benefit by knowing you and the life here." He asks how it is done. I explain that I will bring a camera and start filming. "And I will bring a tape recorder to record what you tell me," I say. "I will pay you a salary. Every time we talk about your life, every time I record you, I will pay your salary." I explain that later a camera crew will come to film more.

I don't have to wait long. He laughs and says yes, "Claro que sí. Vamos a filmar una película." Of course, let's make a movie. He says, "¡Cómo no!" Why not.

A few days later, Ventura and I take a long walk on yet another trail. It seems that much of our time together is on trails. Trails in the Sierra are steep or flat, slippery or rocky, abstract or intentional. I look at how abruptly they ascend to the clouds, and the thought of hiking them is merely a dream, or I find myself clutching stones and scrambling up, hand over hand, simply because there is no other way to get where I am going.

A few times, I walk the trails alone while Ventura rests at home. He explains that they are all old hunting trails. Animals hunt on these trails, humans hunt animals on these trails, and I hunt, too. For what, I am not yet sure. A movie. About what?

We casually talk about the landscape and his life. He takes me on a hike to visit his eighty-year-old aunt, who sits on the ground outside her house with puppies in her lap. Eighty years is a long time for a Rarámuri to live.

We are a day's walk from any other homes. She lives alone. We sit and they speak in Rarámuri. Occasionally she turns her head in my direction. Ventura says she would like to show me her house. She stands and stares straight ahead as she walks. I realize she is blind. We go inside her house. It is a closet-size room made of chinked logs.

It is almost empty. There is an old oil drum for a fireplace and a goatskin in front of it where she sleeps. The only light is what enters through the low door. A sliced log serves as a table and kitchen. Square and center, there is a container for water. There has been a drought in the Sierra for ten years and water is gold.

There are a couple of eating and cooking utensils and nothing else in her home. Ventura shows me a pot she made and asks if I would like to buy it. Of course I would. We make the transaction, visit a little longer, and then continue our stroll.

While we are hiking, Ventura asks, "Can you lie down here on the trail?" It is a weird question. I think he is propositioning me and I am disappointed. I don't want our friendship altered with this. I use the frequently uttered words, "¿Mande? No entiendo." (There is a theory that Cortez, the Spanish conquistador, taught the word "mande" to native slaves, so when he called on them they would answer back to him, "Command me." Now it is commonly used to mean "What?")

Ventura rephrases, "Can you lie down here on the ground to sleep?" I don't know what he is getting at but I say I could sleep on the ground if I needed to. He says he can't. He goes on to explain that he is afraid that if he sleeps on the ground in the dark, animals will come to get him. He wonders if I am fearful like he is. Maybe lions and snakes will come.

He says he slept on the ground in the past when he worked in a canyon stringing lines for an electric company but he never liked it. I laugh. How un-Indian-like. Here we have a macho Indian who chops wood and was governor of his community, and he is afraid of the dark. Perfect. I like him even more.

As we walk, he tells me that his dream is to move to a big city. He says his daughters can be secretaries in a bank. He says they need ribbons for their hair. His son can work in a store. They will have a house with a floor in a neighborhood with *carritos de carne*, street-food wagons. Ventura dreams of living in the city the way I dream of having a vineyard in Italy.

Now I begin to see why I want to make a documentary about him and the life here in the Sierra. As my friend Santiago says, this is a time of magic. It is a time when ceremony is an intrinsic daily companion, not something that happens once a year. When the *bacánari* root affects a person's behavior by cloaking him in a curse. When an individual goes to a healer to speak to Peyote. It is a time when healers intimately know three hundred plants that cure soul and flesh. It is a time when Ventura still remembers the giants that roamed the land, when darkness was as powerful as sunlight.

It is a time before electricity, before the Grand Highway. A time of drought, when a skinny cow lies on its side, panting, thorns blanketing its lips because the only food it can find is prickly-pear cactus. When Rarámuri sons and daughters move to Cuauhtémoc or Ciudad Chihuahua to earn money, never to be seen again by their parents. It is a time to seek the Seven Cities of Cíbola, but Rarámuri style.

It is a time when the only thing in abundance is nothing. No crops, no water. A time to invite foreigners to the canyons, for Evangelists to dig wells, for lumber companies to build mills. A time for the Rarámuri to weave more belts and baskets, fire bigger and more exquisite pots, embroider more shirts, and make more violins for the tourists. It is a time for change that cannot be undone. It is time to leave your land and all you know, and migrate to another country and dream of a life where there is food each day.

CHAPTER 7

NOROGACHIC

IT IS ALSO time to get serious about making a movie. I keep a notebook of ideas, storyboard sketches of camera angles of log cabins and of Ventura's head. I write words I want spoken in the movie but I don't know who will speak them. It is a documentary, after all, and the director is not supposed to put words in a person's mouth. Or is she? As I talk and walk with people, I hear groups of voices. Everyone tells me secrets and I hear choruses of gossip. I see hunger and hardship and lifestyle changes as the Western world bumps its way into a landscape of murmuring voices.

I pick up a pen and write, "Did you hear? What did he say? Who told you?"

A woman's voice says:

She looks at the light bulb.
It is like the moon, but not.
She touches it.
Hot like a match tip, but not.
Something new, but not.
It heals with the same cool mystery as their antibiotics.
She stands in the moving wind, jealous of the way it changes with such ease.
The bulb swings from the wire.
Things will be different now.

Change in the Sierra. And gossip, the key to understanding change from the inside out. Gossip, the telephone line of the mountains. Being a woman, I get invited into a river of information. Not that men don't gossip. I could go on and on about that.

But being a woman, I am not much of a threat in the Sierra. I realize that violence occurs, and women can be vulnerable. But as a woman traveling alone, I find that people want to take care of me. I can't even walk to the conasupo to buy tortillas without a companion. Later, a friend, Imelda, will protect me. She will send her eight-year-old daughter, Susana, to accompany me every morning to buy fresh eggs. I learn that she was sent so I would not be lonely.

In Tucson, months after my first trip when I met Ventura, there was a knock at my front door. A man with a faded red ball cap stood on the porch. It was the same face I saw in the VW on the Sierra road a year earlier. Hearing that I was interested in the Sierra, a mutual friend sent this man to see me. His name is Santiago Barnaby, from Montana.

Hard to categorize, Santiago is a man of three cultures. He lives half the year in Bozeman, Montana, where, for fun, he sleeps in caves that he carves out of mountain ice. When he is not hiking Montana trails, he is home caring for his burros, hinny, and vegetable garden. The other six months of the year, he lives in the Barranca del Cobre, mostly in the pueblo of Norogachic, an area of mixed cultures of mestizo and Rarámuri. He has done this for over thirty years.

Proud of his four-legged friends, Santiago packs his donkeys and hinny and ventures into the Montana mountains in weather I would hide from. To people like me, mules look like horses, and hinnies, well, I had never heard of them.

One of my first faux pas in the Sierra is to tell Hiram, a Norogachic vaquero and friend of Santiago's, that I like his horse while he is saddling up a mule. Politely but firmly he explains the difference. Mules and horses look alike. Except mules have long ears. I have since become a great observer of ears. I don't want to call someone a jackass who isn't. A baby hinny is a special creature, smart and fuzzy, a cross between a female donkey and a male horse. With only a 20 percent chance of conception when mating the two, the hinny is a rare breed.

I am embarrassed that I couldn't tell the mule from the horse. And I hope there are no hinnies around because I don't want to act dumb twice. As Santiago introduces me to Hiram, the quintessential Sierra cowboy, I know right away that I don't want to be a fool in his eyes.

He stands straight, wears a white cowboy hat with a black band, and sports a thick, trimmed moustache. Dimples play around the mouth. He is polite and serious but laughs whenever he gets the chance. That means mostly when his buddies are near. I take notice when I meet him. I mean, he *is* rather handsome. He could have just ridden up to the hacienda on a fine horse in *Soy tu dueña*, the long-running telenovela about love, kidnapping, and intrigue on a fictional Mexican ranch.

After Santiago introduces me to Hiram, Santiago and I make plans to travel through some canyons. We plan what we will pack with us: food, water, and cameras. If there is any one fine example of a vegetarian, Santiago is it. How can someone who just eats veggies be so durable? How can cabbage, chiles, beans, and a few nuts get you up a trail that has the gradient of an elevator? He needs only a topo map, and maybe not even that, to cross the many scabrous mountainsides and canyons of the Barranca del Cobre. He's chummy with the region.

The only reason he doesn't get lost or injured is because he is also smart. As I am returning to the States from the Barranca del Cobre, I give him a ride to the city of Cuauhtémoc. He wants to be dropped off outside Cuauhtémoc at the junction of the main highway and a dirt road so he can bushwhack back to Norogachic, 117 miles away as the crow flies.

Imagine how long that walk is. The topo map is scary. There are just too many squiggly black lines, concentric circles, and contour lines that indicate high mountain peaks and quick drops to lower canyon elevations. In other words, cliffs need to be scaled. If a person can do a hard fifteen miles a day on flat ground, think about the time it takes to hike those canyons.

As we stand outside my truck, in the far distance we see silhouettes of the Barranca del Cobre. Above us, large black clouds roll in. I am concerned he will be in the rain and get washed away down rushing canyon rivers, not to mention that he might get lost. He laughs and says he is headed for a nice dry cave.

I ask if he is worried to be alone. He says that the Barrancas have too many people and he is sure to run into some. So we part. He slings his not-so-small backpack over his shoulder and walks away.

Weeks later, when I return to Norogachic, about two hours from the village of Choguita where Ventura lives, Santiago suggests I stay at Casita Blanca. It is a two-room white stucco house on the hill behind the home of the owners, Gabriel and Imelda, a small hill away from where Hiram and his family live. It has no cooling, but there is a stove to burn wood when it's cold. There is a small wooden table and a bed.

That's it for indoors. Out the door is a balcony where you can look over a wide river, usually dry. On the other side of the riverbed is a mesa with a trail up to the top. Each morning, the sun rises over this mesa, reaching toward me with peach fingers.

Santiago introduces me to the people of Norogachic. Here I meet mestizo cowboys and their families, and Rarámuri who have a more traditional world view than Ventura. The differences will make the documentary interesting. Santiago becomes instrumental in arranging events and people to film for the doc.

Ernesto lives with Pascuala and their ten children up Arroyo Grande, across the big slabs of pale rock. You enter sunlight when you enter their house of canary-yellow walls. On the stove is a pot of beans and a flatiron that has to be heated over fire.

There is no electricity. Pascuala bakes bread in an adobe-and-stone oven. Out the front door, gardens are wild with color. Although they mostly plant food necessary for survival, you can spy a woman's touch in parts of the garden stuffed with flowers the colors of the rainbow.

Over in the pen are black-headed goats. Look a little further and you see the cliff's edge with ropes dropping over it. The family pulls up water from a container at the base of the cliff.

Gabriel lives in the house down the hill from Casita Blanca with his wife, Imelda, eight-year-old Susana, and her younger brother. One afternoon as I sit on the porch of Casita Blanca, Susana grabs her doll and carries it over to me. She sits on the porch wall and watches me brush my hair.

"Your hair is not nice," she tells me.

"Really?"

"If you braid it, you will look pretty like my mother." She brings her doll and sits in a chair beside me. "Like this," she says. She braids the doll's hair, unbraids it, and then hands it to me. Each day, in hopes that my looks will improve, she brings the doll and we braid. The lesson is twofold. I learn braiding and I learn Spanish. Soon, I speak almost as well as an eight-year-old.

Gabriel drives a big truck to chauffer the nuns from the church school to other pueblos in the canyons. Once when going down a steep canyon road, his truck rolled over, the steering wheel coming off; Gabriel flew forward and was impaled by the steering column. His was a recovery understood only if you believe that a man with a metal post stuck through his torso can live. He says he is talking with me today because he believes in miracles.

Imelda stokes the wood-burning stove to cook up a warm breakfast of rice, milk, and raisins. When I go out to the yard to do laundry with her, she explains which barrel has soapy water and which has rinse water as she scrubs away on both a corrugated tin washboard and a special stone for cleaning men's work pants. "Ay qué, Catalina," she laughs as I try to tell her a joke in Spanish. Of course the laughter is not at my sense of humor, rather at my tongue-tied *español*. Susana, who attaches herself to me like a shadow, is my best audience because she thinks that nothing I say makes sense, so I provide endless hours of mirth.

Gabriel's brother-in-law, Hiram, and his wife, Elia, live a half mile down the road. Hiram owns not only his own house in Norogachic but also a plot of land up the mesa, several horses and chickens, and a couple of cows. He and his seventy-year-old father, Lupe, ride horses to tend corn on the land above.

Santiago respects Hiram and tells me I can trust him, too. I walk over to his house. Elia invites me in for coffee and cookies. The kitchen is white stucco walls with photos of kids and Lupe. There is a stack of lace tortilla warmers on the edge of the table, the lace handmade by Elia. She hums as she wraps tortillas inside for Hiram to take as lunch when he rides up to the fields.

There is a nice window in the kitchen that lets light pour across the concrete floor. I smell coffee. As Elia stirs the beans on the wood-burning stove, she simultaneously kneads dough for more sweets. I sit in a high-backed wooden chair next to the sink, across from the table. Off to one side is a bedroom, where the bed takes up 80 percent of the space. There is also a small room for showering and washing hands. The toilet is outdoors. Years ago, they built this house together, side by side, one adobe at a time.

As years pass, I will get to know these hardworking people. I see how, simultaneously tough and generous, they work all day every day; I see how they give what they have, like plates of hot steaming *frijoles de ollo*, but cannot share what they themselves lack, like body lotions and soaps, and scissors and knives for the workshop, and oil for the saddles. Or reading glasses.

Santiago started a reading glasses program in which he gets donations of glasses from people in Montana, then takes them to the people of Noro-gachic.

I learn what it means for families to enjoy each other's company and enjoy each full moment of precious downtime.

I also learn what it means to see the same faces every day your whole life. One morning at Casita Blanca, I hear yelling. Later, I go down to the house for breakfast and see that Imelda has been crying. I just hug her and don't ask questions. She hugs back and puts a piece of wood in the stove.

One afternoon, I go to Hiram and Elia's house. He sits at the table, stares straight ahead. Normally, he invites me in with warmth and pulls out a chair for me to sit on. But this morning, Elia, with a stiff back turned to him, washes dishes. "Siéntate, Catalina," Elia says as she pours coffee for me. But it is a glacier between the two of them as Hiram grabs his hat off the hook and walks out in silence. It is sometimes a malignant togetherness that is healed by the ritual of the day, or the intrusion of strangers. Or a good dance down at the barn.

As in the United States, putting food on the table is stressful. Working dawn to dusk for little money is depressing. I learn that, like with families in my country, it is hard for the poor to stop being poor. But don't call the families of Norogachic poor. They will tell you that they have what they need and more.

Like most of the couples in Norogachic, Elia and Hiram met when they were children. Their families lived near each other; they grew up and got married and have always been together, day after day, year after year. They are husband and wife but also like brother and sister because they have known each other forever. Family is all there is.

In order to make the film, I need guides into the backcountry. Hiram offers. I ride with him through canyons and washes. He teaches me how to mount, how to lean in when the horse charges, and lean back when we slide head-on down a narrow canyon trail. As we ride, he turns often in his saddle to see if I am all right as I follow behind, trying to keep up. When he glances back at me, it feels like a warm hand has just touched my head.

I appreciate his attention but feel silly not knowing how to ride a horse. It's like not knowing how to drive a car.

He teaches me how to hold the reins, how to hold my thighs around the horse, how to listen to what the horse tells me. And how to watch out for low-hanging branches.

I like to watch Hiram. Black hair is tucked under his white cowboy hat; his dark eyes look straight at mine. His muscled hands constantly wrap the reins, rub the saddle, or twist the rope. While his hands move often, his tongue doesn't. He is a quiet man.

One day he takes me to the high country to film more of the area around Norogachic. I have an 8 millimeter camera. I plan to mix still photos and video. Will it work? Maybe not. I pack up some filmmaking equipment and we head for the Arroyo Grande.

As we leave Norogachic, we ride high to the top of a hill. Hiram looks down at a house in the valley. He nods his head and pulls his horse to the left. He doesn't speak, just nods again and motions for me to follow. We ride up next to a tree, closer to the house, and sit the horses, hidden by branches.

From a distance, we circle the small adobe house. A tin roof reflects the rays of sun. No people are around. Finally, Hiram motions and we gallop up a trail and away from the small adobe.

"What were you looking for?" I ask.

"Not sure," he says.

"Should we stay in this area?"

"No, I'll come back later."

"For what?"

"A few weeks ago, two gold candlesticks, a silver plate and cup, and some items the priest uses were stolen from the church. I think I know who did it."

"Should we tell someone?"

"No, the thief is not from around here but his friends are. It will be taken care of."

"How?"

"It just will."

Midday, we stop to *sestear*, to take a rest, and are surrounded by dry cornstalks hanging from oaks like moss dripping off cypress trees in bayou swamps. Rarámuri men store dry cornstalks on tree limbs so they can feed their animals as they pass this trail during the dry time of no harvest.

Cornstalks rustle like ghost speak, so even in daylight you are aware that people and time have passed this way long before you arrived, and will continue to do so long after you pass by. The hanging stalks shift slightly but there is no wind. It is as if someone breathes on them.

We dismount. Hiram walks the horses to the stream to drink. He then builds a small fire, pulls from his pack coffee and tin cups and a bag of tamales made by Elia. We sit side by side and eat the tamales, some stuffed with beans and chiles, some sweet with raisins. He folds two shirts and places them on the ground. He says he will rest. Do I want to rest, too? he asks. I say I am not tired. He doesn't say anything. He removes his hat and stretches out to sleep by the stream. I watch the tiny water try to flow. I guess the earth will absorb it before it gets far. I watch him sleep. I watch the water. I watch him.

After he wakes, we sit shoulder to shoulder and I show him a topo map of the land around Norogachic because I want to know where I am. I point to a spot. "Are we here?" I ask. He doesn't say anything. I say, "Oh, maybe we have come this far. Is this the canyon we crossed?" He says, "Eh." He shows no interest in it and turns away to poke the fire.

It dawns on me that perhaps he can't read the map. Or maybe he is not interested because why should he be? This is his home. He knows every boulder and shadow, dip and turn, within a hundred miles. He knows it the same way I know that there are three steps down my front porch, a young mesquite tree by the street, a right turn at the end of the block, and a mile to a food store.

His first breath was in this land. He knows who was here then and who was here before. It is his land. It is his father's land. It is the Rarámuri land. It is no one's land. It is the land of eagles, of foxes, of blue birds. It is the land that can't be known. It is the land that gave and now takes. It is the unpredictable land where humans hang cornstalks in case the rains that have come for hundreds of years no longer come.

I travel with Hiram in the change of seasons. In times of snow, when it starts to fall off the brims of our hats, I hunker down in the saddle and try to imitate him. I hunch forward to make the tarp I am wearing billow out to cover me more fully. That's what he does. But I have to take care that the camera stays under the plastic. Water and film don't mix.

We are caught in a winter storm. Hiram puts a little plastic cap over the crown of his hat, a cap like a hairnet but not porous. It keeps the precipitation out. I don't have one so the wetness seeps through the weaving and water trickles down my face. The horses step sideways through a rushing stream with water rising near to the knees, and I am so cold but think that when we get back to Norogachic the women will have steaming frijoles, coffee, tortillas, and sweet breads, and there will be a fire to warm me.

I wonder how I would exist out here. Perhaps I would be a failure in the Mexican ranch world. I would rather be out in the snow on the horse and have hot food waiting for me back at the ranch instead of being the one to prepare the food. I am suspecting I wouldn't make a good housewife.

On a warmer afternoon, I learn to ride fast without falling. After a gallop in wide-open space, Hiram rides up and pulls back on his reins, his horse close to mine. He grins with dimples at the corners of his mouth, eyes flashing like mica. He grabs the horn on my saddle and leans over to tell me he likes riding with me. Out of the blue. He says his wife doesn't ride. He wants someone to ride with. A companion on horseback. I think about this. Then I think that age-old question: how does a person stay away from something she wants but can't have?

When I live at Casita Blanca in the warm weather, Hiram drops by to visit after his workday ends. He is the good neighbor who walks over the hill to my balcony at Casita Blanca with a bottle of exquisite tequila and two small glasses after the sun goes down and the sky is full of stars. He is the caballero who sets two chairs on the balcony, pours the tequila, and tells me to look at the moon, our chaperone, hanging over Arroyo Grande. Hiram is the man who moves the chairs close and quietly asks me how I liked the horse I rode that morning. He is the man with the sweet smell of saddle oil and hair lavender. He is the man whose warm arm is next to mine. He is the man who is married.

A few months later in the summer, a photographer friend, Susie, and I hire Gabriel and Ernesto to guide us into remote Rarámuri ranchos to film and photograph. Ernesto packs up two burros with camera gear, Gabriel throws on a barrel of water, the wives wrap up enough food for five days, and we head off toward the canyons to meet some Rarámuri.

Gabriel assures Hiram that he will take good care of us for the week. Hiram tilts his hat forward, shifts from boot to boot, and watches silently as we walk away. Minutes later, I look over my shoulder. He steps forward with the low-slung walk of the Barranca cowboy. For a second, I think he is going to join us. Then he stops. I keep glancing back at him until I almost trip on rocks.

Filming in the Sierra Madre. Photo by Kathryn Ferguson.

Susie looks at the packed burros and says that's not enough water. It is June, 110 degrees, and not yet Día de San Juan, the day the rain arrives. The Sierra is in a decade-long drought. The men assure us we will find water on the way. We all wear hats, Levis, and long-sleeved shirts to shield us from the sun, the men in huaraches, we in our tennis shoes.

As we leave Norogachic, we walk past women washing clothes in the arroyo. They are bent over, wringing out shirts. They lift their heads to watch us as we walk, small smiles on their faces, the beginning of wagging tongues. Two gringas and two *mexicanos*. The voices of gossip gear up. I wonder what it would be like if I were standing with them and not over here. Wonder if I would be gossiping, too.

We walk trails all day. Susie doesn't speak much Spanish so we hang back and talk. The men walk in front, turning around to check on us. We are all polite with each other.

We pass dry arroyos, follow trails up and down steep hills, traverse big flat rocks, pass through stands of red trees, and walk and walk and walk. This is familiar territory, like the Tumacacori Mountains at the border of Mexico and the United States, about sixty miles from my Tucson home. Flat land with sudden cliffs. Dry arroyos. Big sky. And hot.

Sweat steams under my hat and trickles into my eyes. My whole body is wet. We drink water carefully. I worry about the burros. Gabriel doesn't give them any water. He keeps saying we will arrive at a spring. We finally do, but it is dry.

We waste energy searching the area for signs of hidden water. None. We have drunk half the water and it is the first day. We have enough for morning. The men assure us we will find more or get it from the Rarámuri. My feet start to form blisters and it is only day one. No one complains.

We stop to make camp. Ernesto and Gabriel giggle like girls, as exuberant as if they were on holiday. They have never guided gringas before. Maybe it will become a new part-time job.

After a long while, they finally decide on the proper place for the sleeping bags, and to my surprise, the bags are placed in a row, just inches from each other. It invades my space.

Not wanting to be impolite out here in the wild, Susie and I casually adjust our bags so they are farther away from the men's bags. As I come to find out, personal space in Mexico is not the same as in the United States. Ernesto and his wife and ten kids all sleep in one big bed. At my house, *I* sleep in one big bed.

Unabashedly happy, Ernesto and Gabriel laugh and hum as they prepare fire to heat water. They work dawn to dusk every day of their lives, and this business of guiding a couple of unaccompanied gringas for a few days is cake.

Gabriel tosses laurel leaves into a pan for tea. Everything gets quiet and Ernesto glances at us. He suddenly seems nervous. I am perplexed.

He clears his throat. In a surprisingly direct manner for a mexicano, he says, "Why are you women by yourselves? The Barrancas are dangerous. Why are you not here with husbands?" Mmm, wonder how long that thought has been percolating?

One of those questions I choose not to think about. But as he talks, I think maybe he is on to something. Maybe I need someone out here to protect me. Why not? The age-old romanticizing of romance.

Woody Allen couldn't have written the scene better. I explain that Susie's husband is tucked safely at home. They are astounded. "Then why isn't he here helping her?" they ask, as if they always help their wives scrub laundry on river rocks.

They ask why I am not married. Here we go again. I just say I am waiting for the right guy. They laugh. "What does that mean?" they ask. "You just need a guy to take care of all the man jobs. Share the load," they say, nodding at each other, talking to me like I'm in counseling.

Stars come out and I fall asleep to the melody of the Spanish language pouring out of two cowboys, yards away.

When the sun rises, we eat bean burritos prepared by Imelda and begin to walk. Full of food and hope about great images we will film today when we arrive at the caves, I am excited to continue our journey. We each take a sip of water, the burros drink, my blisters don't feel so bad, and I am not worried. We pack up and hit the trail.

The half run, half flap of small two-legged dinosaurs fleeing predators may be what started it. Maybe that was the beginning of flight. Now, the animal we call a bird uses feathered wings to get airborne when being chased by big teeth. In whatever way it works, a six-foot-wide bald eagle taking off in flight is an everyday occurrence for the eagle but an astounding sight for this human whose head it circles. It is large. It is magnificent. For an instant, its darkness covers the sun. I comment on it as we walk. Without glancing up, Gabriel says there is a nest in the cliff above. It is as matter of fact for him as it is for the eagle.

It is the eagle's powerful focus that I am attracted to. I have always loved the hawks and other birds of prey I see around my Tucson home because there is nothing extraneous about them. They are all about focus. Full-body focus, fourteen pounds of rock-hard focus. I wish I could say the same about myself. I am extraneous personified. I make a mental note to focus.

We stop to film the surrounding cliffs, trails, and birds. Susie pulls out a tripod; I start shooting with the Pentax still camera, then change over to the Super 8 camera. Later I will use a digital Sony PD150, which is great with low light and distance. Eventually, the finished film is a mix of mediums and textures, much like the land we walk through.

The rule used to be that a film is created with one type of camera, one style of shooting, one style of editing. That doesn't seem to fit as well as it once did. The layered world we wake up to every day is best described with whichever mediums portray the textured life we live. In film, voice, or love, grainy is as good as smooth.

Our hike gets more difficult. We are thirsty. It is humid and over one hundred degrees. It is the rainy season but there is no rain, no Día de San Juan. There is no point in complaining. It is just damned hot. I sense we are all a little nervous. Susie is right. We didn't bring enough water and have three more days to walk for filming, then four days home.

Since we saw the eagle, I hope we will come upon a river or lake because I remember reading that eagles live near water.

After we finish filming, I sit down in the shade of a scrubby tree. If I didn't passionately desire to make this film, I would suggest we turn around and go home. My mouth is parched. Gabriel says there is water ahead.

We arrive at red dirt. The surface is cracked, like the inside of my mouth. When I bend down to touch it, it feels slightly moist. Or is that my imagination. I scoop it up but there is no touchable water. Like Mars. A beguiling, reddish landscape with a liquid past.

Red, the most powerful of all colors. Red lures, repels, frightens, warns, enrages.

We have orchid red, Chinese red, fire-engine red, blood red, brick red, and sangria red. We have red personalities that are fiery, determined, tenacious, full of vigor, and courageous, and perhaps eagles are red inside.

In front of us lies red in the form of terra cotta—colored earth. It waits for the Rarámuri to claim it and carry it and pound it and mix it with water in order to paint dots and lines on the blank faces of dancers at Semana Santa. We are at a sacred place where there is sacred soil. But all I can think about is a drink of water.

We stand at the edge of a *charco*, a pond that is often dry, where it has blown out to its chalk edges. The inside of my mouth feels like chalk. In the charco center, it looks like mud. With the sun's reflection, it glistens.

I dig around in the mirage searching for moisture, a deep pocket of water. I am so thirsty. I would drink it even though it is red. There is no water of any color.

Later we make a dry camp and the next morning, rise to film at sunrise. It is hot. As we walk, the backs of my hands burn. I turn them over so the palms face outward. The palms burn. I put my hands inside the shade of my

Levis pockets. There are no trees in this area, just a wide, dry arroyo. Gabriel says sit down and wait. He points to some log houses. He says he'll go ask the Rarámuri if we can have some of their water.

Soon he returns empty handed. He offered to pay for the water. They told him they only had enough for the family. We continue to walk.

As we round the curve in the glaring white arroyo, we see a Rarámuri grandfather sitting in the center of the arroyo in hot sand. He wears a bright-orange construction-site helmet. He digs with a large wooden spoon. He digs sand and throws it aside, repeating this motion over and over. His hole is almost two feet deep. He digs for water. We approach. Ernesto asks if he has found any. He shakes his head. Dotting the riverbed are abandoned holes where Grandfather has dug like a badger. We move on.

Another mile, a Rarámuri woman crosses in front of us, leading a burro across the dry arroyo with a rope. The burro's body is draped with a bouncing white bulge, like cats trying to escape from under a white bedsheet. It is a hill of empty plastic gallon jugs piled on top of each other, one tied to the next, piled as high as the burro is tall. They trudge across the sand. Gabriel calls out, "Is there water?" The woman doesn't acknowledge us and moves on as if we all populate a Samuel Beckett landscape. "I can't go on. I'll go on."

Late in the afternoon, we arrive at a junction of two arroyos. This is where Gabriel promises we will find water. There are boulders and smooth river rocks with pockets. We hop from rock to rock. All pockets empty. With effort, we pry up the smaller rocks. Dry. We look everywhere for water.

We climb a hill to have a better view. Seeing no water sources, we continue. We arrive at a second spot of hope merely to walk upon what seems to be a quiet gypsum pond, comfortably containing nothing within its banks. I am suddenly depressed. I think that our dear guides don't know what they are doing. I hope they know the way home.

We arrive at our destination. There stand monolithic hillsides with large animal–size caves eaten into corrugated rock walls, caves that are traditional Rarámuri homes. In front of the large opening, there are empty wooden corrals to keep animals enclosed. In the recessed darker areas of the caves are personal belongings.

No one is home. We hear bells. I turn to see two children herding goats up a hill. Gabriel calls as they hide their faces from us. He calls again, asks where the rest of the family is. A boy says they have gone to another rancho and will return in a couple of days. We rest, then film goats and goatherds, boulders, rock walls, caves, and dry riverbeds. B-roll. It is like taking notes. Jotting down the sound of bells. I know somewhere in the film we will need goats and goat bells. We move on.

I am thirsty. My body doesn't feel right. Somewhere someone is dying in a flood and here we are, thirsty. Weather knows no borders. The drought here in northern Mexico is the same as the drought in New Mexico and Arizona.

A few miles further, our trail takes us near a small, shallow pit. We are at the end of the fourth day. Gabriel and Ernesto quarrel. We feel sick. I say let's go back to Norogachic.

But at the pit, we see a bit of murky, hot, stagnant water. We are overjoyed. Mostly it is a mosslike algae filled with green water.

Susie and I have iodine pills so we throw the whole concoction, water and algae, into a container with the pills, shake it up, and then we are supposed to wait thirty minutes. While we wait, I fear something will come take the container of water—a bird, a bear, a person. I keep my eye hard on it. It is a long wait.

Then we divide it. I wipe fine bits of sand off my mouth before I put the water to my lips. I can't tell if it's cool or hot water that hits the inside of my mouth—it burns for an instant, then soothes. The sip of smooth water goes down my throat like a rocking chair. It gives me chilly goose bumps.

We know that Giardia is present in this part of the Sierra, but we take the chance anyway, hoping the pills work, and we divide the algae into four parts and suck on it. The water tastes like iodine but no one cares. It is good. We scrape up the rest of the algae and repeat the recipe, suck and swallow, suck and swallow, spitting out a few rocks in the process.

The next day we walk, film, and photograph. At the end of the day, we camp near a Rarámuri cornfield where the stalks stand brown and skinny. We decide to return to Norogachic the following morning. I feel an insect in my hair. Then another. I flick it away. It doesn't go away. I look at my fingers. They are wet. I look up. It is rain.

We turn our faces to the sky and open our mouths. We set out our wares—empty cans, tin plates and cups, a big spoon—and we hang up a tarp from a tree branch and then tilt it toward the containers to catch water. A trickle from the light rain rolls to the corner of the tarp and flows down to the cups. Gabriel says we even have enough to give the burros.

We return to Norogachic along the arroyo. More women are washing clothes. They look up to watch us. The gossip must be in full swing. Did you hear? They did what? Who told you?

CHAPTER 8

IN A HANDSHAKE

ZAPAREACHIC IS A small rancho. It is primarily composed of a single house and a few animals. It is the house that every home-decorating magazine wants on its cover. Only journalists don't want to drive three days from the United States to the Barranca del Cobre, then walk miles over dirt trails, boulders, and steep hills, to arrive at the house for a photo shoot.

They want to see beautiful hand-hewn logs that support the stone walls of the grand, thousand-square-foot multiroomed casa, but they don't want to sleep on platform beds under heavy handmade blankets with no heat, and falling snow outside.

They want to take glossy photos of the tiled porch, braced by carved tree trunks, which faces an open patio, but they don't want to jump out of the path of rooting pigs that might get mud on their suede UGGs. They want to imagine living in one of the most beautiful handmade Mexican homes ever built with corbels and rocks, but they don't want to live in remote Zapareachic, miles from nowhere, approachable only by foot or on horseback.

They want to sit around the open patio and drink sexy shots of tequila but they don't want to have to go to the river to haul up buckets of water for chasers. Zapareachic is a slice of heaven, but it's not for everyone.

Built by Maclovio, a mestizo, and his wife, Leonarda, a Rarámuri, the home stands alone in the scrub pines surrounded by white rocks and white clouds. The daughter works at home; the oldest son goes to Guachochic, a mestizo town hours away where he has a radio show, *La voz de la Sierra Tarahumara*.

Maclovio agrees that for my film he will organize a *tesguinado* by bringing in a hundred Rarámuri from the surrounding canyons. They can butcher some cows for a traditional ceremony, feed one hundred hungry people, and help me make a riveting part of the documentary right here at Zapareachic. Sounds good to me.

We gather at Casita Blanca in Norogachic. Hiram, Gabriel, Ernesto, Maclovio and his son, and Santiago, and I are here to make honest-to-god plans to film a tesguinado and a *tutuburi* ceremony of thanks, with help from a PBS camera crew from Tucson.

I sit next to Hiram because I am nervous. His calm is contagious, the natural calm of the natural world on a good day. He places his palms on the table. I mirror my hands on the table like his. I wait for our work to begin.

Spanish is far from my first language. Frankly it's laughable even though at the university I was assigned to write fiction *en español*. Little good it does me here. This is a different education.

I'm also nervous because I am the only woman. In the Sierra, I try to walk the path of a no-see-um and, at the same time, be someone who is capable of hard work and getting things done, like all the women of the land. Which is hard when I am a fool at Sierra life. I have to be taught which rocks are best to scrub Levis on, and which rocks are obviously gentler for cotton cowboy shirts.

Darkness comes early in the canyons. Gabriel lights the oil lamp on the green wooden table. We sit on chairs and barrels carried from the house down the hill. Hiram sets a bottle of tequila in the center of the table. Faces are half shadow. No one takes off his hat. I guess this is the man's world. Making deals. I wish I could aim a camera at this scene.

Hiram opens the bottle and passes the tequila. I take the smallest of sips in order to be polite, but I need to keep my wits about me.

It takes a while to get to the subject. There is talk of planting, of harvests, of drought, of neighbors, of who will be the next Rarámuri governor of Norogachic. The talk is not private talk. There are foreigners at the table, so the talk is that which can be heard by outside ears.

Finally it is my turn. I know this because everyone has stopped speaking. In the silence, they politely wait for me to begin. I say I can use your help. I am making a documentary about the old ways of the Sierra becoming new ways. I could use your help to arrange a tesguinado. Mmhmm, they nod. "I see," they say with interest, as if we have never discussed it before.

I bring up Maclovio's idea about the ceremonies at Zapareachic. He informs me that it will be a great deal of work. It will take all the men at the table plus many more to organize such an event. They will spread the word through the canyons, pin announcements to trees about the date and location. Boulders near the house need to be moved to accommodate space for so many people. Water must be secured. His personal animals must be taken care of because his family won't have time to do the daily chores with this intense endeavor.

Then there is food cost. Maclovio pulls out a piece of paper with a list on it and the cost per item: chiles at 100 pesos per kilo, salt at 80 pesos, frijoles 40,000 pesos, *jabón* 40 pesos, gasoline 500 pesos per liter, *pasta de dientes*— toothpaste? I'm paying for toothpaste? Seems that some items have slipped into this long list perhaps in the hope that I don't know the word in Spanish and it will just pass by unnoticed. I read it aloud. I say, "Oh, yes, toothpaste, good idea," and move on, agreeing to pay for it.

Corn. I must purchase a great deal of corn. In order to make tesgüino, the sour beer that accompanies all Rarámuri social and religious events, we need kilos and kilos of corn in order to ferment the beer, and prepare for the day that one hundred hard-drinking Rarámuri arrive.

Finally, after arguing over the price of several items, we reach an agreement about the list. Where is Giulio when you need him? I yearn for his producing skills, his finesse, and his command of several languages.

Hiram explains that I will have to purchase two cows for the killing ceremony, and they will need the women to set up camp where they can cook and where we will all sleep. We need tents. He says we need armed men to guard the camp. It's true that we don't want the $60,000 Beta camera stolen while we sleep. Actually, the camera will sleep next to the cameraman's head at night. Add another expense for bullets for the guards' guns.

The particulars grow and so does the cost. Hiram had spoken to me the previous day about the two cows. Each will cost $400, and I am going to buy the cows from him.

Then there are logistics. How do we get a Tucson film crew out here to make this doc? There are costs for renting two four-wheel-drive vehicles from Creel, transporting the crew, hotels, food, medical supplies. Not to mention videotapes and as many batteries as we can carry because there is nowhere to charge them—there is no electricity at Zapareachic. We will need cameras, cables, lights, and so on.

For the week it will take to prepare for and shoot the three-day ceremony, the cost will be $1,000 a day just for the residents of the Sierra who prepare the ceremony shoot. The final budget of the one-hour film will be $70,000, including production and postproduction (editing), personnel, and salaries.

But not my salary. I am to be paid if the film is picked up for distribution, after it is completed. In the real world of filmmaking, this is an embarrassingly small budget. No one in the studio system would consider this a real budget, or a real film.

In my personal world, $70,000 is an unimaginable amount of money. My world is the world of Independent Filmmaking, which runs the gamut from student films made with parents' money, to *El Mariachi* made on Robert Rodriguez's microbudget of $7,000, to Dennis Hopper's *Easy Rider*, to Francis Ford Coppola's *Apocalypse Now* tallying in at $31 million.

I think of Sandy, the pilot. She tells me there is a saying that flying is hours of boredom punctuated by moments of sheer terror. I think that applies to my life somewhat. In between fascinating and breathtaking weeks in the Sierra, there are months of tedious grant researching and writing and odd jobs to pay for the trips. Just for me to drive solo into the Sierra and stay for a couple of weeks costs a minimum of $1,800 each trip.

How am I going to get this money? With the help of Giulio, I learn to write grants, and we secure a third of the funds within the first year of production. I think, wow, this isn't bad. Soon I will have all the money I need. But that is not to be. After the initial money, I receive no funding for another year and a half. Then dollars occasionally trickle in.

I must constantly update the budget because scenes, weather, characters, and politics change. But when I go to Giulio with my updated budget, he shakes his head. How does he explain the cost of two cows to our New York funders? And who is going to pay for real bullets?

About writing grants. In order to do this you must be a little like a prostitute. You accommodate the granting agency and write anything they want to hear. The depictions of this film are endless. When applying to women's foundations, you say that the film is an inside view of the life of Rarámuri women. To get a grant from media foundations, you say it is reporting on the current sociopolitical state of the Rarámuri. For humanities grants, it is about how Rarámuri cosmology and music relate over the centuries.

It takes weeks to research which grants are the proper ones to apply for, and then days to sit down to write a good proposal. For that work, you

Kathryn Ferguson films. Photographer unknown.

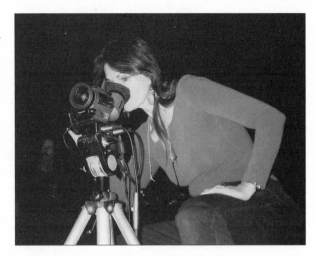

walk to the mailbox several times a week to receive letters that say, "Dear Ms. Ferguson, Thank you so much for your application. Although we find your project fascinating, we do not find it to be a fit for our organization. We wish you luck." Luck, the brutal leveler.

I plaster the wall with rejections and try not to take it personally. But thank god for granting agencies. If it weren't for them, the film would never be made.

So we pass the bottle again. This time I drink. And then drink again. I have just paid a few hundred dollars earnest money and made an agreement with men I barely know to return to the Sierra to shoot ceremonies with a hundred people I don't know at all based on a word of agreement and a handshake. I give them my word; they give me theirs. When I return in three months with a camera crew, will there be a grand ceremony? Or will I arrive to "Discúlpame pero no pude juntar a la gente" (Oh, sorry, I couldn't get it together). There are no phones.

I return to Tucson to write more grants. I sit at my desk and worry. Is this shoot really going to happen at Zapareachic? I have a fear that I will arrive with a film crew and there will be no one home. No hundred people, no camp, no tesgüino. Even though it is just one small part of the film, it is crucial.

When Santiago passes through Tucson on his way to the Barranca, I ask him to inform Hiram that I am coming Wednesday to Norogachic to finalize plans. I need to confirm the organization one more time. So far, every time Hiram gives me his word, he keeps it. How nice it is when you find someone you can trust. He is my Sierra rock and shelter.

After another long trip to Creel, I ride the Rarámuri bus to Norogachic. I am a few miles outside the pueblo, reading a book of Spanish verbs, trying not to get distracted by the passing scenery. The bus stops. I don't look up. I assume it is another stop where passengers can exit. I hear "Catalina, Catalina, ¡ven!" I look up and Maclovio is on the bus, standing by the driver, waving at me to come with him. I think this is nice. He comes to greet me. I wonder how he knows I am arriving. I guess Hiram told him. Hiram was to meet me at the arroyo and take me over to Casita Blanca.

Happily, I reach up to get my backpack and go with him. The bus continues on. Leonarda stands outside the bus with two horses and we greet each other with "¿Cómo has estado?" (How have you been?). Then they inform me that I am going to stay at their house tonight. I say thank you but I can't because Hiram is waiting for me to arrive in Norogachic. They say they will take me to Hiram's house tomorrow.

Leonarda says, "Here, this horse is for you." Then I realize there are two horses and three people. She says she will walk. I protest. I feel ridiculous riding while she walks. Am I going to sit atop the horse like a female conquistador while she walks? Too weird. But I don't seem to be in control of this situation. They strap my backpack behind the saddle. Maclovio hands me the reins and says, "Up." We have a two-hour journey ahead of us.

Leonarda walks behind in her red headband and her long blue-and-red-flowered skirt; Maclovio rides in front. The trail, flanked by scrub pines, sits narrow and flat on top of a mesa and the terra cotta–colored earth is dry and ahead are small canyons with a sky half full of cumulous clouds.

The air smells like pine even though the trees are small. Near a rock, a rattlesnake passes silently, and the horses have not sensed it as they continue with an even gait looking neither right nor left; and there is a stillness and I wonder why I am riding this horse on this unexpected journey. I am not sure this is where I want to be.

As we stop for a break, I realize this break is for me and that they can continue indefinitely with no rest. They are not tired, but my thighs are already sore from being astride a horse. I haven't ridden with Hiram for a few weeks.

I am grateful for the rest. I get off the horse, walk around, stretch, and drink water from a bottle in my backpack. Leonarda and Maclovio stand. They don't drink.

We continue for another half hour and arrive at their home in Zapa-reachic. Neither Maclovio nor Leonarda are inclined to speak often, so Maclovio leads the horses away and Leonarda takes me to a room in the log house where I deposit my belongings. There is a tall bed that fills most of the room. I unload my backpack, walk out to the porch, and sit down to watch the pigs.

I am not sure that this is not a gentle kidnapping. I sit on the edge of the porch, Rarámuri style, not speaking, just waiting. All my friendly chatter that is the custom of my people has long gone. In my culture, we fill the air with talk. Not so in every culture. The sun goes down.

Leonarda invites me to the kitchen, which is in a separate building. She has made a fire to heat the large cast-iron pot of beans on the iron stove. After she lights an oil lamp in the center of the table, she sets down three bowls with mismatched spoons. Maclovio enters, hangs his hat on a nail, and sits at the table with me. He asks about my family. I ask about his. Leonarda serves us, and after we begin eating, she joins us. I ask about the planting and harvesting. He talks about the drought.

When dinner is over, the directness of my culture takes over and I thank them for inviting me to dinner, but why did they bring me all this distance to their house?

Maclovio looks down and says it is about the cows. Then he looks up straight into my eyes and explains that he knows that Hiram and I made an agreement to buy two cows from Hiram to use in the film. He says since it is a film about Rarámuri and not Mexicans, I should buy the cows from Leonarda, a Rarámuri. I wait.

Maclovio continues to explain that Leonarda owns many fine cows and can sell them to me for a special price to use in the film. The man of the family talks business with me but in Rarámuri families it is the women who own the cattle.

I slowly begin to understand the point of my visit. I understand that gossip runs far and deep in the Sierra. I understand that I don't understand the fine lines between cultures. I understand that jealousy occurs worldwide. And I understand that if I want this film made, I need to buy Leonarda's cows.

The next morning Maclovio walks me to the outskirts of Norogachic, bids me farewell, and I find my way alone on the trail into the pueblo and on to Hiram's house. When I enter his yard, he doesn't speak. Elia comes out of the house, wipes her hands on her apron, and says come in for breakfast. I decide to first talk with Hiram.

I find him in the barn. As he hangs a rope on a hook, he looks away from me and says, "We were expecting you last night."

I explain to him about Maclovio meeting me at the bus. He is silent. I tell him I was surprised that Maclovio took me to his house. He is silent. I tell him about our conversation. He is silent. I explain to him that I want to do what is right.

With his back to me, he says, "Tú y yo tenemos un trato." I say yes, I know we have an agreement.

So I end up buying two cows from Leonarda, and I pay Hiram for a cow that he will keep, for a total of $1,200 for three cows. I don't want to harm him. He is my friend. But I want to get the film made. Keeping your word. How is that done, again? I just changed my promise to my friend and didn't buy his two cows. I am less than a beetle. As we know, beetles have no loyalty. I am ashamed.

But on the surface, this seems to satisfy all.

Now how do I explain this slowly inflating budget and this conversation in a barn on a beautiful cool Sierra day with chickens clucking and goat bells ringing to Giulio and the film investors in New York?

The Barranca del Cobre, Chihuahua. Photo by Richard Speedy.

CHAPTER 9

SCOUTING

I FIND I need to do more exploration before the major film shoot. I haven't nailed down all the locations where we will set up cameras.

Heading south in the Barranca del Cobre, we stay in warm mango land, the river town of Batopilas. At first light, we are on the trail. I am barely awake and look straight up. That glance at the switchback is the equivalent of four espressos.

Lois, a good friend from Tucson, and I travel with Santiago. We hike with his companions, Librado and Librado's son Maxi, to visit Santiago's friends in Santichique, a Shangri-La ensconced in steep canyons above the Río Batopilas.

Santichique is a Rarámuri community that entertains no one. It is a gated community, enclosed by impenetrable sheer rock walls. It is probably the most traditional enclave on the continent.

I am here to explore another part of the Barranca del Cobre and scout for another location before I bring in an expensive film crew. Santiago arranges for me to sample bits of the Barrancas so we can make appropriate selections to tell the story. He is comfy anywhere so I grab a camera and note pad and follow him. Although we are shooting important parts of the film in Norogachic and at Zapareachic, I want to see other options in the vast canyonlands.

Lois, petite and feminine with her mane of blonde hair, moves like a cat over the dramatically ascending trail. She is a private person in a public job, a personal assistant to a federal judge. Her preference in lifestyle is not the visible high-powered life of courts and legal intrigue. Instead, she prefers the mix of an Australian Shiraz or a tequila followed by a well-sung corrido in a Batopilas cantina.

The trial, I mean trail, we are about to climb is damp and slippery. Like the worn steps of Aztec pyramids, indentations are carved out of the mountainside, small smooth steps in the mountain created from years of use by Rarámuri feet.

On the road, we see a forty-year-old man carrying a post literally the size of a telephone pole that he chopped from a pine tree, carved, and now carries across his shoulders to the town of Batopilas to sell at a new hotel under construction. He has navigated this trail to bring the pole down the mountain, sometimes rolling it, sometimes carrying it on his shoulders.

Librado and Maxi are mestizos who live in Batopilas and are Santiago's longtime friends. The three of them guide visitors through the Sierra. They make expedition-type hikes from the subtropical thorn forests and sands of the Río Batopilas, up and over a 7,600-foot-high pine tree ridge sprinkled with rare white orchids, down to the Río Urique—a journey of several days.

The journey is not for the faint of heart, nor is it friendly to the quadriceps. Librado and Maxi, lifetime arrieros (muleteers), make the fire, cook everything from *caldo de queso* to cinnamon pancakes, and herd burros and patrons over awesomely rugged mountains.

Librado, thoughtful, quiet, lean as a piece of jerky, has taught his son well. They both laugh without making much noise, and Maxi takes cues from his dad. Librado almost imperceptibly nods his head in Maxi's direction, and Maxi jumps up to stir the fire or gather some wood. Seems that they speak a language that doesn't require sound.

We alternately walk along the edge of a riverbed, and then when the trail calls for it we drop down into the river, scaling boulders taller than we are. For eons, powerful water has roared through here. I think about what it will be like to bring the big camera here. The scenery is magnificent. But a camera, no matter how good, can only absorb what is in the frame, not the periphery. I think of all the great Westerns like Sam Peckinpah's *The Wild Bunch* that were shot on 70 millimeter, sometimes using six cameras for one scene.

At last, walking becomes normal. We reach level, dry ground, pine trees, and filtered sun. We rest under the trees, eat apples and nuts, and move on. As we walk, the trail narrows and the edge of the mesa appears.

I whistle in surprise as we round a corner. The safety of the tree canopy and flat land abruptly opens onto a sharp exposure of sky, a six-hundred-foot sheer drop, and a river far, far below. One moment we hike through a meadow, the next we nearly step off a cliff. As we hike the Sierra, terrain changes like morphing dreamscapes.

With another turn and one unstable step forward, I am on the edge of a cliff. I inhale sharply. Librado is in front, Lois behind him, then me, followed by Santiago and Maxi. We walk in file because the trail is a thread along the cliff's edge, with a mountain wall rising on our right and on the left a river so far below we can't hear it. We move forward.

Abruptly the trail ends in front of us. Looming ahead is a scree slope. The cliff at my right becomes an incline of erosion made of loose shale. It lists upward 50 degrees. We are separated from our trail on the other side by a ten-foot spread of whopping rockslide. On the left is the shear cliff wall that drops to the river.

There is no more trail. Nowhere to go. Fear flies at me like a demon, freezing me to the spot—muscle and thought immobile. She haunted me as a child climbing trees; she haunted me changing light bulbs from two-story ladders in the PBS studio; and today she roars back for a visit.

Everyone stops. The last thing I hear is Librado calling, "*Vámonos.*" Let's go. Then I hear nothing. I'm in a vacuum. In slow motion, I see Librado step forward in his huaraches and float over the sliding shale. In front of me, Lois hesitates. Then she swims over the rockslide, her mermaid hair floating behind. It is my turn. I can't move. I want to go back. I want to go home. I want to have a glass of wine with my Airedales on the patio. I want to read a book. I want to light a log in the fireplace. I want to put flowers in a vase. I want to start the day over, like in the movie *Groundhog Day*. I want to not be here.

I turn around. Santiago is close behind me. I say, "I can't. I'll go back to town, you all go on." He says, "No, you can't go back alone. You can do this. Just don't stop in the middle. Go."

I turn back to the rockslide. I can't move. I barely hear, "Catalina, *ven.*" From far away, Librado's voice calls. He has already leaped the gap. He says, "Come," and in the distance waves his fingers, beckoning me. I can't move. I think if I reach for his hand, I will pull him over the cliff as I fall. I try to breathe but can't seem to remember how.

I hear a whisper. "*Ven,* Catalina." Librado is standing next to me. He smiles, holds out his hand. He speaks softly to me as if I am a beloved burro that he coaxes. He forces me to look at his eyes. I take a step. He holds my hand. He walks backward. I walk forward, close to his body, an inch from his checkered shirt. I see only his black eyes. I can't look anywhere else. He puts his foot inside my foot, like we are waltzing. We take another step. We step again but I know what is ahead. A torn trail.

I don't know how long it takes or what happens but I am on the other side. Air suddenly whips around me and I can hear people talk and everything is very loud.

I hear rocks crunch and fast footsteps and I turn to see Santiago and Maxi run up and across the slide, then down toward us. I hear rocks slip over the edge. As they run, they slide downward but are on the forward trajectory toward where we stand. Their feet move but seem to go nowhere, like the cartoon roadrunner. Then blessed traction takes hold and suddenly, they are standing beside us. Rocks continue to slide behind us, where the essence of Santiago and Maxi hangs. Now they are here but could have been riding the rocks down to the river. I don't like this place.

We turn to walk. I stay close to Santo Librado. Tears start down my cheeks as we move forward along the trail. He is too polite to turn and glance back at me.

As we enter Shangri-La, the unroaded village of Santichique nestles in a narrow corridor of unclimbable, sheer red cliff walls that shoot up 1,500 feet. They are smooth and shine like petrified wood.

We are in a deep, narrow canyon, but the trail widens as we walk through an orchard of oranges. Ahead, the corridor opens to a more forgiving landscape of a running stream and *trincheros*, low stone walls that contain narrow plots of corn and keep goats at home.

Above Santichique are bubbling springs that spill over into a swimming hole, where we sit and eat more oranges than I thought possible. I can't stop eating them, because they taste the way oranges are supposed to taste, not like the ones in my neighborhood grocery store.

Nearby are velvet-blue and -black magpie jays, whose photos adorn the cover of every book about Mexican ornithology. Occasionally a reclusive Elegant Trogon stops in to visit.

For twenty years, this has been Santiago's special home. When he is in the village, his friend, the first governor, invites him to be part of tribal council meetings. And Santiago is godfather to the second governor's three children.

We are fed well and treated like royalty for the day. When it comes time to leave, we are gifted so many oranges we look like walking citrus trees on the trail.

We return to Batopilas, where word on the street is, don't mess with the pueblo of Santichique unless you want your ass whooped. Back in the day, the Rarámuri were known as powerful wrestlers. Those of us who see only what we want to see wrote the popular description of the Rarámuri people as being shy and quiet. Fortunately, the people of Santichique are as quick to tell a joke as to toss you to the ground—two efficient ways to handle intruders.

But after being in Batopilas canyons, I think this is for a future movie, not the one I am making. Like the trip with Sandy and the Mexican Navy, I like the idea of filming here but not the actuality of it. I need to narrow my focus and just stick with the land and people around Norogachic. The documentary will be better with Ventura and Hiram, and not overloaded with too many locales. Besides, I like hanging out with my friends.

I return to Tucson to do paperwork. I type at my desk. The phone rings.

"Hello," I answer.

Crackling noise, pause, then, "Will you accept a call from Ventura Pacheco Leon?"

"Yes, of course."

A few moments, then "¡Bueno, Catalina! ¡Catalina!"

"¡Ventura, qué sorpresa! ¿Cómo estás?" What a surprise! How are you?

"¿Así me recuerdas?" So you remember me? he asks. I had seen him three weeks earlier.

"Qué loco eres, Ventura." How crazy you are, Ventura.

"Llamo de Creel." I am calling from Creel.

"What are you doing in Creel?" I am wondering why he is calling. I gave him my phone number when we first met and told him to call collect whenever he wanted. Something's up. It is a big effort for Ventura to leave his home and travel five hours on a rickety low-geared bus over rock-strewn dirt roads just to get to the town of Creel to find a phone.

As usual, we don't get to the point right away. We talk about the weather, what is going on in Creel, how is the family. Finally he tells me that Bob, the Evangelist in charge of the religious group in Choguita, knocked on Ventura's door to talk about the film I am making. (The last time I was there, Bob told me to take the damned camera and get away from his house, which, perhaps he had forgotten, is Ventura's house. At the time, I thought Bob to be merely a grumpy guy.)

According to Ventura, Bob stood at the door of Ventura's house and told him that I am exploiting Ventura and his family. That when the documentary is complete, I will earn a million dollars for the film. The documentary will go to Hollywood, then screen in theaters throughout the United States. And Ventura and the Rarámuri people will receive nothing.

"¡Dios mío, Ventura! Andas preocupado?" My god, Ventura, are you worried?

"Dime, Catalina, ¿es la verdad?" Tell me, Kathryn, is it true?

Of course not, I say. I explain that all I am doing is spending all my money to make the film. I explain about grant money, which I told him about previously. If grant money arrives, I turn around and use it on the trips to the Sierra. I tell him I also work extra jobs to pay for trips.

I tell him that in my culture I am on the bottom of the ladder economically. I say that when the film is finished, if no one likes the film, it will sit on a shelf in the closet and all the work will be for nothing. If a distributor picks it up, I will be lucky to even earn back what I have spent. I say that most people have a misconception that all Americans are rich. I blah blah blah and run out of words and am stunned at what black seed has been planted in his mind.

I ask if he is unhappy with our financial agreement or the filming. He says no, he is not unhappy. I remind him that we will show the finished documentary in the Sierra.

We end the conversation on a friendly note but my stomach hurts for days. I just want to give Ventura a big hug. So I plan another trip to his house to make sure he is all right. It means I have to do a few housecleaning jobs, get a dog sitter, and pay someone to teach my dance classes. But he is a great guy and I don't want to lose a friendship over a stranger's strange words. Sierra gossip is powerful.

As much as I love being in the Sierra Madre, I begin to dread the trips. Unlike the first few trips, it is not so much a grand adventure where every turn in the road is new and exciting. It becomes a difficult and repetitive journey. It costs a lot to make the trip and I get exhausted driving alone for ten hours at a time. But I feel I have to go see Ventura out of friendship.

After more preparations and a long drive, I finally arrive at his house. His wife makes coffee and we sit on a bench. Ventura pulls up a chair across from me, settles into it, and reaches for his Bible. I think, uh-oh, have I misbehaved so badly that I deserve a sermon? I wonder if this has to do with the conversation over the phone.

Ventura opens the black leather Bible with *Santa Biblia* written in gold letters on the cover. It reminds me of the Bible that door-to-door salesmen tried to sell my mother. We ended up with several in our house even though they were expensive because she just couldn't say no to those earnest, slick-haired boys who talked of salvation.

Ventura opens to the middle of the book. Instead of reading, he pulls out a photo of Max, my Airedale. In the photo, I sit in a chair under a bougainvillea-covered ramada at my house with oversize Max sitting next to me.

Ventura says he looks often at this photo. He likes Max. He says he never saw a dog like Max. With black and tan wiry curls sprouting around Max's face, his head is larger than mine. When he sits next to me, he is as tall as the chair I sit in.

Is he good for anything? Ventura asks. Yes, he is a good watchdog, I say. And in Wilcox, a town a couple of hours east of Tucson, a Chinese man raises Airedales for hunting, then hunters rent them to catch bears. The Airedale trees the bear and with unyielding tenacity keeps the bear up the tree. I say that Max also has a good sense of humor. I point out that he behaves just like Ventura.

Ventura says he hopes to someday meet the Chinese man. He hopes to someday leave the Sierra forever and go to the city to live, maybe Tucson or Ciudad Chihuahua. He wants a better life and knows that the city is the answer. His Tuscany.

He explains that his children can get jobs. Maybe he can find a dog like Max to guard their house in the city. I don't mention that Ciudad Chihuahua is full of Rarámuri sitting on the sidewalks begging for coins.

He tells me he is going to cross the border and meet me in the Arizona desert. He tells me I can come get him and take him to my house. The desert is not the Sierra. How will he find his way? I ask. This kind of talk makes me nervous.

I read in the Tucson newspaper of growing migrant deaths on the Arizona desert. It is a death no one wants. You die of dehydration, a slow, agonizing shrinking of organs. It can easily be a sixty-mile walk without water. It is impossible to carry enough. A gallon of water weighs eight pounds and a person needs a minimum of a gallon a day walking in extreme heat. A body can lose up to two quarts of water per hour hiking in the desert in the middle of the day. The walk from the border to Tucson can be more than twelve days, depending where you start, an additional weight of at about a hundred pounds. I tell him not to cross; we will think of some other way.

We drink our coffee and make plans for the day in Choguita.

CHAPTER 10

FILMING THE FESTIVAL

FINALLY THE TIME arrives. The crew—a cameraman, a grip, and a gaffer—arrive in Creel. I thought we would be shooting this the first year. Four years later, we're ready for our first big shoot.

Bill Yahraus, a filmmaker friend from Los Angeles, joins us to advise me as a director, take production stills, and just be an all-round pillar of experience. He and his wife, Robin Rosenthal, make documentaries. Bill edits major motion pictures, was executive producer of Sam Shepard's *Silent Tongue*, and has a bit of dry British humor tucked into his ancestral map.

I have arranged for an extra jeep and a local driver. With all the gear packed into two 4x4s, we leave Creel and head out to Zapareachic on a road so rough it takes five hours to go fifty miles.

After about an hour and a half on the boulder-strewn dirt road, we smell heat. Our driver is concerned. A little smoke rises from under the hood of the jeep. We get out of the car to inspect. Water drips from the radiator. The jeep is not well and needs to go home. The driver says he can fix it. He asks if we have soap. I just happen to have a bar of almond soap. He rubs it hard over the fins of the radiator core, stopping up the perforation where water seeps out. It is a little less useful than smearing gum all over the radiator.

The soap stops the leak for a few more rugged miles and then water gushes forth with a fury. End of journey for the jeep. Where is chewing gum when you need it, I think, as I try to figure out what to do next. And I am embarrassed. Bill, a real producer, probably thinks I am a yoyo not to have preplanned for disaster. But he smiles and relaxes as he sits down on a rock to watch the first dilemma.

Since we have two vehicles, we decide to send one ahead to the site of the fiesta while the driver gets the broken jeep back to Creel to exchange it for

87

one that works. There is no room in our other vehicle for everyone, so Santiago, his friend Chandler, and the driver stay behind to take care of the disabled jeep. Bill, Dan the cameraman, soundman Jacobo, and I leave them standing by the side of the road in the middle of nowhere. I wonder if we will see them today or the next. So begins the shoot.

After a few hours, we arrive in Choguita to give Ventura a ride to the festival. He grins, ready to see his friends from the hinterlands, whom he hasn't seen for a long while. He is groomed, wears his favorite blue shirt and a cachucha covering his thick white hair.

We hear the sound of drums coming from a neighbor's house. Dan wants to see the drum, so we walk to the neighbor's house. A short Rarámuri woman who weighs about 250 pounds sits on the ground playing a large round tambor. It is a wood frame with goatskin stretched over it. Little black goat hairs wave across the stretched skin.

Dan says he likes the drum. She smiles. Like many Rarámuri women, she speaks her language and not much Spanish, but Dan, fluent in Spanish, gets his point across. She says no deal. He says OK. We start to leave.

She says wait, maybe her son has one he would like to sell. Dan asks how much. "How much can you pay?" she asks. This goes on for a while. They agree on a price. Her daughter runs, literally, over a hill and disappears. The woman tells us she has gone to get the son's drum.

We wait. I am anxious. We need to be at Maclovio's. I still don't know if the festival is arranged, if there are people there, if the film is going to happen. My stomach is in knots. We sit on the ground and wait.

At last, a young man strolls over the hill beating a drum with a deep *da doom da doom*. We stand up. The woman remains seated in the dirt. Her son hands her the drum. She tells Dan that it is no longer for sale. Oh no, I think, not now. We have to leave.

Dan says, "I thought we had a deal."

She says, "What else can you give me?"

He says, "What do you need?"

She says, "A dance."

He looks perplexed.

She says, "Dance for me, then you can buy it." She settles her full body on the ground into a mountain of folds in her skirt, discreetly covering her outstretched legs, takes the drum and drumstick from her son, and beats the goatskin. Dan looks at Ventura, who has no expression, and then at me, then he shrugs and starts dancing a samba. He's an Anglo who lived for years in Brazil and dances a mean samba.

The woman thinks this is the funniest thing she has ever seen and lies on her back in the dirt and laughs, still playing the drum over her ample belly.

Dan gets his drum, the woman gets her laugh, and we jump into the jeep.

We drive up the road as far as we can, get out of the vehicle, and walk toward Maclovio's house. I smell wood burning on a fire. With greatest relief, I see vaqueros clearing camp, women stirring humongous pots of tesgüino, and a few Rarámuri men hanging out together smoking cigarettes. It is happening. After all this time, it is actually happening. What we agreed upon moons ago with a handshake in Casita Blanca is happening. I'm so happy I could dance a samba, too.

Smoke of burning pine directs my eyes to a bonfire as big as a bedroom, which will burn down to a smaller fire that will eventually cook carne asada, frijoles, and tortillas for more than a hundred people.

It's a circus. At the edge of the scene, Maclovio gathers compadres to move large boulders to finish a little yard work. He wants a small wall built to surround his property while there are men "in town" to move heavy rocks with crowbars and muscle.

In another area, amid much laughter, men use small sticks to dot little spots of red ochre over the white-painted bodies of the *pascoleros,* two men whose entire bodies are painted with colored clay and black ash, after being ritually washed. This washing is usually closed to outside observers because it is a religious ritual overseen by "true believers," those men with little white crosses on their foreheads.

While the pascoleros are painted, a gourd of tesgüino, fermented corn beer that fuels a variety of Rarámuri activities, is passed around. With tesgüino in tow, they build houses, cook meals, and gather for religious ceremonies. My culture sees drinking as a vice. The Rarámuri regard tesgüino as both common and sacred. Vice is a concept created by my inventive people.

Women carry a small wooden table outdoors to be used in the middle of the night for the tutuburi, the owl ceremony. After steers are sacrificed, the scalps are removed. Later during the night, scalps will be set on the table altar. Behind the altar, three human-size crosses stand side by side, covered in gauze fabric. Out of the darkness, fabric hangs like a shroud behind scalps

Tutuburi *ceremony. Photo by Bill Yahraus.*

of blood and fresh hair, and soon a low voice will chant, gourds will rattle, and I will expect ancestors to appear.

Later when we film this, I will feel nervous in the cold night. Beyond the glow of fire sits darkness that has waited at the edge since early man first danced, as three men will dance tonight. I am told that the shuffles and stomps keep bad spirits below ground. But I wonder if good spirits might appear in their stead. The prediction is for a spirit kind of night with moving clouds, shadows, and whispers from beyond the edge of vision.

But that is to come later. Right now, above us is a clear blue sky. As I look to the hills, I see a white trail snake from a dense line of trees. Here they come. Like the flame-breasted fruit dove, red flickers from headbands as Rarámuri walk out of the pines, down the trails toward Maclovio's house.

They are really coming. One or two at a time. Then a family. A few men and children ride horses with long-skirted women walking behind. More than a hundred Rarámuri walk from homes days away, through mountains and canyons to join the festival.

We are finally going to film three age-old ceremonies: the painting of the pascoleros, the tutuburi, and the killing of the steers. Rarámuri families arrive for days of celebration and thanksgiving at having survived murderous conquistadores, droughts, crop-killing freezes, and tourists.

Leonarda's daughter, a dark-haired beauty who always dresses in traditional clothes, walks toward me carrying a bundle in her arms.

"We have a gift for you," she smiles.

I unfurl the bundle. It is a Rarámuri blouse and skirt, mostly bright green with scores of tiny yellow and red flowers traversing the fanlike pleats.

"You must wear it for today's ceremonies and then take it home with you."

Hmmm. What a lovely gift. But my mind is jagged with details of the shooting schedule, if we have enough tape and batteries for three days, should I check the audio again, where is the boom mic, will the sunlight be too bright all day, where did I put the aspirin, and where should we shoot the conversation with the women? Putting on a dress and eyeliner and fixing my hair is almost beyond me at the moment.

I say thank you and go into my tent. I can't stand upright because the tent is low. Bent over, I change into the skirt and blouse. The only shoes I have are either sneakers or boots, not the handsome huaraches worn by Rarámuri women. Thank goodness I shaved my legs. But gracious, are they white! Somehow the green dress doesn't look as nice against pallid skin. Bent over, I comb my hair back into a ponytail, adjust the skirt, and feel stupid. How am I going to direct a film and maintain the respect of an all-male crew in this getup? But of course I have to wear it.

I finish grooming and return to the center of activity. I wear the boxy blouse, wide-pleated skirt, and boots, feeling lost in volumes of fabric. Like Alice when she became tiny.

"¡Oye, Guapa!" Hey beautiful! yells Ventura, followed by a bellow of a laugh. A grin from the cameraman, giggles from the women. Bill snaps a photo. Most people don't say a word.

Hiram nods approval, walks over to me, and whispers that he always wonders why I don't wear dresses. Apparently, he had disapproved of my Levis all these years. They are not as fine as dresses, he explains. He likes his women feminine, his horses true. Yes, all mestiza and Rarámuri women in the Sierra wear skirts or dresses, whether working outside, cooking, chopping wood, mopping, climbing hills, or giving birth in the field.

As I look around at the activity, I realize that everyone has toiled long days in preparation and will continue the labor for a few more. They have carried huge cauldrons in which to ferment the tesgüino, but I have no idea how they got them to the house. Everything is carried on the back or on burros.

Someone has cleared the land around the home of plants and boulders so that a hundred people can sit together. Dishes and tables were carried long distances for food preparation. Horses and burros are tied to posts and trees. Drums beat, smoke rises, laughter rings, and people arrive.

It is time to film the ceremony. A steer has been brought to the side of Maclovio's house. Under glare from a round sun shines a light that is not round but spreads over us like a blanket of mirrored dust, a sunlight that flashes from knife blade to eye. Two vaqueros move to their positions. They walk to the mottled-skin novillo, the steer. One loads a shell into the chamber of a .22 caliber rifle. One throws a loop around the novillo's neck and backs away to the end of the long, slack rope. The skinny animal jerks his head and casts a wary glance skyward at the empty air above him, distracted by whatever invisible affair cattle might be perturbed by.

The vaquero with the rifle standing twenty yards away straightens his spine, lifts the rifle, aims, pulls the trigger with a sharp pop, and misses. The novillo bolts at the sound. He pivots on his rear hooves, shooting puffs of dust into the air. The other vaquero tugs the long rope and pulls the novillo into place again, to the spot where he is to die. A crowd of Rarámuri stand around to watch, kids sit on a boulder poking each other, women eat tortillas, men shout advice.

The vaquero aims again and shoots. A second time, his bullet misses the mark.

"¡Qué mala puntería!" What a bad shot, a man calls out.

"No sabes desperar." You don't know how to shoot, another man calls. "The steer doesn't want to die," shouts another.

A man walks over, takes the rifle, steps closer to the novillo, aims at his head, and fires the tiny .22 bullet. The novillo lets out a cry and jumps in the smallest way. He turns quickly, stops, and looks confused. In slow motion, he turns his head toward the crowd, and then tilts his head down. He lifts his hoof, takes a momentary step forward as if nothing happened, as if there is no bullet in his brain, then begins his doomed run for life away from the direction of the humans. He hurtles forward, lurches sideways, and sprints as the man drops the rope. Vaqueros and children run after him; men whistle and shout directions to the novillo like "Stop!" and "Come!"

Dan the cameraman, a consummate professional, follows the novillo, filming every twist and turn. With the heavy Betacam aimed close, he runs alongside the animal, who charges with amazing speed in his quest to hold onto life.

The novillo, moving as fast as he can, runs headfirst into a pine tree. Dan says, "Jesus!" as the novillo ricochets off the tree and resumes running, one knee buckling under him. He rises, stumbles, and runs.

He passes through sunlight and tree shade, zigzagging like a captive fish frightened by his reflection on the wall of a tank. He passes through sunlight and shade from life he knows toward death he knows not. I run beside the cameraman. Hiram runs beside me. I say to him, "Can't they just shoot him again and stop all this?" He shakes his head. Even though this is the way of the neighborhood, I see by the shake of his head and the set of his mouth that classy Hiram thinks this is not well executed. But it is not *his* neighborhood. The Rarámuri live here.

Eventually the novillo falls and doesn't rise again.

Hiram and Maclovio prepare a second novillo. As the vaqueros approach, it trots away. A Rarámuri man chases the animal on foot, twirling a riata. The lasso sails through the air and lands around the animal's scrawny neck, as it should. Hiram, Maclovio, and Ernesto charge the novillo from the front, causing him to run side to side in bewilderment.

As the novillo pivots, the Rarámuri digs his heels into the ground and wrestles it down to its side with a thud, professional-rodeo style. The novillo struggles. Hiram, Maclovio, and Ernesto rush in to triangle the legs and bind four hooves together as the novillo's bony rib cage heaves, his torso attempting to leap off the ground.

The men pull back, running out the ends of the ropes, tethering the novillo in the fashion of the little people who fasten Gulliver to the earth. The choreography moves according to history's plan, the dance of food from blood to mouth from caveman to cowboy, the dance of the hunt since the Paleolithic.

Leonarda brings a tin bucket to the scene and sets it down by the novillo's moist nose. Hiram pulls out a boning knife and bends low to the novillo. Like a surgeon, he makes one swift slice across the novillo's throat. With a small jerk, the animal twists his head up to look at Hiram. In slow motion he lays his head back to the earth, one side of the face up toward the sky. As blood moves with the moon, rises and falls with the tide, so it rolls from throat to bucket, not a trickle but a wave. The novillo watches with a single eye, a bulging ball, which rolls from top to bottom, watches as if this were not happening to him, as if he were separate from the blood running from his neck.

Maclovio, in ceremonial headband, dips his metal spoon into the bucket of blood and faces east. He sings a thank-you for the many blessings his people have received. He tosses the orchid blood onto white stones. He stoops again for another spoonful of blood. He faces north to speak thanks, then repeats to the west and the south, each time tossing the blood high in a crimson-tailed arc. The song of thanks hangs in the air like a prism as golden blood splats to the ground like the pot of gold at the end of the rainbow. All will eat today.

As if we are in a dissection laboratory, the ground is cleared and swept to prepare for the lengthy operation. The animals are laid out on the ground side by side. For each carcass, the heart is removed and blessed by Maclovio, and organs are placed on a platter. The horned scalp is removed and taken to the table, made sacred for the night's tutuburi.

Hiram makes a shallow slice and the skinning begins. With keen fingers and sharp instruments, he flays the length of the animal, removes skin from membrane. Long after orders are barked to his assistants, followed by focused silence and rapid wrist work, slabs of meat are ready to cut and cook.

After hours of filming, I stand in a circle with Rarámuri and mestizos. Leonarda hands me a plate of carne asada and beans. Maclovio tells me thank you for providing today's food. Hiram stands next to me. He smiles at me and nudges my elbow. I realize that I am supposed to take the first bite. I can't. After watching the slow killings, I can't. But I do. I say thank you and chew the meat, as tough as Cuauhtémoc's fighting heart, the novillos' revenge. It is the last meat I am able to eat for two years.

CHAPTER II

VENTURA'S HOME

AFTER FILMING THE ceremonies, I return to Tucson to begin editing. I am on the last leg of the documentary, compiling more than six years of film, video, photos, and audio. I need to spend even more time on editing and marketing—who would ever have suspected that this would turn into a seven-year project?

For almost a year, I work side by side with Sean Sandefur, an off-line editor recommended to me by Giulio. We hire a translator to transcribe Spanish, English, and Rarámuri. We transfer still photos to video, hammer scenes together, and create and shoot needed B-roll in Tucson: necessary footage of dirt, gravel, chairs, swatches of color. And at a sound studio we record a preacher's voice and a female chorus of gossip that play a major part in the finished documentary.

We send Super 8 film stock off to Boston to be transferred to video. We discover "found footage," meaning we accidentally observe that a few seconds of footage we had discarded adds depth if juxtaposed with another moment we find on the cutting-room floor. It is like putting together a puzzle that never ends until you finally say, "OK, OK, this works."

Since this is a nontraditional documentary, we want to test it on an audience to see how it plays. I invite some acquaintances—an anthropologist, a man seeking his PhD in film, a Cherokee filmmaker friend, and a few people who merely have an interest in the Sierra—to my house to screen the rough cut.

An acquaintance, a Belgian chef, offers to help with the screening. In Spa, Belgium, where kings and queens used to submerge themselves in the town's famous fountain of youth, the Belgians believe that a tasty morsel should be given to guests on all occasions. So the chef whips up royal plates of food for my guests. He and Sean and I prepare for the big day of our first screening.

Sunday afternoon, we set up a screen and projector, place chairs around the room, set out the food, plates, and silverware, and wait for the test audience. They trickle in. We tell everyone to help themselves to food. Only one person takes a plate of hors d'oeuvres. No one else is interested. Most are in a hurry and have other places to go, they inform me. It's beginning to feel more like an In-N-Out Burger event.

Everyone grabs a chair and we briefly introduce the rough cut, explaining that the documentary is a hybrid of traditional and experimental, and not yet finished. We would like feedback.

We show the film. When it's over, no one says anything. A very long pause. "Any observations?" I ask. The PhD candidate says, "You need a map at the beginning." I say, "A map of what?" He says, "The places where the film occurs." The last thing I want is for an audience to see yet another documentary about Indians that begins with a map. I thank him. No one says anything.

Finally, a woman says, "It needs a voice-over explaining everything." "Everything?" I ask. "Pretty much everything," she answers. The Cherokee filmmaker says, "You need to show the lineage, the history of the Rarámuri." I say, "Oh, that's been done in every other film I have seen about them. Do you think it needs to be done again?" "Absolutely," he answers. And so the afternoon goes. Everyone hates it. Only the anthropologist says, "It is the way it is down there. This film feels like when you live there." Shortly after that, everyone scampers out. No kind words, a feast of untouched food.

Sean and I can barely talk or even look at each other. I say, "I'm sorry. It's my fault. I'm not a filmmaker. I'm sorry I got you into this."

He says, "I guess I'm not an editor." I know he is an excellent editor so that reinforces my role as a bad producer, bad scriptwriter, bad director, and all. How pretentious to think I can make a movie. We sit without speaking. Then we agree we are going to drop the project.

It is a terrible afternoon.

I go to my room for about a week and don't talk to anyone. I am sad that after all these years the film doesn't work and I have no way to fix it. There is no reason to spend more money to finish a bad movie. For the first few days and entire nights, I try to rework the film in my head and on paper. I take 8½-by-11-inch pieces of white paper, write titles of scenes, words, music, and draw images on them.

I boil tea on the wood-burning stove in the living room. I put my face over the pot. I inhale vapor to drown the scorpions in my head. There are shadows in the corner and snakes on the couch.

For the past few years, I have spent time alone waking to dawns of ideas and sunrises of clarity. But now I am alone in the mud. I want to fill my mind with cities of revelers and continents of creativity, make a Felliniesque film of passion and life. Instead, I tape pieces of white paper to the wall of an empty room.

At 11 p.m. of the third night of my solitary confinement, I discover how it will work. I lay all the paper around the dance-studio floor and have a vision of the final film. Soon I am taping papers to the wall again like pieces of a puzzle with music written on top of riverbeds, cornfields rolling by under Ventura's explanation of the owl of death, and so on. I can see the entire film.

The next morning, I wake, drink coffee, walk into the dance room, and look at the walls plastered in paper. What was I thinking? This version is terrible. My grand plan is confusing as well as redundant. It is an even worse movie.

At the end of the week, I give up. I sit in a long, hot bath until the water turns cold, get out of the bath, put on a warm bathrobe, and drink a bottle of wine. The next morning, I wake up no better than at the beginning of the week. And with a hangover.

Finally, I look at my phone messages and return one of Sean's eleven calls. He comes over to the house. He says, "This is crazy. We can do it. Let's just start."

So we do. We slog through the rough cut for another eight months, sitting side by side reworking the entire film. After it is finished, we take the rough cut to online master editor Henry Rubin, who works his magic using a high-tech editing suite and shapes the piece into a fine finished production.

It works as a documentary and as a piece of art. I'm not sure how it happened, but I know it never would have happened if it hadn't been for Dan the cameraman, Bill Yahraus, Sean, Henry, Ventura, Maclovio, Hiram, Santiago, the women of the Barrancas, the singers, and Giulio and Claudia and the Screening Room, and many more. A movie is a people process.

But while all the editing is rushing along, I make another trip to Ventura's to show him photos of the ceremonies and get some much-needed, final B-roll of ranchos and his home that will put the icing on the cake, the last piece of the puzzle that will make the film pop. I need a shot of the burro that stands inside the door of Ventura's house, his daughter's dollhouse made of Saran wrap, and a riverbed with round, white rocks.

That is the luxury of making a documentary. You can add one more ingredient. In feature films, you can't add another scene because movie sets are created at great cost, production is allowed an allotted number of weeks in order to meet a budget, the film is shot, and the crew strikes the set. If you discover in editing that you need one more perfect shot, it's too late.

It feels good to get out of Tucson again. After two days of travel, I arrive at the crest of the hill. I look down into the valley toward Ventura's house. No smoke. That is unusual. There is always smoke from the wood-burning barrel, smoke that floats into the sky from the stovepipe on top of his roof. I drive down to the house. No one runs out to greet me.

I get out of the truck and walk around calling his name. I bang on the front door even though there is a latched padlock. The house the Evangelists rented stands empty, too.

I walk up the hill to a neighbor's house. The man explains that Ventura and his family moved to Ciudad Chihuahua. I knew he wanted to leave the Sierra and live like city people. A step up in life, more opportunity for his children. I guess he finally reached his dream. Funny that he never mentioned he was moving.

The neighbor doesn't seem to know anything else other than that he is taking care of Ventura's burro and goats; more likely he just doesn't want to talk to a gringa. I walk over to another neighbor, who gives me the name of a minister in Ciudad Chihuahua who is an acquaintance of Ventura's.

Armed with a skinny slip of paper with a couple of names on it, I finish the shooting I need to do and go to Ciudad Chihuahua. I'm excited to see Ventura's new setup. After a tiring drive out of the Sierra, I enter the city, which is only about seven hours from Ventura's house. But it seems that the drive takes a week.

As I move through Ciudad Chihuahua's convoluted street system that connects rivers, three hills surrounding the city, colonias, municipal buildings, businesses, museums, and heavy traffic, I finally realize I am lost and tired and take a hotel for the night. The next morning I drive around the medieval European–style "one-way" maze of streets and eventually find the small curbside church of the Evangelists. I talk to a volunteer who knows

Ventura. They give me another slip of paper with an address located in a huge barrio at the edge of the city.

As I drive past old colonial buildings and the big cathedral, I feel I am on a journey through the maze of Mexican history. During the colonial era, Ciudad Chihuahua was a place where missionaries met to strategize battles for souls of the Rarámuri. The colonial-era missionaries would slowly travel to and from the nearby Barranca del Cobre with plans to save the souls of the *cimarrones*, the unbaptized Indians.

Why is it that someone is always trying to save these people? And what is this idea about "unbaptized" people? Does being baptized make a person more "holy" or "unholy"? I find the terminology insulting. As I drive, I think maybe we should call the film about Ventura *The Unholy Tarahumara*. One reason is because of the confounding and arrogant belief that the Rarámuri people were pagans and needed saving, and another is because Ventura is a standout devil's advocate, a one-of-a-kind, no matter what culture he is from. And we should use *Tarahumara* instead of *Rarámuri* because the former is the common name. I'll run it by Sean.

The next day I look for the house where Ventura is living. I find the colonia, then the street. A few women walk down the road with plastic bags. Dogs wander. It is a regular Mexican barrio, with many small houses jammed against each other. Of course there are no numbers on the houses so I start asking. Finally a man says, "Oh, you're looking for the Indian with one leg? He lives over there." One leg. "¿Qué dijiste?" What did you say, I ask, thinking I misunderstood. He repeats, shrugs and walks away. I am worried.

I cross the dirt street to a small frame house with a few rocks lying in front of the door. The outside walls are coated with gray plaster, and a track of cement drips down a dusty window like a termite trail.

Jutting up from cinder blocks of an unfinished wall is the ubiquitous metal rebar seen throughout Mexico like fields of yucca spines. A doll with a half head of curly blonde hair lies in front of the door on hard-packed dirt. I knock. A face looks out the window. The door opens and Catalina, Ventura's daughter, steps back, simultaneously smiling and looking at the ground. She wipes long bangs from her eyes.

I look into the room. Ventura sits on the floor with one and a half legs splayed out in front of him. I say, "¡Ventura! ¡Soy Catalina!" He smiles and says, "What took you so long?" His booming preacher's voice no longer booms.

We are all so surprised to see each other. I'm surprised I found the house. Ventura and his family are shocked I am here. We haven't seen each other in months.

I sit. His wife brings me water in a chipped coffee mug. Ventura says something in Rarámuri to Catalina. The fifteen-year-old girl walks through a door and returns with her newborn son. They are all proud. Ventura revives. Gaining more energy than when I first entered the house, he beams.

He tells me to hold the child. I hold the baby, who starts peeing on me. They bring a dusty shirt for me to wipe the warm liquid off my chest and dry my wet blouse. A young man with a bowl-cut hairdo who looks to be about sixteen years old walks in from the other room. He sits down and doesn't say anything. Ventura says he is the father.

I can't believe his leg is gone.

"¿Qué pasó?" I ask, nodding toward the missing leg.

"*Es el diabetes.* They said I didn't have a choice. A doctor here volunteered to do it, so we came to Chihuahua and he took my leg. I don't know where he put it."

"Do I look like a beggar?" he adds. Lying near him is a polished wood stick, not really a cane. With help from his wife and the stick, he gets off the floor and sits in a chair.

"No, Ventura. Not like a beggar; like a king with your scepter." I don't know the Spanish word for scepter so we fish around languages a bit as Ventura returns to his familiar personality as teacher. He waves the stick and starts ordering his family to do this and that. I relax a little.

We talk for hours. The family has been in the city several months. It is not what he thought, he says. "There is no way to get money here, either. And no way to travel around the city. You have to depend on others to find your way. And so many people. And so expensive."

"I am too old to be here," he explains. "The city is for young people. I want to return to the rancho."

I don't know what to say. This all makes me sad. I don't know how to make it better.

After spending a warm time with Ventura, I leave his house happy that I saw him but disturbed at his situation. I return to Tucson. A few months later, I walk to my mailbox in front of my house. I pull out the mail, flip through a couple of bills, and see a handwritten envelope addressed to me. It is from Santiago, postmarked El Paso.

I stand by the mailbox to read the three-page letter written in longhand. Ventura is dead, Santiago is sorry to inform me. I reread the sentence. The rest of the pages don't matter, something about how the doctors wanted to remove his other leg, but, instead, Ventura wanted to go home to the Sierra. They did indeed wrap him up like a piece of cheese, tying the brown burlap around his corpse with rope like an item in the *carnicería*, the butcher's shop. They lowered him into the ground.

Months later, I feel a need to be where Ventura lived and died. I return to Choguita to find the little white cross with his name painted in black letters, Ventura Pacheco León, marking his spot of earth on the hill above his home. It is next to other little white crosses. I stand above his home looking down the hill at a barren spot of earth where his log house used to be. Nothing remains. The tin has been removed from the roofs of his three buildings, each log has been taken, and the outhouse wood is gone. There is simply nothing there. A few weeds flourish where the kitchen stood. It is as if it never happened. Eight years never happened for me. A life never happened for him.

At home on my desk, I have a Rolodex full of dead people. The dead sit there among the living, indistinguishable. I can't throw away those little dog-eared cards with addresses and most recent phone numbers and intimate notes jotted from conversations with people that are gone. If I throw them away, they will be gone forever. On Ventura's card I had written, "likes oranges."

It is like what happened to my friend. Her husband left a humorous recording on their telephone answering system, telling people to leave a message. After a long illness, he died. My friend kept replaying the message to hear his voice. One day as she was replaying it, she accidentally erased it. She panicked and tried to retrieve it, but his voice was gone forever. She slipped down into a crevasse so deep she couldn't eat or drink or think, learning what it means to be alone as she banged into walls along her downward spiral.

We hold tight to threads of voice, or a dog-eared Rolodex card with a name scrawled on it, in an attempt to defy the cold blast of forever. For months I am sad about Ventura. We were a generation and two languages apart but he was a special man.

The final time I see him I am asleep. I am in a house that has partial walls and a roof. Wind blows through the rooms. The house, the desert outside, the small scrub plants, everything including me is the color of a camel, and the sun rides low in a bronze sky.

The house is made of wood with screened porches, and fine powdered sand blows through the screens. Ventura walks into the house with no announcement. I am surprised and happy. I say, "I thought you had died." He laughs and says, "No, I feel good," and sits down. He tells me I should dust the table as he sits in a wooden chair and pushes my grandmother's oil lamp to the center.

"¡Qué bárbaro!" How barbarian. "Don't you have electricity?" he asks. We talk about this and that, and as we gossip I notice that sand swirls around his feet.

Eventually he says, "Let's go outside." I think we are going to take one of our long walks where we just stroll around and hang out. Instead, he walks ahead of me rapidly. I see through the back of his head that he is smiling. He is relaxed and walks in an unhurried way but I can't catch up to him. I call out, "Wait, Ventura." I walk faster. A brown dog appears and follows Ventura into the desert through mesquite shrubs. Everything is covered in sand. I call to Ventura, "Don't go yet," and follow him. He keeps walking. I run after him. "Wait!" I call. I can't keep up.

In front of him, all the air is a sandstorm that floats to the corners of the horizon. He walks into it. His clothing cracks into small crystal flecks, as his physical being breaks apart into fine grains of sand like a puzzle coming undone. I can no longer tell the man from the sand. The dog trails him, following nothing. I wonder if he knows Ventura is gone.

CHAPTER 12

THE UNHOLY TARAHUMARA

WHEN *THE UNHOLY TARAHUMARA* is completed, I return to Norogachic to show the documentary. Of course, I go a week early, traveling from home to home to announce that it will be shown. More notes are tied to trees in the Sierra so the gossip line can reach families living far from communities to notify them about an event "in town." I make several short exhausting trips to the Barrancas. About a month before the screening, I am in Norogachic to announce the event and to test equipment. I test the TV set at the Catholic school to make sure it works. All is well.

I announce the film in Choguita, too. But I choose to hold the screening in Norogachic, which is the only pueblo that has electricity. Electricity arrived in the Barrancas for the first time as we were finishing the film. Two places, the Catholic school next to the church and the mayor's house, receive power. There are electrical wires strung through the pueblo for anyone who wants electricity, but no one can pay for it, so dead wires hang above white-washed walls, swaying over painted advertisements for politicians who promise a better life.

The day arrives for the screening. I have brought all the cables and connectors and adaptors I can think of. We are going to hold the event in a big barn of a building where I went to a dance the first week I was in Norogachic. Much has passed since that first dance. I walk to the church to get the TV.

Even though the TV from the school was promised to us for the screening, since the last time I was in Norogachic, the TV has stopped working. Now what.

The only other person who has a TV is the mayor, Marta, a friendly no-nonsense woman. I walk over to her house. Her husband is watching TV. I bypass him and ask if we can use her television. She knows that today is the big day and says it is for the good of the community so she tells her husband to carry it to the barn. He protests but weans himself away from the telenovela and, with the help of a Rarámuri man, carries it down the dirt road, over the bridge across the dry riverbed and up the hill to the barn.

Inside, there are no electrical outlets; only one bare bulb hangs high from a rafter. After a little head scratching from the men, Hiram enters the barn and takes stock of the happenings. He quietly takes over. He climbs a ladder to hot-wire a bundle of wires, and after a few flying sparks we are in business with a TV monitor and a video player. Some men go to the church plaza and call out that it is time for the *película*.

Slowly, about a hundred people fill the barn. At first, Hiram and his friends stand around the walls of the barn like they are teenage boys at a hoedown, shyly toeing the boards in the wood floor before asking a señorita to dance. Years ago, the first night I was in Norogachic, I went to a barn dance. I remember that Hiram leaned against the barn, one foot planted on the wall, either because it was cool to stand that way or to get literal support at a big social gathering. The only man who seemed comfortable was Gabriel with his jokes.

Then, as now, there weren't many women, and they stood in a group separate from the men. Today, as more people enter, everyone jockeys to find a spot, men in front, women in the back, looking for a place where they can see the TV monitor that perches on a tall bench.

The documentary is mostly in English with Spanish subtitles, and some Rarámuri language. But not many in the audience can read Spanish, or even read. So at first they stand quietly and watch. Hiram and his mestizo friends giggle, and the Rarámuri in the audience don't change expression until they appear on screen. Then laughter bursts out everywhere. The mestizos poke each other, the Rarámuri grin. For the seventy minutes of film, no one leaves and no one sits. They stand until the credits role. I am so pleased. The only thing missing is the star of the show, my dear Ventura.

II Arizona Trails
Hunted

Photo by Paige Hilman.

CHAPTER 13

AL OTRO LADO

IN MEXICO, WHEN they talk about going to the United States, they say, "Voy al otro lado." I'm going to the other side.

Now I am on the other side. I spend most of my time here at home in Tucson. I finished *The Unholy Tarahumara* and am searching around for another film to make, or another reason to return to Mexico.

In my kitchen, I have a new addition to the room. He is six feet two inches tall and takes up most of the small space. When he stands at the sink, we can't open the oven door. His name is Valentín.

"*Mira*, look, I straightened my hair. Do I look like Angelina Jolie when she played the Russian spy in the movie *Salt*?" I ask.

"En tiempos de hambre." In times of hunger, he smiles. "Oyes, voy a hacer chorizo. ¿Quieres?" I'm going to make chorizo. Want some?

"Depends," I answer. I don't really like chorizo but I don't want to say no because I like our Sunday mornings together. It is the only morning we are together, then hang out all day. He sure is old fashioned. Maybe it's the difference in cultures. Lately I am always saying that. It's a cultural difference. Hmm. Not sure. It's the man-woman difference. Hmm. Not sure. It's the early stage of a friendship difference. Hmm. Whatever it is, it is a difference. Chile and Chocolate. That's us.

His eyes are a stereotype. You know, the black eyes behind the bandit's mask. The eyes like Cairo. Eyes you can't read. Omar Sharif's eyes behind the white muslin cloth shielding his face from Sahara sands in *Lawrence of Arabia*. Eyes like magnets that draw you in and get you into a caravan of trouble.

The Latin jazz trumpet screams as Rafael, the bandleader, and his sister dance salsa while belting out "Carnaval" into the handheld mikes at the

Tucson nightclub. The drummer slams his rhythms and the whole room jumps. Everyone stands at bistro tables, dancing in place while they raise margarita glasses and shout, "¡Dale!" The small dance floor is full. My friend Robin and I sit at the bar. She says she has to go home, gives me a hug, and leaves. I just bought a glass of cab and decide to stay to finish the drink.

I see the *ojos*, eyes, walk into the crowded room. I am spellbound. I think to myself that those have got to be the greatest eyes I have ever seen. But with looks like that, I am sure the guy is a jerk. You know how it goes. Accustomed to getting all the women. So I announce to myself I am not going to speak to him. There are two hundred people in the room and I am clear that I won't permit Ojos to walk up to me and start a conversation.

He sits in the only vacant seat in the room: the one Robin has just left. Next to me. Oh my god. I am not going to talk to him. If he tries to talk to me, I will just look the other way. No, I will be polite and say, sorry, I am seeing someone. Whoa. Too much. I will nod and say I am just finishing my drink and going to leave. No. I will say . . . oh forget it. I am not going to talk to him.

Ojos gets the bartender's attention. He orders cranberry juice. He doesn't say anything to me. I swivel my seat to watch the musicians. He doesn't speak. He swivels his seat, too. I focus on the stage. I watch the dancers. Neither of us speaks. I don't dare turn my head. The music set ends and Rafael walks over to say hello to me. I have gone to listen to his band for years. I love to salsa to his music. He says, "¿Qué onda, Valentín?" and slaps Ojos on the shoulder. He came to talk to Ojos, not me. They joke around in Spanish, then Rafael turns to me and says, "¿Qué tal, Kathryn?" How are you?

"Hi, Rafael."

"I didn't know you two knew each other," Rafael says.

"We don't," I say.

"Oh, this is Valentín, *muy buena gente.*" Good people. Rafael introduces us.

Ojos turns to say, "How do you do?"

How do you do? No one says "how do you do."

"Con mucho gusto," I say.

Ojos and Rafael talk a while. Then Rafael returns to the stage to sing.

"Do you go hear his band often?" I ask. I had never seen him around before. Uh-oh, that was a mistake. I just spoke to him. Oh no.

"A leetle," he says. Heavy accent. Like Antonio Banderas. Low voice. I don't say anything else. Long pause.

"And you?" he asks. And me what?

"Uh, yes, I like to dance to his music."

"Do you know how to dance?"

"Yes, a leetle," I say. He laughs. "I teach dance classes," I go on. "Do you dance?"

"No." Long pause.

"¿Dónde naciste?" I ask. Where were you born?

"Oh, you speak Spanish," he says.

"Unas palabras. Mi español no es increíble pero es suficiente," I say. A few words. My Spanish isn't incredible but it's sufficient.

He laughs again and says, "Can I buy you a drink?"

So we talk in my silly Spanish and his medium English. It is painful at first. He is so polite and very quiet, sort of shy. He is from a small town in northern Mexico. I know the town and the politics and we have a lot to talk about. He is here on a visa so goes back and forth. An hour later we still talk.

Finally, I say I have to go home. He says maybe we can get together. I say maybe. He says, "If you teach me how to dance, I'll teach you how to speak Spanish." It's a deal, I think, and a line. He asks for my phone number. I fumble around for paper. He gives me his card. Then he says, "Can I walk you to your car?"

I say no. There is this book my mother wanted me to read when I was a child. *A Tree Grows in Brooklyn*. In the book, the mother works long hours so they can buy food. They are poor. On Sundays, they are allowed to have cream in their coffee, a special treat because they couldn't afford cream for more than one cup a week. So the girl would make the coffee, add a spoonful of sugar, and pour in the dense, white, special cream. She would carry it to the table, eat her toast, and save the coffee with cream for dessert. Then she would finish breakfast, pick up her coffee cup and go to the sink, and slowly pour the tan coffee with thick, delicious, real cow's cream down the drain. Every drop. Even in poverty, she could select. That's how I felt about Ojos walking me to my car. I could say no and pour his eyes down the drain. No one wants to be subject to wanting.

But he doesn't call the next day. I wait all day. I keep checking the phone. I wait all day Monday. He doesn't call. All day Tuesday. No call. A girlfriend once told me that after meeting a man, he must call you by the third day. If he waits later than that, don't accept the call. It's too long. Forget him. That was my friend's three-day rule.

On the third day, I am at home, running out the door. Phone rings. I grab it. "Ello, may I speak to Katreen?" And that's that. Now he is in my kitchen cooking chorizo. The kitchen smells like the border. The smell of fire with tortillas browning on the flames, red peppers grilling with onions. Unlike the perky smells of cottage cheese and lettuce, odors of my pre-Valentín kitchen.

"¿Qué haces?" he calls. What are you doing?

"I'll pass on the chorizo. I'll join you in a minute for coffee. Let me just finish writing down this thought," I answer.

Él tiene la mano, as they say in Mexico. He has the hand, meaning he is a good cook. As he drops whole garlic cloves, spices, and water into the blender, I enter the kitchen to ask a question about Spanish translation for a sentence I am writing. He translates as his hands pummel ground beef with red chile powder that rises from the bowl like sorcerer's smoke. The powder is so pungent it makes me sneeze, and I leave the kitchen as I hear him cough from the fine chile in the red air. I call out a few more grammar questions. He calls back, "Por favor. Déjame en paz. Soy un hombre humilde . . ." Please, leave me in peace! I'm just a humble man who wants to eat a quiet breakfast. So I type silently. I hear the chorizo sizzle, then he sits to eat. I type.

Then "¡Dios mío!" he yells. My god! "¡Está enchiloso!" It's hot! He keeps eating. "Oh dios mío," he groans. He keeps eating, finishing every last bite. "Oh dios mío," he rasps. I walk into the kitchen. With tears in his eyes and a smile on his lips, he sits at the table with a glass of Alka-Seltzer. "Best chorizo I ever had!" he whispers. I sit down for coffee. Best *café con leche* I ever had.

I return to my computer to write.

I've finished the film about Ventura, and can't find a groove. I am floating. I try to write a story but can't form an idea that is interesting enough to write down. I need a new project.

And I miss my Sierra Madre friends. What do you call a friend you never see anymore? A ghost, a memory? When you make a documentary about someone, you learn to know that person in a manner that is different from normal. I knew Ventura and Hiram in a heightened way because they were in my daytime thinking and my nighttime thinking. They were in a film that absorbed my every moment for seven years.

I thought about them far too much. They were attached to me like my shadow. In the editing process of the film, their photos were pinned to my wall, along with photos of burros, log cabins, and panoramic views from Sierra trails. If I fell asleep on the couch in my editing room, they were the last things I saw.

There is a photo of Hiram standing next to his father, Lupe. They are in front of an adobe wall. Hiram's shining black eyes have a little glaze on them. He is serious, the way all men were serious in old-time photos of the American Wild West. But I snapped this photo, so I remember all the giggling involved getting these cowboys to stand still while I tell them to say "tequeeela."

There is a photo of Hiram's back as he saddles a horse. I will always know his back. He is turned toward the horse, with an outstretched hand high on the horse's neck; his back and arm muscles move through the checkered cowboy shirt as he reaches for the saddle. I keep this photo on my dresser.

There is also a photo of Ventura in a snappy black turtleneck sweater, surrounded by his daughters in traditional skirts.

I just plain miss those guys.

But in a way, it feels like they are with me, like two ravens, one on each of my shoulders. You know ravens—smart, untrusting creatures that only infrequently allow the approach of strangers, yet they are playful. And they help each other when a predator comes on the scene. Ventura and Hiram, protectors, and reminders at my shoulder of how to live the straight and true. How to sit tall in the saddle.

As I daydream about them, I glance out my window. I can't figure out what I am seeing. Hanging from the laundry line are large handkerchiefs pinned to the clothesline, or maybe they are strips of cleaning rags. But they don't float like fabric. They hang heavy. Oh, I see. It is *carne*, meat. But there are no flies buzzing around. Maybe the salt keeps them away. Or the cold weather. I guess we are going to have *machaca* for lunch tomorrow. Valentín's handiwork.

The more he is here at the house, the more I learn about hanging meat, misinterpreted foreign words, how to cook *mole*, and how to dance the *cumbia* at midnight. Valentín is from the northern tip of the Sierra Madre range, not a Sierra cowboy, but he brings his "Sierra" to me.

He is a mix of other things mexicano. He builds computers but has childhood memories of ten kids in a two-room house as he grew up. He is as modern as an Intel chip, and as old fashioned as the carved wooden saint, San Judas Tadeo, whom he prays to every day.

Speaking of meat, I need to go to the store for groceries. I look for the car keys.

I ask Valentín, "Where are the keys?"

He says they are *en the keechane*. "The key chain?" I ask. "Sí," he responds, impatiently turning his attention back to the work on his desk. I leave his *taller*, workshop, which is adjacent to the house, and walk back inside to search.

I look around for the key chain. It is not in its usual spot on the nail by the door. I can't find it. I go to the living room, no key chain. I go to the bedroom, no key chain. I go to the bathroom counter. No key chain. I look all over the house, and then look again. I go to each room twice.

Exasperated, I walk back outdoors to the taller. I tell Valentín I can't find the key chain.

"Where is it?" I ask.

He looks at me incredulously. "You don't know where is the keechane?"

"No, I don't."

"Are you *loca?*" He looks at me, not believing what I say. "It is where the *estufa* is (the stove), where we cook," he explains. Oh my god. The keechane. The kitchen. The keys are in the kitchen. Again I walk back to the house. And sure enough, there they are on the table, partially hidden by the newspaper.

Next day, the radio is playing in the kitchen. *Los hijos de la mañana*, a KCMT radio show, plays a song. Valentín stands up, does a pirouette, all six feet of him spinning with unusual control, and then he grabs my hand and we dance a cumbia. He says all that exercise makes him hungry. Let's go get burritos for dinner.

Later, we head out for the Taco Shop. After we eat, we walk out of the restaurant laughing, stuffed with a heart-attack meal of carne asada burritos and creamy flan. It is 11 p.m. and a good day has ended.

We get in the car. As Valentín backs out of the parking space, he notices there is less light at the rear of the car. He gets out to check. The left taillight is out. This is a problem. We can't drive the fifteen minutes to the house without a taillight. I can drive without one, my friends can drive without one, and if a policeman stops us, we might get a written warning to repair the light, but usually just a few spoken words telling us to fix it.

If your name is Lorenzo, Juan, María, or Valentín, and you live in Arizona, you can't do that. It is probable deportation even if you carry a visa. At a minor traffic stop, city police call the Border Patrol and the wheels of deportation roll.

This is new in my life. During most of my youth, the Southwest welcomed people from Mexico and Latin America. This land used to belong to Mexico. Historically, our U.S. border only recently moved to where it is. As the great historian Lupe Castillo says, ours is a history of south to north, not the U.S. history taught to me in school about how Americans moved from east to west.

Not only have we always needed the labor of people from the south, we actually liked them. Except when we didn't. In the 1920s, we rounded up "Mexicans" whether they were U.S. citizens or not, and we put them on trains and deported them. This seems to be how we behave during times of economic downturn and schizophrenic political policies. But for most of my life, my friends and neighbors have been people from the other side of the border.

As Valentín and I sit in the car, I think about the newscast I recently saw on NBC. Four thousand people who are U.S. citizens, or have legal status to be in the United States, have been deported or are in the process this year, an increase over the previous year. How can that be? I wonder.

Valentín looks in the glove box for a bulb. None. We sit. Who can we call to come get us this late? There is only a Labrador at the house.

He pulls out his cell and looks up phone numbers for auto parts stores. We find one that is open until midnight. It is on the other side of town.

I drive. Even though I am driving, we don't want to be stopped and go through identification interrogation. They question not only the driver but passengers, too, and deport them if they don't have papers on them. We're tired. I drive the back streets, ending up in cul-de-sacs, backtrack, and eventually have to drive the main streets. I watch for police, sheriff, or Border Patrol vehicles, and I try to drive the exact speed limit, but not too exact, so as not to attract attention.

Finally arriving at the store, we buy the bulb, install it, and drive home. What a relief. With much at stake, Valentín is easily the most careful, law-abiding driver I have ever ridden with. No mistakes allowed. We have an uneventful drive home, but by the time we arrive at the house it is 12:30 in the morning.

This becomes a way of life. We live with a nagging in the heart each day. The reality is in the numbers. This year alone, forty-four thousand people were deported from the United States for traffic violations. Altogether, two million people have been deported under the Barack Obama administration. The greatest number for any administration in U.S. history. And the most common violation is when the tiny light above the license plate doesn't shine. Who even knew there was a light above the plates? We live in fear that our little bulb will go dark.

Valentín and I don't go out for a normal drink the way couples did in the past. When we first dated, I noticed he always drank cranberry juice. I thought he was a recovering alcoholic. I would have a glass of wine, he his cranberry juice. Always very sober and serious. It wasn't all that fun.

I learned later that he simply never wants to take the chance of being stopped by the police after having a drink. The specter of deportation has a way of taking romance out of a date.

CHAPTER 14

WATER

LEAVING VALENTÍN IN town, I take a trip alone, an hour south of Tucson, for my rendezvous with the sun. Near the Mexican border, it is an angel's landscape and a devil's lair. But above all, it is beautiful. The Buenos Aires National Wildlife Refuge. I have hiked this area much of my life. I have seen the mountain lion print. I know where the big owl lives. I like to sit quietly on a hill to watch the sun set over one hundred miles of Sonoran desert and the sacred Baboquivari Mountains.

But of course I am never alone here.

The dark night arrives and I watch as gold stars from her mantel fill the sky, roses by the hundreds decay at her feet, and the night-blue veil spreads across the land covering bones of those who walked. Under her cloak lie hundreds of bodies, the children of Juan Diego Cuauhtlatoatzin, the man who first spoke to her. The Virgin of Guadalupe keeps watch this evening, her dark skin the color of mixed offspring born from violent conquest by Europeans over natives.

And who lies on the desert floor under her cloak? When I was a child, it was "wetback," "mojado," "spic," "beaner," "greaser," "naco," "drywaller," "gravel-belly," "nethead," or "latrino." Now the word is one that is filled with equal animosity but fits contemporary society, a word that easily rolls across the tongue and enters the conversation with no repercussions. You know it. We all use that word.

As I listen to sunset sounds, I think about early years that I traveled back and forth to make films in Mexico. My desert was an open, free place. I traveled without fear. But I began to hear about increasing numbers of bodies found in the Arizona desert. The remains of people who come to the United States to look for work or find family. I constantly worry about Hiram,

Gabriel, and Ernesto in Norogachic. Parents with little money will work hard and travel anywhere in order to feed their kids.

Hiram told me once that he had crossed years ago to work on a ranch in Colorado.

"Did you like it there?" I asked.

"Yes, it was America."

"What does that mean?"

He shrugged. "It was a mythological land. *Una vida nueva* (a new life). And I earned twice the amount of money in one day that I earn in a week in the Sierra. I could afford to buy things we need, and still send money home to Elia and the kids."

"How long were you there?"

"Ten months. They were good to me on the ranch."

"Why did you go back to Mexico?"

He shook his head at the silly question. "*Es mi tierra.*" Because it's home.

As a polite afterthought, he told me, "It's good to work in your country. We can't make enough money here. But I'd rather live here in Mexico. I like my way of life better."

And then he added, "But probably I will cross over again soon. We're having a rough time."

"Don't," I said. "It's dangerous now. You have to walk in scary canyons and desert with no shade. Get a visa."

I know it is dangerous to cross the desert. I also know that I hoped he would arrive in Tucson. But not on foot. Like most people who think about making the journey, Hiram doesn't think about hours walking under a violent sun, he doesn't think about getting lost, or about dying.

"I can't get a visa. I don't have enough money. You have to prove that you have $1,500 U.S. in the bank, and that you own property. Your government wants to be sure that we have deep ties to Mexico and will return to Mexico . . . besides, I'm from the Sierra. I can handle the trails."

This evening, as I relax in my favorite spot on the hill and watch the stars come out, I think about numbers. Numbers of stars. Numbers of bones under the Virgin's cloak, numbers of miles of walls, and numbers of fighting politicians. Twinkle twinkle twinkle.

Mathematics and data. I read history and look up information. Anyone can. But just because it is public information doesn't mean that we know what is happening. I do a little research.

I am interested in the fourteen bodies of recent history. A scandalous number of dead people—fourteen. In the early 1990s, fourteen bodies were recovered each year along the U.S.-Mexico border. They were lying on the desert, distorted. Or bloated, floating face down in the Rio Grande. People were aghast at the large number—fourteen.

After 1994, in the span of a decade, three thousand bodies were recovered. Three thousand. A more outrageous, scandalous number. And those are only the bodies that were seen. Bodies lie secretly at the bottom of a canyon, or on a trail that goes nowhere. Or in plain sight to buzzards but never to be seen by human eyes. The desert is big.

Each year, the number of desert deaths equals the number of people on an airplane. As the local saying goes, it is as if an airplane crashes in the desert every year and everyone is killed. Unlike in a plane crash, nothing is done about these deaths. Unlike in a plane crash, these people often die as a result of dehydration under a white-hot sun.

Death is, at the beginning, the enemy. He is a sly shapeshifter. And quiet. You barely notice when he first takes your tongue. It becomes heavy and rough, like a dead log. You mistake the feeling as a familiar thirst. You have known thirst before.

Next he takes your throat as it shrivels, then pricks like cactus spines. With his sleight of hand, you become so thirsty you suck on anything—your tooth, a rock—to find saliva. You rage at your thirst, then at the thought that he is near. If you are loud enough and say the right prayers, he will go away, as do all spooks.

He whispers to you that he can wait, that in time you will learn to love him. He will become your only friend. Then he torques the muscles in your legs. As cramps grab you like a vise, you bend over to dig thumbs into calves to stop the pain. You beat the calf with a rock. As you lie on the ground rubbing muscles, you think of those you love. You are afraid here alone. Death takes your tears, so your sobs are deep and dry.

Sitting on the desert floor, you begin talking to your wife. You forgot she was here. Then she speaks. You look up to her face but it is not hers; it is the face of your new companion. You are confused. Death nudges you, like a cat with a lizard under paw.

Then he takes your belly. Cramps. You roll in the sand, arms clutching your abdomen. You hear the drumming. It is your heart. It will not stay in its cage. It wants out and it will come out. It will explode. Death sits close,

*Death-map poster.
Photo by Tim
Fuller; map by Ed
McCullough; pro-
duced by Deborah
McCullough and
Kathryn Ferguson;
designed by Stephen
Romaniello; La
Muerte: Baldemar
Peralta.*

to toss you to his other paw. He has all the time in the world. There is no rush.

You go unconscious. When you awaken, you see that you are lying next to a pond of water. With joy, you roll over to lick the glistening sand. It tastes so good. You swallow it. Your throat fills with dry dirt and teensy hot rocks. You choke. Your heart pounds. Your body spasms. Death licks your head. He is no longer your enemy. He is your only friend. You want him to take you. You beg. He tosses you to the other paw, then puts you between his teeth and carries you away.

No one is interested. We hear of no politicians attempting to stop this tragedy, and the media is bored with the subject. Death is no longer sexy. "We covered that last year," journalists say.

Before the 1960s, the United States was sleepy, and Mexico was primarily agricultural. But Mexico's politicians wanted to develop oil, industry, and tourism, not farming. Farmers stopped producing basic crops, and Mexico began importing food. As the world became glutted with oil, Mexico could not sell its petroleum.

But for many of us, numbers are boring. We are just too busy in our lives to worry about the economy, much less about the economy of a friendly country to the south.

In the 1980s, there was peso devaluation, making the cost of tortillas out of reach for most Mexicans. In 1994, NAFTA was created to increase trade between Canada, the United States, and Mexico.

As NAFTA permitted foreign banks to easily enter the Mexican economy, it killed small Mexican businesses. Since the oil industry was not doing well and staple crops were imported, rural Mexico emptied. Greater numbers of people made the long walk north. Numbers everywhere you look.

I recall one of my early trips into the Sierra, when I saw that semitrailer covered with the words *Frutas y Verduras* on the outside, but instead of fruits and vegetables, it was filled with all those faces staring at me from inside the open door. I remember how startled I was to see them, and they to see me. At that time, I had no understanding of thirty bodies in a truck, other than that it was phenomenal. Or of NAFTA, or the policy of deterrence.

At Casita Blanca in Norogachic, sitting around the table with the vaqueros, we agreed what price I would pay to film the ritual slaughtering of two steers for *The Unholy Tarahumara*. Months later, Hiram took me aside and asked me to agree to pay them more money. The peso had been devalued by almost 50 percent. He asked me to pay the new dollar/peso value. His crops and cattle were worthless. I paid more, and for a brief moment, my tiny movie was the only income for this small spot of Sierra.

So the sleepy United States, now wide awake in trade negotiations, implemented stronger border enforcement, perhaps knowing that NAFTA would force a tide of humans north. Coincidentally, at that time they started building the wall.

I had never heard of the policy of deterrence. It was created to close off all urban ports of entry from Mexico to the United States. The plan was to funnel people into the Sonoran Desert, which would be a geographical barrier, forcing migrants into deadly terrain that would deter their attempts to cross. Or they would be forced to cross the Rio Grande.

If enough people died, our government thought, word would get back to their hometowns and migration would stop. But the Border Patrol was wrong. Men, women, and children walked or swam across the border on the back of hunger.

Pick a number: 180, 203, 196, 179. Deaths skyrocketed. One year, a record 252 bodies were found in the Arizona desert alone, about fifty miles from my home.

The Pima County Coroner's Office had to purchase an extra $60,000 refrigerator to store the overflow of bodies.

Imagine you have a farm in Mexico. You work daily, sunup to sundown. You take your corn to market. But suddenly no one wants the corn. Week after week this happens. You hear about something called NAFTA. You aren't sure what this is. You don't realize that your own government has made an agreement that allows corn from the United States to be sold at cheaper prices than Mexican corn. You do realize that no one buys your corn.

Imagine you can't find work and your family is hungry. Imagine your son decides to help the family. Or maybe he is your friend and his name is Ventura, or Hiram. He walks to the bus station and the whole family kisses him good-bye. He rides the bus for two days to Hermosillo, Sonora. Then he gets a ride to the small dusty pueblo of Altar.

Imagine he stays in the priest's shelter for migrants. Father Prisciliano Peraza García, known as the cowboy priest, a courageous man with enough love to fill a desert and the last outpost of kindness, advises him against the looming journey, and protects him from the *polleros* literally gnawing at the priest's padlocked gate. The padlock behind which your sweet guy lies on a bunk trying to sleep, but can't because he is waiting to take that first step into America, where he will drop to the ground and hide on command when his guide spies armed U.S. border agents on patrol, and his guide shouts to his chickens, "¡Agáchense!" Get down.

In a temporary haven, away from hovering narcotraficantes and cartel eyes, the padre advises him that if he is going to make the journey, he shouldn't tell his plans to outsiders. The padre is known to say that since fish die by the mouth, it's best not to talk.

But your friend decides to cross the desert anyway. Imagine that from Altar, he takes a "taxi" crammed with six strangers along a rough road, full of potholes and *narcos*, to the border town of Sasabe. In the night he walks across the border into the Arizona desert. Imagine you never see him again.

✦

¡Ajuuuaa! Eres un animal. You are an animal. *¡Échale, Daniel!* You are a dirty chicken. The policy of deterrence pops up in the most unexpected places. But not where you and I would see it. Our government wants to deter people it has already deterred.

In Tucson, Daniel was stopped for too much smoke emitting from his tail pipe. Since he was living here undocumented he was placed in a detention center for three months and was headed for deportation even though he has a wife and U.S.-born son here.

He tells me that in detention, a looped *migra* corrido, a Border Patrol "ballad," plays twenty-four hours a day, even when prisoners try to sleep. The song says, "You are only a chicken, you are not welcome in the United States. The only way you can get here is to pay. You are illegal, go back to the

Father Prisciliano Peraza García, the "Cowboy Priest" of Altar, Sonora, at a quinceañera *in the pueblo of Pitiquito. Photo by Kathryn Ferguson.*

country where you came from." "Son como una plaga porque . . ." You are all a plague because you bring the plague.

Daniel says the singer then barks like a dog. The singer is Mexican. Daniel, also Mexican, can tell by the bark and by the accents. No American could sound like this, he says. The migra must have paid a lot of money to some poor man to make this song. Daniel, a musician, says that no amount of money could make him sing such a song that would be played in a prison full of Mexicans and Central Americans.

The song was pounded into his head in the detention center at Swan and Golf Links Roads in Tucson. The same place where the Border Patrol's Tucson sector chief invites humanitarian groups to meet. Perhaps we are in an upstairs conference room with floor-to-ceiling windows, hammering out our right to be in the desert, sitting in leather chairs around a polished wood table, listening to the chief, while next door the corrido plays for prisoners. Little do we know.

I leave my beautiful hill after dark and drive back to Tucson. I hear that people walk at night because they are not as easy to spot then. I wonder if they are walking now.

The next morning, I make a cup of strong coffee. I pick up the *Arizona Daily Star* and see a local news item about organizations that go to the desert to prevent deaths by taking water to migrants as they walk the trails. I try to picture this. Perhaps volunteers in hats and sunscreen sit in chairs on a desert trail and hand out paper cups of water as people walk by. Like a lemonade stand.

I am curious to know how it is done, who the volunteers are, and if this work is effective. In Norogachic, Hiram told me he was going to cross to find work. If he dies in the desert, I will feel as if he died in my front yard. I will be responsible for my friend's death.

As I read more, I see that a new group called No More Deaths is being organized. They are setting up a temporary tent in the desert for the first time. They say, "Join us Sunday at 1 p.m." at a church, drive to the desert, and stay the night at the tent. This is appealing. I love camping. But what if they are a bunch of religious loonies?

I know the desert around southern Arizona pretty well and I know that if the camping situation gets too weird, I can get back to Tucson. So I take a backpack and a sleeping bag, join a group of strangers, and ride with them to a camp in the desert.

Leaving Arizona's Interstate 19, we drive twenty-three miles on a curvy road from the one-street town of Amado to the bigger one-street town of Arivaca. After driving a convoluted dirt road with potholes the size of buses, we cross a wide wash. A trail parallels the wash. We notice footprints on the trail. We all study the trail and assume that the fourteen different shoe prints must belong to border crossers since we can think of no other group of people who would be walking in the middle of nowhere.

A few minutes later, we arrive at a camp fifteen miles north of the Mexican border. We are in time to cook up some food and sit around a fire as the sun drops. The camp consists of a tiny trailer and a shade-providing tarp the size of a postage stamp.

Since this is the first official night of the organization, no one knows each other. In the cool evening, sitting close to the flames, as each person introduces himself I meet a nurse, a minister, a businessman, a grad student, and a physical therapist.

After spaghetti, we put out the fire, and I climb into my sleeping bag on a cot. A couple of people sleep in their trucks.

In the night, I hear footsteps. Maybe it is a migrant, someone in distress. "¿Quién eres, necesitas agua?" I whisper, not wanting to disturb my fellow campers. A female voice laughs and says in English, "No thanks, it's just me and I don't need water." It is the physical therapist out for a 2 a.m. pee.

I stay at the camp a week, and then later I periodically supervise the camp for week-long stints. We walk trails and drive roads looking for people. Our only relief from the hellish summer heat is an inverted water bag hanging from a tree that streams tepid water onto your head and naked body. This "shower" is the closest thing to heaven I have known.

Eventually, I begin to volunteer with another organization, Tucson Samaritans, because they search the desert 365 days a year rather than having only a seasonal presence. They were formed two years prior to No More Deaths, so are more experienced with the desert.

Samaritans, a ragtag group including nurses, doctors, teachers, artists, students, scientists, and business owners, are an assortment of shapes, sizes, and ages who comb desert trails deep into the mountains, laden with backpacks loaded with water, medical items, and food. They hike endless miles searching for desert crossers.

In the future, I will learn of more volunteers in Arizona and across the southern border. But I have never been fond of ubiquitous words like "humanitarian" or "activist." They are worn on the chest like a badge. What I am drawn to are invisible people behind the scene. I see hundreds of unheralded women and men who pay no attention to nomenclature. They require no fanfare. They slip back and forth between borders, slide between groups, work round the clock, year after year, simply trying to do some good, and they receive nothing for it.

Ed McCullough, a geologist and former dean of the Department of Geosciences at the University of Arizona, volunteers. He has discovered, walked, and mapped more than two thousand miles of trails that migrants use when they head north. A few of us tag along and pretend like we help him.

He created a GPS system for searches. These two thousand miles of trails between the Mexican border and Arizona Highway 86 are a pinky fingernail on the unmapped body of trails in the landscape.

Ed, a quiet man, easily walks twelve miles, eats nothing, drinks water occasionally, consults his GPS. He looks about him as he walks. He sees the lay of the land as if he were looking down from above. Even though he is standing on the earth, he sees it as if he were flying over. He understands the flow of water even though there is none; he understands the tilt of the incline rock even though we can't see the cause; he understands where desperate people would walk even though he himself is not desperate.

He understands the inclination of the earth's axis when it tilts toward the sun to create summer. He understands the axis of the earth's rotation, and at what point the sun will kill. He hikes, records, plots GPS information into the computer, and informs.

He wants to get to people before they become corpses. He wants to place water where a woman can find it, and drink. A woman who walks hours at night from the international border through steep mountain passes. A woman who climbs a fifteen-foot iron-bar wall, shimmies up the poles by wedging knees between bars, hand over hand, until she reaches the top, and then jumps fifteen feet to the ground, arriving with a jolt in the USA.

A woman who spent the previous night among strangers trying to sleep on the floor of a bare room in Altar, waiting for the pollero to come and say now is the time. A woman who leaves her home near Norogachic or in Chiapas, where there are no men because they have gone north. Or one whose husband in Kentucky works for minimum wage at a racetrack, or one who leaves her nine-year-old son with her mother so she can make the trip, perhaps a trip with no return. A woman who is told to take birth control pills in case she is raped on the journey.

Ed looks around for a spot he can plot, record, and transmit, a place to set water for this woman who will arrive. A well-thought-out spot, a place where she will see the white gallon container and drink.

Trails are seductive. Tethered to a dream by a dirt path, we are promised safety; civilization is just ahead. When searching for people, we leave bread-crumbs on the GPS to find our way home and keep ourselves from the ovens of the witch. Often, trails peter out. Like cobwebs, they ensnare their prey.

Another volunteer, Bob Kee, finds three bodies in three weeks. But we don't say bodies now. We say human remains. I think this is out of respect for fam-ilies of the dead. Two are found a few hundred feet apart, between trails.

Bob rights wrongs with gentleness, the way Zorro fights injustice with his sword. He hikes a dozen miles in rugged country with as much ease as if he's going to the corner store for milk. He has the stamina of a wildebeest, which can cover two thousand miles of the Serengeti during drought, but unlike the wildebeest his beard is short and he never bellows. He is a steady man. And his empathy for our fellow humans is far greater than mine.

In the Tumacacori Mountains a few miles north of the Mexican border, Bob and three women volunteers from Samaritans drive a dirt road eight miles west of the interstate, find a trail, and hike four strenuous miles up and down canyons. They carry backpacks of water and medical supplies. It is noon in March. The weather is an unusually cool seventy-eight degrees and so pleasurable that Bob almost forgets why he is walking.

The group passes debris at old hunter campsites cluttered with tires and rusted cans and a few small bones near a mesquite tree. They walk through ocotillo fields. Bob decides to bushwhack in order to reach another trail beyond Coyote Tank.

As they inch their way through a cholla forest, careful not to disturb the tiny cactus thorns, which maniacally seem to jump onto your skin, Bob looks up and sees a white globe reflecting sun like a fortune-teller's ball. It lies 150 feet away in sand and scrub. He suspects what it is. The group approaches. It is a human skull and lower jawbone.

He sees that the vertebrae and hipbone are in correct position, and one leg has upper and lower bones attached at the knee. The other leg has escaped the skeleton and wandered twenty feet away.

Human remains discovered in the desert. Photo by Bob Kee.

The group circles the bones and finds no clothes. This puzzles them. Normally, people die in their clothes unless they are in a final state of heat exhaustion when they remove clothing so that nothing will touch the body's nerve endings.

Later, the volunteers learn that these are the bones of a small woman. After being deported, she walked into the desert to return to her family in the United States. Most of her is in one place. Her skull is here, no longer protecting her brain. Her ribs are scattered, no longer protecting her heart.

Where did she go, the mother, the thinking woman, and how is it to spend her last moments here with hard rocks and small sounds, and who guides her on this part of her journey? Does a coyote wander by in the dark night to counsel her on leaving the earth, or does she let go her last breath as the hawk passes the sun in the white of day? She is in the place of no time. She lies beneath the Virgin's cloak, in the exhale of our borrowed life, and there is no reassurance in bones blown across the desert floor.

Upon encountering a body, you are required by law to inform the sheriff's department. You are required by law not to touch things, not to pick up a baked-white bone, turn it over in your hand, feel the smoothness at the femur head and a rough spot on the smooth, dry shank, and feel where the attached ligament crosses a muscle that expands and contracts and cramps as the woman inches her way up the steep, rocky trail at night, worrying that, in the light of the full moon, she might be seen by someone waiting to rape or arrest her.

You are not allowed to rub your hand over the rough roundness of the skull or blow dust off the skull and breathe life into the eye socket where the eyeball darts back and forth in fear, skin on the brow sweating like a hunted thing, because we hunt our own kind in the desert night, but not quite our own kind, because the skin from the south is dark and separates this woman from those who have light skin like snow that blows from the north.

In the Tumacacori Mountains, cell phone reception is spotty. After several attempts, Bob reaches the Santa Cruz County Sheriff's Office. A deputy agrees to meet him. Bob and one of the women hike out to the road, where their car is parked, leaving the other two women to wait near the skeleton. It is four miles of rough country back to the road.

When more deputies arrive, Bob gives them empty backpacks and suggests they fill them with water because they will get thirsty. A deputy says they don't need the water, so Bob adds some to his pack just in case.

Late in the afternoon, Bob drives the Samaritans' 4x4 vehicle back toward the site of the skeleton. The deputies follow. They travel a rough road to Coyote Well, about a mile west of Coyote Tank, where the women wait. The road shaves off some hiking time, and a deputy wants to drive even closer to avoid too much walking, but the road becomes a pit of boulders.

Moving rapidly, they see another set of bones that Bob had seen earlier, which he had believed to be animal bones. The deputy says, "Let's take a closer look on the way back."

A deputy says he has never heard of Samaritans but has heard that people were taken to federal court for leaving gallon water jugs on migrant trails, a charge of federal misdemeanor of littering. Bob explains that Samaritans' purpose is to look for people in distress in the desert, but today he and his companions have come across this skeleton.

The deputy sympathizes. Finding them walking is better than finding them dead, he concurs. The hardworking deputy says that a few months ago, when the temperatures were in the cold thirties, he and his buddies discovered a body.

They had to wrap it up and carry it out on an ATV. They had to throw it on a metal frame like in the old Wild West, when a cowboy threw a body over the saddle and slowly walked back along dusty roads to a small town of wooden buildings and laid down the body in a saloon. But now the deputies fold it up in a plastic bag. Instead of a horse, they place it over a rack on an ATV. But the corpse doesn't rest easy on the ATV, as cumbersome body parts crumble or flop over the edge at will, so they wrap it up tight.

By the time they get back to where the skeleton lies, it is 6 p.m. and the sun is going down. The other volunteers worry because it has taken so long for Bob and the deputies to return.

The women have marked the placement of each set of bones so they will be easier for the deputies to spot. In the fine sand, not finding rocks to mark where body parts lie, they remove items of food from backpacks and place them around the skeleton. The food packs, full of carbs, protein, and salts, are made to give sustenance to hungry travelers. Usually used to nourish the insides of a body, today items are used as place markers for what remains of the outside. They set a can of applesauce at the skull, a box of raisins by the wrist, a pack of socks at the pelvic bone, a can of tuna at the far-flung foot.

The deputies quickly get to work. They take photos and record information. The first deputy, with holster, gun, and radio on hip, says they need to wrap it up fast because he wants to finish before dark. It is dangerous, he explains. Bad guys come out at night. They place the bones in a bag and start walking back to the vehicles.

As they hike, a half mile away from where the woman's skeleton had lain, the group sees the other small bones. The deputy says let's check this out. They find more bones, a shirt, pants, a belt, and shoes. The flesh is long gone, a snack for vultures and coyotes. Perhaps this skeleton knew the other skeleton.

But the deputy thinks these bones have been here a year or two, and the other bones are more recent. With no identification found, the remains of both these beings will be recorded as *desconocido*, unknown, joining bagfuls of desconocidos at the Pima County Office of the Medical Examiner, Forensic Science Center, in Tucson.

Thousands of mothers and fathers lying in small drawers.

When they reach the vehicles, Bob and his group climb into the car and the deputy follows. As they drive in the last light of dusk, the deputy sees a silhouette near a shrub. It is dark. He isn't sure if it is human or not. He slows down, backs up.

A man stands immobile. The deputies carefully get out of the truck to question him. He answers in Spanish. Where are you from? Mexico. Are there any others with you? No. He is lost. They pat him down for weapons. He doesn't even have a wallet. Get in the car, the deputy says. Ahead on the road, Bob notices that the deputy's headlights are not behind him. He turns around and goes back. When he realizes what is happening, he gets out of the car to take food and water to the stranger.

The man sits silently in the seat in torn clothes. He is nervous, exhausted, waiting for the ride the deputy will give him to Border Patrol agents, who will put him in detention and then deport him back into Mexico in the middle of some night, into a border town he has never seen where cartel narcos hang at the corners, waiting to conscript him. He is not yet bones in the desert.

Three weeks later, Bob finds a third set of human remains. About fifty miles northwest of where he saw the first two skeletons, he hikes with more volunteers in the Altar Valley. They are at an intersection in a housing development at the edge of the desert. They stop the car at the corner of two dirt roads, Stagecoach and Pyle. Preparing for a hot hike, everyone loads backpacks as Bob walks a few yards away to investigate a dry wash.

In the sand, he sees a round shape, gleaming like a dental hygienist's sink. He can't believe it. So close to houses. And only three weeks after he saw the others. It is a stark white bleached skull with specks of reflected sun that ricochet off the skull like glitter. Huge. Human. A big man, Bob thinks. If this neighborhood had been developed just a little more, the skull would lie in someone's backyard.

As in the Tumacacoris, Bob marks the placement of each set of bones, this time using rocks. A Pima County sheriff's deputy arrives. He sees a skull and jawbone, and ten feet away, a spinal column with the pelvis attached, and one leg.

The hips are still attached to the vertebrae with dark connective tissue that looks pliant. It seems as if one were to bend it, it would slowly return to shape. Although what we know as a man is gone, if you look carefully, you will see his pain tattooed on the desert floor.

Under the vertebrae is a dusty jacket. The deputy thinks the body has been here a month or so. Two hundred yards from the road, he dies here in a wash, a forty-minute drive from a job in Tucson.

The deputy calls the Border Patrol, who sends an agent to take a look. The agent says that he, also, has found human remains. The deputy takes photos. He tosses the bones into a large bag, the kind you would put trash in. As with the woman found at Coyote Tank, Bob will return with friends next week to say a few chosen words and give the large man a formal good-bye.

CHAPTER 15

SPIDER WEB

SING ALONG TO the tune of Old MacDonald. "Uncle Sam, he had a wall, ee i ee i o. At this wall he had some Tonks, ee i ee i o. With a Tonk Tonk here and a Tonk Tonk there, here a Tonk, there a Tonk, everywhere a Tonk Tonk, ee i ee i o." Put your right foot in, take your right foot out, turn yourself about and dance a cumbia.

Tonk is what U.S. Border Patrol agents call people from south of the border. "Tonk" is the sound made by a club when it hits the skull of a Mexican. They also refer to Mexican, Central American, and South American border crossers as "bodies" or as "forty-eights." On their radio, they call to another agent and say, "We've got nine bodies here." Or they say, "We've got nine Tonks."

As I continue to weekly scour the desert with Samaritans, I learn many things. Some is hearsay; much I learn firsthand with my own eyes and ears. When I started volunteering, we had scanners tuned to the Border Patrol's radio frequency. They now scramble the frequency so we can't hear them.

But before, we heard everything. They were supposed to use language according to protocol, but these agents are mostly young guys and just can't help speaking the lingo or giving opinions. On a Sunday morning, a nurse, Helen, and two other volunteers and I were searching in our vehicle with a red sign that says "Samaritans." We drove past a Border Patrol vehicle on a blacktop desert road. We had the scanner on. We heard one agent call another and say, "Those Samaritans just passed us. If they think they are so holy, why are they driving around here on a Sunday morning? Shouldn't they be in church?"

Or we see uniformed men scattered around the desert in their trucks. I talk with an agent who sits for lonely hours in his BP vehicle. Inside the truck is a

Kathryn Ferguson hikes on a trail. Photo by Linda Vogel.

screen and various equipment. On top of the truck is a twenty-foot tower with a rotating camera that surveys the landscape. From inside the truck, when the agent sees an image of people walking through the desert on his screen, he can focus a green laser beam from the top of the tower onto the group.

The agent then notifies others. They don special goggles that enable them to see the green beam. No one else can see it. The ground crew follows the beam to the migrants, then moves in to capture them. Our true border wall is green dots floating above human heads, not miles of metal stuck in the ground.

Mike Wilson, previously with Special Forces in the U.S. Army, explains that the military was creating this war technology when he was in the service in the 1970s. He says that once the beam hits its target, it remains with a person until he is removed from the sights of the laser.

And, of course, it is far more sophisticated nowadays. Laser designators can be shot from airplanes, trucks, or handheld devices. And from drones. In 2006, while driving on Arivaca Road with John Fife, I saw an early drone. Low flying, pewter colored, no window, no cockpit. It flew low, seemingly alongside us. Now drones come in all shapes. Personalized. Go to the Internet and watch as drones with lasers are used experimentally in the Arizona desert at the border. You can sit back in your living room, put your feet up on the coffee table, and watch people get captured.

Can you imagine a green laser trail attached to your being, a beam of violence that you don't know is there, directing a band of armed men to capture and harm you?

The agent who sits in the truck explains that the migrants have the advantage, though. He says that because agents carry guns, Tasers, and equipment at their hips, they cannot run quickly. It is easy for the migrants to run away because fear makes them run fast. They are lucky to be afraid, he says.

Valentín and I prefer the word "Tonk." It has a nice ring to it and makes a good beat for dancing. When our mood is somewhere between giddy and outrage, we dance to our song. But sometimes we just don't feel like dancing. Monday before breakfast, Valentín calls from his sister's house.

"Can you drive to Swan and Glenn and check the intersection? I hear there is a roadblock."

"OK, I'll call you when I get there."

On Spanish-language radio, the traffic reporter announces to her audience the locations of the police activity throughout the day. It is code for alerting people to roadblocks by police who are checking for identification papers. In Tucson's shadows, dark-skinned people keep an ear to the radio.

I drive to the intersection. There are no barriers, just a white unmarked car parked on the side of the intersection with two men in suits in the front seat. I drive past them but can't see much. A half hour later, I return. They are still there.

Police randomly set up blockades throughout the city at unannounced times and locations. Lines of cars slow to a stop. When we arrive at the barrier, we have to show ID. They ask for nothing else, then tell you to move on.

After I verify that there is no blockade, Valentín drives his usual route to my house, where we begin a peaceful day.

Each weekend, he places a tent at the Swap Meet to promote his business. On Saturday at 9 a.m., he gets a phone call. The caller says the Swap Meet is full of Immigration and Customs Enforcement agents. Stay away. He says that early in the morning agents gathered in the parking lot, guarding every entrance. At 6 a.m., they stood outside the gates in all-black clothing, donning black flak jackets and carrying assault weapons. On command, they ran into the "alleys," the little streets in front of the stalls, shouting for everyone to halt—¡alto!—knocking over tents, tables, and wares. People screamed.

As soon as the caller hangs up, Valentín's phone lights up again. Like gossip in the Sierra, the message travels fast around the city. Did you hear, where are they, who told you?

Since it might be dangerous for Valentín to go to the Swap Meet, I drive to see what is happening. Like a waking lioness, I begin to feel a need to protect him. I set my toe into the no-exit web of politics. Almost unconsciously, the politics become personal. It is my small beginning of no return.

In the Sierra, I felt protected by the cowboys and Rarámuri. But what if Hiram and Ventura were here? Would the tables be turned? Would I be the one in charge? If I were with Valentín in the Sierra, would he be protecting me? Does a border change the role of men and women? Who hunts, who is hunted, and who protects? I feel the ravens on my shoulders shift from claw to claw.

Until now, I have always been able to walk away. I could walk away from the Sierra, walk away from filmmaking, walk away from Samaritans. That will change. Silk thread by silk thread. The spider's thread and love, the strongest fibers known to man, will wrap me so tight that I will suffocate.

An hour after the phone call, when I arrive at the Swap Meet to investigate, everywhere I look are black T-shirts emblazoned with the letters "ICE." Agents drive trucks down the alleys in front of stalls; armed, they walk in twos and threes.

It is a strange scene. Many stalls are empty; no one has arrived to work them. There is some business as usual, as a few vendors wait on customers.

A handful of people walk around as if it is an ordinary day. It is quiet. There is no norteño music, which usually blasts from CD players.

Adjacent to stalls doing business are other stalls that have been destroyed. Awnings have been knocked down, tables turned upside down, boxes of clothes flipped on their sides.

I turn a corner and see a stall with the naked butts of five female mannequins facing out to the alleyway. The mannequins have been perched across a table in a line, breasts facing the table, their backsides facing the little street where I walk. Two are clothed in shirts. The others are not clothed.

Six ICE agents move around in the stall. They are between twenty and forty years old, tall with bulging muscles, and they laugh hard, enjoying themselves. One agent wears a girl's flower-print blouse over his black T-shirt. He twirls. Another agent picks up a woman's blue silk blouse and rubs it over his crotch and chest and face. He pats the mannequin's butt. His colleagues agree that he is hysterically funny. They can barely continue their work because they laugh so hard.

A five-foot-tall woman stands by a broken pole. Her awning tilts toward her, ripped at the corner. Two of her display tables are turned over. An agent throws clothing into the back of an ICE truck parked in front of the stall. She stands to the side. She watches as they dismantle her merchandise and play with her mannequins.

I ask the woman if this is her stall. She says yes. I ask her why they are doing this. She says she doesn't know, that they ran in, shouting at the people who were setting up their stores early in the morning. She says that they started tearing things down and that trucks drove by to confiscate merchandise. I say this is shameful. She doesn't respond.

I call a journalist friend to tell him what is happening. I ask him if he knows why there has been a raid at the Swap Meet. He says he will investigate. He says he needs witnesses to talk to him, or no one will print a news report.

I ask the woman if she will talk to a friend of mine who is a reporter. She hesitates and says she doesn't speak English well. I tell her we have Spanish interpreters. She agrees to be interviewed and gives me her phone number.

Later, the reporter calls me. He says an ICE spokesperson told him that the raid was intended to confiscate counterfeit merchandise. I hear from vendors that agents demanded to see identification papers and took people away to Border Patrol.

The reporter wants an interview with the woman. I call her and get an answering machine. I call again. No luck. I leave a message that my friend will call her. She never answers. He never gets an interview with anyone, and the story doesn't run.

I relate the story to my friends at the weekly Samaritan meeting. At each meeting, we discuss experiences like the Swap Meet. We discuss the politics of the desert as well as experiences from the trails. From each other, we learn things about the border that are never broadcast in public news reports.

At one meeting, Brother David Buer, a Franciscan friar who tends to the needy in many capacities, tells us about his recent search experience with Samaritans on a desolate trail near the town of Ajo.

The town lies in the upper part of the stunning and treacherous Arizona-Sonora Desert. Forty-three miles north of the Mexican border, it sits at the edge of Organ Pipe Cactus National Monument, which receives 7½ inches of rain in a good year. It claims twenty-eight types of cactus, none of which you would want to bump into. Six varieties of rattlesnakes live here, along with scorpions and Gila monsters.

The most significant detail of interest is that there is no shade big enough for a human in this part of the desert, and no water. If you are crossing the desert, you will walk at night to avoid the sun and men with guns, but in the dark you will not see the snakes, thorns, or trails. You will become lost in a hundred-mile-wide bowl of boiling hot rock.

On the trails, Brother David, a tall man with a long beard, wears his floor-length brown habit, tied at the waist with a cord, and hiking shoes. Imagine the surprise when a border crosser sees Brother David walking the lonely desert, approaching him with love and water.

Brother David and his companions were hiking when a small, fifty-year-old man appeared. As the man walked toward Brother David, he collapsed to his knees and pitched forward, facedown into the dirt. A tin pie pan fell from his hand and clattered onto the trail. He had carried the pan to hold his urine, which he had been drinking for four days. He was lost from his group and had found no water. Brother David and the volunteers gathered round him and sat for a long, quiet time. With water and food, he slowly revived.

At our meetings, we are inundated with stories like this. Meeting after meeting. The stories numb you. The numbing starts inside, creeps past the heart and settles in the brain. So instead of feeling, you get busy collecting.

Collect socks for migrants with blisters, fill food packs, fill tires with air, buy gallons of water, take notes, create committees, vote on what kind of sausages to put in the food packs. Organize fundraisers to help those behind bars. Get on computers to commiserate and complain. Write articles. Protest. Fill out legal forms. Bide time.

Otherwise, if you really think about the boys who are shot in the back and killed by the Border Patrol, the people who suffer heart attacks, those who are out there dying while you sit in an air-conditioned meeting, when you fully understand that even with the politicians' "immigration reform" the dying won't stop, when you fully consider the senseless deaths, you freeze. You are embalmed with uselessness.

A few days later, we attend yet another meeting. When not in the desert, life seems to be a clothesline of meetings, one agenda pinned to another.

"Our desert will never be quiet as a graveyard," says the commissioner. He likes that line. The lines he likes we will hear again. We are now at a meeting with the U.S. government. We are with the commissioner from the Department of Homeland Security, at a gathering he has called.

Two walls of the room are floor-to-ceiling glass, with cool-blue glare proofing that keeps the conditioned air close about us. The other walls are ice-castle white. Outside, the sky cracks open as passenger jets pierce heaven. This is a down-and-dirty meeting at the airport, an obligatory meeting for Homeland Security to show the American press how it includes humanitarian values in its agenda, a quick meeting before the commissioner catches a plane back to Washington, D.C.

In the room, Homeland Security's people and Border Patrol sit side by side at one end of the table. No one wears a true uniform. After all, dress makes the occasion. They have come to speak with the common man—us. We are a collection of nine representatives from humanitarian organizations.

The woman officer is casual, the two men are in dressed-down browns, and the commissioner is in a navy-blue flight jacket with the half-inch-high letters "DHS" on the pocket.

The man by the door casually wears wires. A small black one loops around his ear. He texts. Outside the door, there is a proliferation of uniforms. Local police. Secret Service. When I enter and exit, they look me over, head to toe. I have never experienced such scrutiny with no sex involved. It's more like I am a potentially dangerous cow. Their eyes start at the top of my head, penetrate my eyes, continue down to my breasts, waist, crotch, legs, feet. I see three men do this. Nothing personal.

Beneath their expensive jackets, at the waist lies the barely perceptible bulge of a weapon. Beyond them, casually placed near the waiting room bar at the Saguaro Cantina, are a slew of plainclothed gentlemen.

The commissioner says that he has called us together for no reason. Just friendly conversation. He wants to hear what we think. He talks of greed and drugs and says that it is illegal to step into the United States with no papers. He likes the borderlands, spent his life in the borderlands, calls himself a *fronterizo*, rolling out the Spanish accent as if he uses the language often. It is the only Spanish word he uses during his time with us. Perhaps the only one he knows.

Fear is personal. When it is not personal, when it is another person's fear, to speak of it requires many syllables: short-term detention, vulnerable populations, fiscal responsibility, quantifiable success rate, complaint process, community relations, jurisdiction, problem assessment, demonstrated mastery of firearm skills, shoot-to-kill considerations, and lateral repatriation.

We nine guests sit around the table. It begins to feel a little like Alice's territory. You know, Alice and the Cat. Like a Tim Burton movie.

It is our turn to speak. We ask the commissioner, "When a person is in short-term custody and is abused by an agent, is there a person we can call, can we have a specific name and phone number that we can call, in order to report abuse?"

The commissioner frowns; *abuse* was not an agreed-upon word. He doesn't like the tone of it. He says, "There have always been proper channels for your clients." Although he knows there are no lawyers present, he chooses *clients*. We continue to explain that there was a problem in Border Patrol detention, and what could be done about it?

"What problem?"

A migrant was in a cell, ill with an asthma attack, and an agent took away her medicine. Someone in the cell explained that the prisoner desperately needed it. The agent said, "Let her die," and took the medicine out of the room.

Like the Queen of Hearts, the woman at the head of the table tells us, "Oh, there is no problem, we have proper channels for such action." The Cheshire Cat grins and says, "Migrants have rights." The Mad Hatter says,

"The detainee can simply say she wants to see a supervisor, and it will be handled. We have signs on the wall explaining this." The Queen's court looks pleased. The commissioner nods with his only smile of the hour.

Another guest asks the commissioner if he has had time to respond to the abuse-report document compiled by No More Deaths. The commissioner says that he has never seen it. The guest says it is a written record of fourteen thousand individual cases of Border Patrol abuses against migrants. It is the record of migrants' testimonies over a two-year period, you know, the one that I handed you at the last meeting, says the guest. The commissioner says he never received it.

The meeting ends. The commissioner has met his public relations obligation. Satisfied that he is doing a good job, he smiles tightly and exits. The wired man still texts.

I feel dirty for having been here. I go home and prepare for my next documentary. Cleaning the drawers in my messy desk seems a better way to spend my time.

CHAPTER 16

CHASING RITA

STILL DISTURBED BY the pointless meeting from yesterday, I dust, sweep, and mop my office. When feeling useless, the best remedy is to run ten miles or to clean. Cleaning is less difficult. I don't recommend cleaning when you get a divorce, however. That is Crazy Angry Cleaning and you might rub the sink so hard that, in your madness, you splash Clorox in your face. What I do today is Depressed Sad Cleaning, which is not so dangerous.

I sit down at the desk, file papers or toss them into the trash. I am overall uncomfortable. I think I just need to get busy. I have no idea why I want to make another documentary since the last one was so difficult. But I search my mind for an interesting subject.

The phone rings on the desk.

"¡Hola, Catalina! Habla Susana. De Norogachic." Susana—Gabriel and Imelda's daughter. The little girl who was determined to improve my hair. I haven't seen her in years.

"I live in Phoenix with my husband now. We would like to visit you. I got your number from Santiago."

"It would be great to see you! A husband? Wow. Congratulations." She must be eighteen.

"Yes, he was in the army when I met him in Ciudad Chihuahua."

"So you live in Phoenix? Can you get down to Tucson and come visit?"

"Yes, and I want to show you my jewelry. I started a little business."

"I'd love to see it and you. How about day after tomorrow at 1 p.m.?"

"Perfect. We will be there. This is my phone number."

I go shopping for our little party. I make a chicken salad and buy a cake. The 1 p.m. hour comes. No Susana. But they do run on Mexican time so I am not worried. I just keep the salad in the refrigerator, ready to pop it out when they arrive. I am excited to see her jewelry. I wonder what materials it is made from. I should have asked more questions.

It is almost 2 p.m. No Susana. I call the number she gave me. No response. Maybe it is not a cell number. 3 p.m. and no Susana. I call in the evening and the next day. She never calls and never arrives.

Weeks later, I hear from Santiago that she had "immigration problems." I didn't understand at the time. Only now am I becoming aware of how often deportations occur. Many times a day in every city of our country.

Deportation. An easy enough word to pronounce. Impossible to comprehend. Raids. Most of us would say, "That never happens in America."

The skeleton of it is this. You are jolted awake by a banging on the door. It is *always* between 3 a.m. and 6 a.m. You go to the door in your bathrobe. You don't want to open it but a man screams that he will break down your door. As you open it, he pushes in, shouting, demanding to know your name. As you glance outside, you see that bright lights and uniformed men are in your yard. You are grabbed and handcuffed. Your small son runs into the room, frightened. He runs to you. A uniformed woman reaches for him. He runs away into the bedroom and crawls under the bed. Two people go after him.

You call out, "Please don't hurt him." A uniformed man laughs and says, "Pliz don hoort heem." Another says, "Speak English, for Christ's sake." They crawl under the bed and grab your son's bare foot. He yells. They pull him into the room. You try to go to him. They grab your handcuffed wrists and twist. They start to drag you to the door. You say, "Can I get dressed?" They don't answer. Instead they pull you outside into the lights. They take you away in your bathrobe.

To be deported is to be ripped away from people we love. "Rip"—a short word for a long pain.

I think about Susana. Surely that could not happen to her. I knew her as an eight-year-old girl when she was determined to improve my appearance. She was the braider of hair. She was the girl who giggled. She escorted me to the tienda each morning to buy eggs. She was my four-foot-tall, self-appointed Sierra guardian.

Working with Samaritans, I hear more about deportations and raids. A big percentage of people we find in the desert are deportees attempting to get home to their families in the United States. I worry daily that it could happen to Valentín.

Every few weeks, Valentín receives a call that another one is gone. After work, in the kitchen, he tells me, "Roberto's space at the Swap Meet was empty tonight."

"He is gone?" I ask.

He grabs a beer and with a blank face and says, "Yes, I talked to his wife. He is gone." Always the same words, always the beer, always no entrance to his face. I marvel that the corners of his mouth give away nothing. Like a performing magician, his eyes cannot be penetrated. I never see a reaction when he speaks of deportation.

It is as if the blankness is a premonition. A dissolving into what came before. Which is that, before I knew him, he didn't exist to me. Is this a premonition that what is to come is what was before? Nonexistence? Will he disappear? Will he be deported? A phantom undoing.

In the language of Homeland Security, "gone" translates as "forever." He is deported and can never return to his family. Let that sit in your heart for a few minutes.

After I finish *The Unholy Tarahumara*, Valentín and filmmaking start to take equal parts in my life. Valentín and I work, hike with dogs, go to movies, cook together, and dance. I am looking for a quiet life, but at the same time, part of me wants to make another film. Maybe if I just stay busy . . .

After a midday meal of Valentín's machaca, tortillas, and Mexican wedding cookies, those little cookie balls covered with confectioners' sugar lovingly known as *pedo de novia*, bride's farts, I return to the process of formulating the next project. I go to Borderlands Theater to see a play.

Rita. A red skirt flares out around her like a crinoline, women's fashion from the 1950s. But this clothing is different. The skirt is pleated with little black, green, and yellow flowers wandering across tiny folds. Her blouse is yellow, also covered in flowers, and hangs over her torso like a packing box with large puffy sleeves.

Her dark hair is cut square at the shoulders and the brow. Her cracked feet spill over the edges of sandals laced up her ankles, not because the sandals are too small but because the dark feet are flattened out with hard use and are engraved with little cuts, and considerable muscle bulges at the edges of the sole. She is still and looks straight ahead. She sits on a metal hospital chair.

It is Rita, played by Mexico City actress Luisa Huertas. I am at a Tucson's

Borderlands Theater production of *The Woman Who Fell from the Sky*, directed by Barclay Goldsmith. It is the first production of the play outside Mexico City.

As I sit in the dark theater, I find my next film. I am certain that I want to make a documentary about the real Rita.

She is a Rarámuri Indian woman who was placed in an American mental institution for ten years because she spoke no English. The authorities described her speech as the "guttural noises" made by those who are mentally ill. In fact, what they heard was Rita speaking her native tongue.

The story is that Rita is found in a kitchen, eating from the refrigerator of a woman's home in Manter, Kansas. She is considered a vagrant and is jailed by the sheriff of Larned, another small Kansas town. The sheriff says they simply didn't know what to do with her.

She can't speak English, and beyond her own language, she speaks only a few words of Spanish. No one knows how she arrived in Kansas. When doctors ask where she comes from, she says "Arriba," above. She repeats the few Spanish words she knows. They interpret "above" to mean the sky.

In the Sierra where she lives, canyons away from Hiram and Norogachic, people walk steep cliff roads. They often stop to greet each other saying, "Where are you going?" They answer "above" or "below." It is the same answer when questioned, "Where do you live?" "Up" or "down," meaning they live in a vertical landscape at the top of the canyons or at the bottom.

So when the hospital staff asks Rita where is she from, she answers "Arriba." They interpret it to mean that she thinks she comes from the sky, and thus must be mentally ill.

When the play ends, I attend a soiree for the playwright, Víctor Hugo Rascón Banda, who is in Tucson for opening night. I ask if I can I have permission to use a little of his play in a film. He graciously says yes, and introduces me to Miguel Giner.

Miguel, originally from Ciudad Chihuahua, is a social worker living in Kansas. He discovered Rita when he visited the mental hospital in the town of Larned. After Miguel told his longtime friend the playwright about meeting Rita, Víctor Hugo wrote the play.

I can tell that making this film will be a bear. As far as I can connect the facts of Rita's journey, I see her as another hungry, misplaced person who wants to come to the United States to work. But I am not sure.

In order to make the film, I have to stitch together Rita's journey. Rita can't speak. For ten years in the mental hospital, she was given psychotropic drugs, Navane and Thorazine, to keep her pliant.

These drugs cause tardive dyskinesia, a condition in which the tongue swells and a patient loses the ability to speak. It also causes the patient to lose control of physical actions, so Rita throws her arms about and jerks her torso, which adds to an image of insanity. Since she can't speak to tell her story, I need to find family and friends in the Barranca del Cobre who can give me insight.

How am I going to make a film about a migrant woman who can't tell me anything about herself? I decide that I will trace Rita's 1,500-mile route that she walked from the forests of the Sierra Madre through the Chihuahuan Desert into the flatlands of Kansas. She walked. I will follow.

I realize I have to do a serious amount of research. And when I return to Chihuahua, I will be alone again. I'll be mountains, canyons, and towns away from Hiram and my other buddies.

I think about Ventura often. It seems to take death a long time to find its rightful place in a person's mind. It leaves a tiny gasp in my parade of thoughts as I catch it stepping out of order, shuffling to the right, shuffling to the left, like Ventura dancing circles in that red headband he would remove when I approached. The one he didn't want me to see because it made him too Indian. Not modern enough. Tell me again, what is the process of discarding the past?

And Hiram. Horses and cowboys—every girl's dream. But he's not a dream. He's real. For Americans, the cowboy is a deep-rooted myth, an image of independence from society. The brave loner. But the original cowboys who ran cattle from Mexico to modern-day Kansas were Mexicans and Native Americans from Mexico who were conscripted by the Spaniards during the 1500s. From those vaqueros, Americans appropriated the "cowboy" who has become our national hero. Ironically, our hero became the lanky Anglo anti-immigrant cowboy who fights against Indians and Mexicans in our movies and novels. Zane Grey could have taken a lesson from Hiram. I miss Hiram. Heya, cowboy, move 'em on out.

When Santiago travels to and from Tucson, he passes me little messages of well-being from Hiram. Like, "When are you coming again?" or "Our house is always open to you." I wonder if he crossed into the United States, or if it is still merely a plan.

Ventura and Hiram, ravens on my shoulders, just out of reach.

Those ravens. Black as the void. I am told that First Raven saw humans fishing in darkness. Humans did not know light. First Raven traveled through the black cosmos and returned with a box of light. Raven, bird of creation, the one that brings illumination from where there was none. Thanks to First Raven, humans now fish in daylight.

But I am not fishing. I am simply starting a film that will take me across borders again. However, I have a foreboding. I don't know why. Something is changing and I can't put my finger on it. I must be watchful. My days are not as light as they used to be. Friends invite me out for a *copa de vino*, but I decline.

Instead, I go to where I am comfortable. I start to frequent a dark cave inside myself where yellow eyes peer from the corner. The ravens enter with me. *Whoosh* go the wings. *Caw* goes the call. I am in the Seven Caves of Chicomoztoc.

I brush up against a wall of wet algae. There is a bat on the ceiling, blind spiders in the shaft, slugs on the floor, centipedes under stone. *Cree crck sst, cree crck sst*—the marimba band of cave music. The masked serpent in the corner, the jaguar standing on two legs.

And something is growing, incubating in the sinkhole of my cave. A cell is multiplying, is spreading, is not part of me but will cling to me. A seed is growing. I must wash it off me. I don't understand what I see. I stand in a blind cave, surrounded by the future, and can see nothing.

Ravens—ace pilots of the feathered beings. Ravens of the keen eye. Ravens of black magic. Ravens of the quick joke. But my ravens are tinged with human. My ravens walk with a red headband and the limp of old age, or the tilted hat of *vaquero macho*. Yet they stay with me, my protectors. "¡Caw, qué bárbaro!" screams Ventura as he flies to me, Hiram close behind. Skinny claws grip each shoulder as they steer me to the light of the open road, and I drive to Mexico. Sit tall in the saddle, they say.

I leave my cave and begin my research in Ciudad Chihuahua.

While I am there, I attend another production of the play. I sit in the dark theater in a comfy velvet seat. At the end, I move into the lobby for drinks and hors d'oeuvres to celebrate the Chihuahua premiere by Mexico's beloved Víctor Hugo. The governor of Chihuahua speaks. Near me, I see women sip champagne as real diamond pins flash from hair coiled in ballerina buns. Chihuahua's upper crust is in attendance.

And the media. Flashbulbs pop. Although Mexicans love their celebrities like Víctor Hugo, they are a little confused about the play. I overhear much discussion about Rita's plight and her treatment by Americans.

Near the olives stuffed with *queso menonita* and tiny pimientos stand a couple of men, managers of maquiladoras (Mexican factories owned by Americans or other foreigners). They are privy to internal government policies that signed Mexico onto the NAFTA bandwagon, so they talk about the trade agreement. And over near the Mexican flag are long-haired artists talking animatedly with hands slicing the air.

What the theater patrons don't talk about is Mexico's role in the migration of its people. Why can't it support its own people and keep them at home with food on the table? Like most political questions, I guess the answer is the money trail.

Mexico makes millions on remittances when its citizens work in the United States and wire money back home to families in Mexico. Americans make billions on border security. Since private companies manufacturing war-machine technology no longer earn billions in Iraq and Afghanistan, they have moved much of their business to the U.S. border, inventing increasingly sophisticated technology to detect travelers passing through the desert.

Migrants are then shipped off to detention, which is another billion-dollar business that places captured people in private U.S. prisons and enforces deportations. Lots of money for a few people.

All around me in the theater lobby, I hear discussions about poverty. Apparently, poverty is confusing. If you live in poverty, it is a maelstrom that never stills no matter who is in power or what words are spoken. If you are at the theater seeing a play about a woman who is poor, poverty is an hors d'oeuvres to be eaten with champagne and chatter.

I decide to start the long process of seeking filmmaking funds.

In Tucson, I set an appointment with Giulio to pitch my plans. When you pitch an idea to most producers, you have to hook them in two sentences. Then your time is up and you are out the door. If they are interested, they ask questions about your project. If not, they say, "We'll call you."

I enter Giulio's office and sit. He is usually on the phone or typing on the computer. He says, "Buongiorno, have a seat, I'll be with you directly," the Italian greeting followed by a British accent. I notice the coffee is hot in the pot. I help myself. I pick up a heavy black mug with a white logo of the Arizona International Film Festival. It is a stylized drawing of a coyote standing upright behind a reel film camera on a tripod.

The walls are covered with photos of fire-eaters, four-foot-tall film posters of *The Wild Bunch* and *Pixote*, and colorful posters of Australian, Chinese, European, and American films that have screened at the Arizona International Film Festival over the past years. There are shelves of DVDs, videocassettes, and reels of canned 16 and 35 millimeter films. Giulio is calm but doesn't stop moving, belying the fact that he may have been up all night directing assistants to set a meeting, or e-mailing a filmmaker in Tibet.

He then turns his attention toward me and says with drawn British vowels, "We had to take our Dobie to the vet yesterday but it was only an ear infection. All is well. And how are your dogs?" We speak dog, then move on to documentary talk. I tell him about ideas for *Rita of the Sky* and about trips I plan to make through backroads of Sierra badlands to find relatives who knew Rita.

He asks how I plan to find funding and wants to see a film proposal, budget, and timeline. Then he wants to hear about the first trip into the Sierra, the bottom line in cost, and where I will go. I tell him about organizing a trip to the canyons near Porochi in the Barranca del Cobre. I plan to travel with people who come to me by way of good reputation, but I haven't met them.

"Traveling with people you don't know?"

"I have no other choice."

"Hmm," he says.

Then he asks, "How is Valentín?" They regard each other with mutual respect.

"He's great," I reply.

Giulio is sympathetic to Valentín being from the old culture where mother is Number One, family is Number Two, and a pot of hot food on the stove is Number Three. A woman running around Mexico alone is not Number Four. Being a modern man, Valentín understands that women work outside the home, have careers, make movies, or own businesses, but deep down he likes his women to be well groomed and take care of family matters first.

Giulio says he will inform the board of the Arizona Media Arts Center and will let me know if they accept the Rita project.

"Tell me again, where are you going in the canyons?"

"I'm not sure. There are communities on the map, near Cerocauhui. We'll be there."

"Nothing more specific?" he asks.

"I won't know until I get there."

"I'll pass your proposal to the board. Take care," he says as he returns to his computer.

A few months later at another meeting, he tells me he had been quite worried and had told his wife, "We may never see Kathryn again. She is going to the mountains of the Barranca del Cobre alone, and doesn't know the men she hired or where she is going or what she will learn, if anything." Curiosity, and stupidity, killed the cat and Kathryn.

I receive formal approval from the board of the Arizona Media Arts Center (AZMAC) to use the center as my fiscal agent, and Giulio becomes executive producer. It is necessary to connect with a 501(c)(3) like AZMAC, allowing funders to benefit from the organization's tax-exempt status.

Once again, I seek money with a vengeance. I research national funding organizations, write slews of grants, and receive mostly rejections. It seems that no one is interested in old, crazy Indian women. I have endless lunches with strangers hoping to find funders, join women's groups in order to "network," send hundreds of e-mails, write to senators, make long-distance phone calls and talk my head off. I do extra part-time jobs of any sort.

I even enlist the aid of a Gypsy bruja. One night I walk the aisles of the Tucson Swap Meet, or the Swap Mall as Valentín calls it. A sign with a large palm attracts my attention. Beside the palm is a statue of Santa Muerte, Our Lady of the Holy Death, a popular Mexican sacred figure of a skeleton clad in a long robe—a "saint" that is popular with drug cartels but abhorred and unrecognized by the Catholic Church. Next to that is the Virgin of Guadalupe, adored by the Catholic Church. All bases covered.

Inside the stall, a woman in a long skirt with waist-length black hair leans on a counter talking to a man. She turns, takes one look up, and says, "I see sadness." I look behind me. There is no one there. Oh, she is talking about me. "Come in, come in," she says.

We go behind a burgundy curtain. She looks at my palms, says that someone has cursed me and that I need the cure. Not normally a believer in superstitions, I would laugh at the notion, but she speaks so matter-of-factly about curses and sadness that I feel maybe she is on to something that I don't know. I am desperate to get funding, and a little wobbly in my understanding of man, the universe, and beyond.

She asks my profession. I explain that I teach dance.

"What kind?" she asks.

"Well, my studio has teachers for salsa, tango, flamenco, and oriental dance."

She stares. "What's oriental?" she asks.

"You know, the Orient, like the Orient Express to Cairo. The Orient versus the Occident. Belly dance." She smiles. She says her daughters love to belly dance. She tells me that she can come to my studio and give me the cure in exchange for belly dance classes. Perfect.

I think after the first lesson, she will enroll her daughters in my classes and I will make more money for the film. But for this initial exchange with the fortune-teller I have to pay ten dollars.

She arrives at the studio with two daughters in tow. All the lights are on and wall-to-wall mirrors reflect the brightness. She walks around the room and says, "I see darkness."

She says, "Bring me a raw egg." I go to the kitchen and get one.

She lights a candle and whispers something. She walks around with the candle. She moves the egg in circles over my head. Then she cracks the egg, pours it into a glass of water. She lights incense. I sneeze. She whispers more words, then looks directly at me and tells me that I am clean. Things will be better. We dance. Her daughters are earnest and dance wholeheartedly. I never see them again.

Back to the drawing board, then back to Mexico. I continue to send out proposals around the United States and get a thumbs-up from Aeroméxico airlines. They will pay for two round-trip international flights for Luisa Huertas, the Mexico City actress who will appear in the documentary. They do this in exchange for listing their name in the credits.

But the next trip I make has to be in my Nissan so I can drive canyon roads to search for Rita's relatives. Armed with my little Sony PD150 camera and a tripod so old that I have to use a quarter to tighten the plate where the camera attaches, I pack the rest of my luggage with boxes of digital tapes, voice recorders for people who don't want their image recorded, microphones, batteries, a still camera, film, and rainproof bags for the gear.

As I pack, I go over my carefully written list. I can't afford to forget anything because there is nowhere in the canyons to purchase penny-size camera batteries or digi tapes or the many other items needed for making films. And then there is the truck. I take my Nissan to my beloved shade-tree mechanic, who makes sure the brakes won't fail me on steep canyon roads and that there is air in the spare, that there *is* a spare, that I have extra cans of oil, that the radiator has no leaks, and so on. I toss a shovel in the back.

I carry as few clothes as possible because they are heavy and I will have to wash them while I travel. Since I will be on the road for a few weeks at least, I take two pairs of Levis, three T-shirts, a warm jacket, underwear, socks and tennis shoes, a hat, sunglasses, a sleeping bag, rain gear, and a backpack.

Of course, I pack a small bag with lipstick, eyeliner, lotion, a hair ribbon, a pair of earrings, toothpaste, and almond soap. I like to pretend that I look like the earthy *Vogue* magazine model Lauren Hutton, in a safari jacket with a $900 Louis Vuitton travel bag hanging from my shoulder as I stand near the campfire.

But, alas, it is not to be. When in the Sierra, it takes exactly 1.3 days for me to look like a bedraggled woman from Dorothea Lange's Dust Bowl photos. I am waylaid by dirt, little sleep, cold-water sponge baths, steep trails, and worries about where I am going and what shots I need in order to tell the story.

Not to mention, I need to clarify what the story *is*, exactly. I pack a notebook to jot down thoughts. I worry about whether my equipment will work properly, if I will have car trouble, if people who say they will meet me will actually be there, and I am confounded keeping track of the tiny digital tapes that can fall out of my pocket if I sneeze.

A year earlier in Norogachic, while working on *The Unholy Tarahumara*, I shot a Semana Santa ceremony for four hours. I returned exhausted to my room at Casita Blanca. I had stood on a wall surrounding the church for a couple of hours, balancing and shooting so I could get a view above the crowd. My leg muscles cramped from gripping a balance on the wall, and my back and shoulder muscles cramped from holding the camera in one position for a long time.

When I returned to the room, I set down my camera and tripod to discover that I was missing the most important tape. They are black, about two by two and a half inches, and a quarter of an inch thick. I had just shot an hour of crucial footage in which the Rarámuri dance and burn Judas and his wife on a big bonfire. It is all on that one itsy-bitsy tape. Thank you to Japanese Technology of the Tiny.

When I couldn't find the tape, I ran over to Hiram and Elia's house to enlist their help. Since Elia was cooking, Hiram, his son, and I walked over to the church courtyard where four hundred people milled about during the ceremony. We scoured the grounds for the digi tape. I asked strangers if they had seen it. Hiram asked his friends who were hanging around the plaza. We retraced steps across the bridge, down the arroyo, along the dirt road back to Hiram's house. He deposited his son and walked with me to Casita Blanca.

I sat on the bed, exhausted and depressed.

He put his hand on my shoulder.

"Is it so important?" he asked.

"Yes," I said. Why does no one take this filmmaking seriously? Is it because it is a small budget; is it because I am a woman? Was I being too sensitive? For people in the arts, it is not a hobby. It is necessary to create; it is somehow necessary to our survival. Creativity is inherent in all humans, but some of us must do it or we wither. We are hardwired to it. As Émile Zola wrote, "If you ask me what I come to do in this world, I, an artist, will answer you: I am here to live out loud."

I was not sure Hiram understood my need to create, any more than I understood his need to be an in-charge macho. Even though we were different, he still had concern for me. Even though I didn't like skinning a cow, I cared deeply for him and respected how he skinned. I guess that is friendship.

"Catalina, I'll ask my friends to search again this afternoon," he said, as he left to return to his house.

All that work for nothing. Although I had other hours of tape, that one had the most exciting footage. I was sick to my stomach.

I sat on the bed, bent my head down to rest it in my hands, and saw the tape on the floor under the leg of the bed. It had fallen out of my little plastic film bag when I came into the room to unload equipment. I breathed deeply, curled up on the bed, and took a nap.

Now a year later in Tucson, I pack my belongings and begin another long trip to Mexico to work on the Rita film.

After hours on the road, I stay in Ciudad Chihuahua at the home of

Rosario, Miguel's sister. She introduces me to Hector, a photojournalist who has agreed to accompany me to the canyons. The more men, the safer, Rosario advises. A woman alone on Sierra backroads is not wise, she informs me.

Hector and I drive toward the mountains. Simpatico and gregarious, he speaks no English so we have an adventure in the land of language. Eventually I get attuned to his rapid sentences and slang. And to help me understand better, he moves his arms in large gestures as he drives my pickup. I sit in the passenger seat, ducking his arms' whopping circles that nearly knock off my hat.

I arrange to meet Samuel in Creel. He will drive us through canyons to look for people who knew Rita before she disappeared into Kansas. Samuel, who owns a motel, used to drive a lumber truck, so he knows Sierra roads that have never been inked on a map.

We arrive in Creel and find his home. Creel is a small town with few primary streets, so it is not hard to find his house. Samuel, a tall, lanky man, greets us at the door of a wood-frame house, invites us in for coffee, and introduces us to his wife and son. We sit at a table with a white lace tablecloth covered in plastic. The table takes up most of the room, with only a few inches to squeeze by the chairs should you want to leave the room. If you have a big belly, you may never be able to leave. A Virgin of Guadalupe sits in the corner.

Samuel's wife brings coffee and we talk about the film, what we want to accomplish and whom we want to interview. We plan our drive to Cerocauhui to rent a cabin while we look for Rita's half brother, Epifanio, who lives far from any town. We learn that we will have to carry the film equipment on miles of canyon trails.

We think we will be traveling for a couple of weeks. Samuel pulls out an old map to show us where we will go. Now I start to get excited. I love maps and can visualize details of our trip for the first time.

Samuel goes outside to look at the Nissan to make sure it is in good order. He will drive, with me and Hector squeezed into the cab beside him. Satisfied, he returns to the house and then directs Hector and me to our rooms. We unload our bags and head over to the restaurant on the main street for dinner. By now it is late afternoon and we are hungry.

We eat steaming-hot chicken *caldo* with chiltepines and frijoles de olla with fresh *tortillas de maíz*, and then head back to the motel for a good night's rest. As we cross the bridge over the arroyo, red clouds fill the sky as the sun starts its descent.

Hector and I talk about why most of Mexico was Catholic but now families have switched over to the Evangelical churches, or many to Santería, and how he doesn't go to church often; he wonders how many religions there are in the United States. Across the street, we see Samuel's front door. We are almost back to the motel. As we walk, deep in angular discussion about Catholicism, I barely notice the truck coming toward us from the street to the right.

I see headlights, and there is still enough daylight to see the gray truck, but I don't think much about it. I hear *kaboom boom ping*, and the next thing I know, my face is in the dirt, I am lying on my belly, and Hector's heavy body is on top of mine.

I don't speak. I wait. I hear tires screech, someone yells, and the truck speeds away. The weight of Hector's body increases.

My spine is pushed inward. I feel sand in my gums and eyelashes, and little sharp rocks jab my cheeks and belly. I don't know how long we lie there. It is like seconds and hours. I wonder why Hector doesn't move. I listen for his breathing.

Just as I am wondering, I see the heel of his palm push into the dirt next to my eyes, and he pushes up his big torso. He slowly rises to peer over the three-foot adobe wall he has shoved us behind. Neither of us speaks. He looks around carefully.

At the last moment before being shoved to the ground so we don't get killed, I remember a glint of a gun in the man's hand, the guy in the passenger seat. His arm and head were out the window, the pistol aimed at us. But it didn't register because it happened so fast.

And besides, who would want to shoot at us? I don't take it personally. Why would they be shooting at me? I don't even know them.

We are about fifty yards from Samuel's house. He is opening the door to walk toward us. We get up, wipe off the dirt, and explain what happened. He says he heard the shots and came out to see what was going on. He didn't recognize the truck. They're not from around here, he says. More strangers come to town nowadays, he adds. Most of them drive new black trucks with black-tinted windows.

I go to my room and lock the door. I walk to the bed and sit on the edge.

I get up and return to the door to make sure the handle is fastened and the bolt is secured. I walk over to my equipment, check my camera gear, check the list, and finish packing what we will need for the next week or so.

I get into bed, thinking about what you see and don't see during a nano-second of danger. I wonder what is rational in a time of confusion and conclude that nonrationality is part of our core. Order is a nice thought, but maybe the human is not really a creature of order and reason. As I put my head on the pillow and try to sleep, I think how we spend a great deal of time calculating right and wrong and make predictions up the yin yang, but in a moment of irrationality, time jumps the track and, poof, comprehension gone. I listen for sounds at the door. My night's sleep is a mess.

CHAPTER 17

INTERNATIONAL

I CONTINUE TO come and go from Ciudad Chihuahua and the southern part of the Barranca del Cobre to film *Rita of the Sky*. Miguel Giner introduces me to the real Rita while he himself becomes a key figure in the documentary. With Miguel's assistance, I film in Kansas where he works, and in Chihuahua, his home state.

In Larned, Kansas, where Miguel lives, the Yellow Brick Road really exists. It is a trail unlike those of the desert. Larned is the home of Dorothy and the Wizard of Oz, the Tin Man with no heart, and a few of his offspring whom I meet in Kansas.

As I drive on flat interstates that connect even flatter towns, I see a tornado in the distance. At first it creeps toward me. I pull the Nissan off to the side of the road, grab the tripod and camera, and start shooting. I know somewhere in the film I can use this. I am favored by the Lightning God and given a front-row seat to film an astounding show.

As the tornado moves toward me, however, the tripod trembles. Then I realize it is not the tripod, but my hands. I am afraid. They shake so hard that I throw the gear into the truck and drive. The tornado comes closer. I hadn't bargained on this. I turn the truck, driving as fast as bombarding rain will let me. Then I hear it. But I don't know what it is. Then I see it. Golf ball–size hail hits my truck and makes troughs along the camper shell. The tornado roils and finally rolls off toward the horizon.

I find Miguel's apartment and stay with him until his workweek is over, and then we drive to Ciudad Chihuahua.

Winding through hilly streets, Miguel, Rosario, and I look for a barrio. We arrive at a cinder-block house where Rita lives with her Rarámuri nephew and his wife.

As we drive through city streets, I look carefully at faces, wondering if I will encounter any of them on a desert trail. By chance. Chance. What are the chances that Rita would end in a Kansas mental hospital and I would end up here at her house in Chihuahua?

As we park, the house across the street roars. Dogs bark, running back and forth on the rooftop edge, telling the neighborhood that strangers are present. Dogs live on the roofs of this barrio. They are probably very intelligent. I wonder how many have fallen to their deaths before the smart ones figure it out.

Arnulfo, the nephew, opens the door for us. We enter a two-room house. Arnulfo seats us, then introduces us to Rita. She sits, white hair, skinny and slumped, but straightens and looks up at me with electric blue eyes. I am startled. For an instant, I wonder if this is really Rita.

What I see is a husk of a human, unable to speak after years of drugs doled out by the mental hospital. It is hard to believe that she is the woman who walked 1,500 miles from the Sierra.

Rita lives with Arnulfo's family. In Kansas, when Miguel was trying to repatriate her to Mexico, he was required to find a family member for her to live with.

At the same time, he discovered that she had spent three years in a Mexican prison for killing her husband. Her Rarámuri husband was found dead outside their house, his head smashed in, perhaps with a rock. There was also a hatchet lying nearby. Both a rock and hatchet are items that would normally be found near log houses. According to Rita's relatives, her husband often tied her outdoors and left her leashed for a few days while he visited other ranchos.

No one saw the killing take place, and many believe that what she had been drinking at a tesguinado the night before the murder was spiked with ground bacánari root. The Rarámuri tell me that the bacánari is a living being, which, if mistreated, captures the soul and holds it for ransom.

I see her story and other migrants' stories as the mystery of human identity. How do we behave when confronted by individuals who appear out of nowhere, with no point of origin, with no identifiable language? We lock them away in a mental hospital. Or label them as enemy, as lunatic, as terrorist. Or we build walls the length of the nation in order to keep them out. Or deport them by the millions.

In our country, we don't react well to women who migrate. Why would a woman walk alone through a deadly desert? Some call her a vagrant, some call her crazy, and some call her aggressive. I call her a brilliant survivor. Imagine walking and walking and walking through mountains and deserts for weeks, alone.

Rita's story illustrates the powerful connection between who we are as human beings, and the place and time that produced us. Without those geographic and blood boundaries, we are at a loss to know who an individual is, because he or she is not us.

A New York educational film distribution company rejected the finished, award-winning *Rita of the Sky*; they said that, because Rita had killed her husband, she was a menace to society, and they didn't want to represent a film that glorified such a woman.

Rosario and I go into the backyard with Rita so Rita can smoke a cigarette. Rosario lived in Kansas for years. When she heard about Rita, Rosario helped with the repatriation. She walks over to Rita. As she leans in toward Rita, together they begin singing "Amazing Grace," a song taught in English to Rita in the Kansas mental hospital. Rosario sings in perfect pitch; with her overly thick tongue, Rita sings *ahhh eggg aa ththhhthh* and in good tune.

For the next two years, with the help of excellent cameramen, we film in Ciudad Chihuahua, in the Barrancas, and in the desert sand dunes that lie south of Juárez. We film the road into Kansas, and the highway that passes Manter where Rita took a detour to find food in a kitchen. Was she just walking along the highway in her Rarámuri dress and head scarf?

While we were trying to determine her routes, we were confounded by the distances and difficulty in traveling such harsh terrain. We heard that she had crossed the border more than once, through a legal port of entry. It is on record that on one occasion, a car hit her as she crossed a road, and her arm was put in a cast.

Arnulfo says that after coming to live with him, she ran away several times. They would find her on the highway outside the city. He said she always carried a plastic shopping bag with onions and water, and a sweater. And she was drawn to the north. Some think she was looking for Aztlán.

After a few years of coming and going, I finish the last processes of the film at home.

In Tucson, my life starts to take different turns. I spend time volunteering in the desert, and I spend more time with Valentín. Life changes in both subtle and glaring ways. The M word pops up. Marriage. Seems like a good thing to do. A little later. Marriage—buoyant as an April cloud or as cumbersome as parliamentary procedure or as durable as a diamond or as forever as death. Something to consider in the future. I have a couple of things to do first.

In the years I traveled to and from the Sierra to film *The Unholy Tarahumara*, I started to become aware that as I made a north-to-south journey across the border, migrants were making a south-to-north journey to look for work or rejoin families. Our lives were intersecting. And I felt safe during those years.

But changes start to occur in Mexico, as well as across the border in my Arizona desert, that affect my day-to-day choices, and I begin to be watchful. I am an artist, not an especially political person. But I begin to pay a great deal of attention to international politics.

The planet is on the move. It is a time of mass exodus from Mexico and Central America to the United States. By the thousands, people leave Tajikistan to seek work in Russia, Turkish people move into Germany to earn a living, and Africans flee genocide by crossing the Sahara into Libya in order to take small boats across the Mediterranean, grasping for the closest rocks— the shores of Malta, Spain, and Italy.

The bodies of 92 abandoned mothers and children are found sprawled in groups in the Sahara as they attempt to cross the desert from Nigeria to Libya. And 365 people drown near the Italian island of Lampedusa as they try to cross the water from North Africa to Europe.

Once people traverse the desert and reach the shores of the Mediterranean in Libya, 50 percent of them then die while crossing the sea in rafts. In the middle of the night, they are taken to a beach, handed a compass, told to keep it pointed north. They get into a tiny inflatable boat and are pushed off into the dark water by "coyotes" of Libya, much like the "coyotes" of southern Arizona who are paid to direct migrants across the night desert.

I sense this is the future, people no longer staying in one place but moving about the world when life is at stake, passing through cultures, walking or riding or crawling to survival. I am coming to think that our concept of nation-states is obsolete, that all peoples have begun to move in ways we have not known before. Of course, I wonder how I would live with only what I can carry on my back.

Pastor John Fife invites several members of social justice organizations to Berlin and Malta. John is a visionary, a longtime voice in the borderlands, with boundless ideas about fighting injustice. In the 1980s, he started the Sanctuary Movement in response to people from Central America fleeing U.S.-supported death squads.

We are invited on behalf of his acquaintances in the German ecumenical groups Asylum in the Church and International Fellowship of Reconciliation to exchange ideas and information with churches and politicians about world migration. They had visited Samaritans in Tucson and had accompanied us on desert trips.

"Why would you want to go to Berlin?" Valentín asks.

"To see what's going on in Europe about migration. And I will be traveling with some great people, and besides, I know Berlin and love the city. Want to come?"

He declines. He wears the face I can't read. It is not an unhappy or angry face. And it is not blank. It is just a face that is not available. As he so often is. Is it the cultural barrier, or the man/woman conundrum? Whatever you call it, it makes things interesting. I think of the Chinese curse "May you live in interesting times." I pack up; he takes me to the airport and gives me an airport good-bye.

When I arrive in Berlin, I wait for my luggage at baggage claim. I wait and wait. I am that last person watching one lone bag travel in circles on the carousel. I go to an office and learn that they don't know where my bag is. I stand there in the only clothes I have. After waiting a couple of days for the luggage to arrive at the house where I'm staying, my hostess takes me shopping. I buy one pair of Levis, two T-shirts, socks, chonis, and soap. That's it for two weeks in Europe. I lose my luggage, but I know that somehow I can get clothes and that eventually I will return to a safe place. Wonder how I would fare as a clothesless wanderer with no home to go to.

Nine months and twenty e-mails later, my bag is returned to me in Tucson. Each item of clothing reeks of cigarette smoke.

After spending a week in Berlin, our little group flies to Malta to learn how the Maltese handle an accidental influx of migrants.

The eye watches us walk around the boat. An eye with a thick braided brow, the Eye of Osiris, is painted on either side of the small boat's bow. Watching for danger, the eyes warn fishermen of impending evil. I am in the port of Marsaxlokk, southern Malta, with our Tucson group, a German guide, and Franciscan friar Dionysius Mintoff.

Friar Mintoff proudly points out the details of Maltese life as we walk along the port with fishing boats painted in circus colors. Eighty years old, he has worked half his life in Malta, bringing peace to the world, one person at a time. A skilled speaker of several languages, when asked if peace is coming, he gesticulates silently with hands moving in circles, adding an Italian shoulder shrug and a big smile. "It is always with us; it just gets interrupted," he says.

He proceeds to tell us that he has a place for us to live if we want to stay in Malta to help. As I look around at the mysterious grounds and think about the great history of Malta, I am tempted to stay. "We will be very busy," he explains. Making peace is a busy job. Then I think, do I really want to have a busier life?

We drive from the port to an old villa overgrown with vines and tall trees, stuffed with plants, flowers, goats, canaries, chickens, pigs—the sorts of things you might expect of a Franciscan. Also on the grounds are Africans walking around in traditional clothing from their various countries, and a small room housing a Doctors Without Borders clinic.

Outside the peace lab is Lister Barracks, which houses twelve thousand undocumented immigrants who arrive in Malta by the skin of their teeth and whose relatives die in dark waters.

As we walk between the bunk beds where a couple hundred men are crammed, we speak with nervous, angry, lonely African refugees, some missing an arm or leg lost in war. They gather close around us with big energy. Words tumble out as if they hadn't used them in a while. They ask for help. I feel like that dream you have when someone starts to fall and you reach out to catch them and realize you have no arms.

Like people crossing the Arizona desert, they leave their countries for economic and political reasons, and when, or if, they arrive in the new land, they are put in prison.

Our group returns to Berlin. We make presentations about migration in the Arizona-Sonora Desert, and then learn about the *Cap Anamur*, a converted freighter sailing under the German flag that rescued Africans in the Mediterranean Sea.

In 2004, the ship picked up Africans who were fleeing war in Sudan. The ship rescued more than thirty people who were sinking in inflatable boats. As the *Cap Anamur* later tried to dock at a Sicilian port, Italian helicopters and frigates forced the ship back to sea. The Italian government says that no refugees can step into Italy. Picture a sea of tiny bobbing boats holding thirty people who are rescued, then pulled on board a big ship, and now the big ship bobs around with nowhere to land.

After eleven days at sea, the *Cap Anamur* was allowed to dock, but the captain and first officer were arrested for "people smuggling," the Italian government confiscated the ship, and the Africans were packed into a detention center to await deportation. After a three-year trial, the captain was acquitted. International message: Do not assist those who cross borders.

As time comes to leave Berlin, I Skype Valentín.

"What are you doing over there?" he asks in a quiet voice.

"I'm not sure but it is getting clearer. It seems to be another version of the Arizona desert. People are moving across Africa, the Mediterranean, and Europe. All over the planet."

"Well, they don't need you over there. Just come home so we can do a little moving ourselves."

"Soon. Very soon." He looks great sitting there in his workshop, in his black T-shirt and spiked black hair. I miss him. Maybe he gets tired of my talking about migration all the time. He lives in two cultures. I live in one and what do I really know about life in other places? I like to think I am a citizen of the world but I am really a tourist. And a tourist in the land of love.

When I return to Tucson, Valentín says he wants to walk trails with Samaritan volunteers. He wants to help. But he says he doesn't need to go as far as Malta. He wants to take water to his compadres who are dying in our own desert.

After consulting with a lawyer, we realize that is not wise. Having only a visa, or even a green card, is legal but risky in an anti-immigrant atmosphere. He can be detained and deported by the Border Patrol seemingly on a whim.

Valentín says, OK, instead of going to the desert, he will write his memoirs so gringos can understand the real life in Mexico. I hand him a pen.

He also says he has a surprise for me. He has been busy while I was gone.

In the early part of our relationship, he had inquired about my parents. I told him they had died when I was in my twenties.

"Where are they buried?" he asked.

"Here in Tucson at the big cemetery."

"I never see you go there," he said.

"I can't remember where they were buried. When I was young, after they died I went back but couldn't find the gravestones. I don't know where they are."

"*Mi amor*, that's loco. Are all gringos like this?"

"I don't know," I said. I rose from the table and walked to the other room.

So today he tells me his surprise.

"Your parents want you to visit them."

This is out of left field.

"How do you know?"

"Because that is what we do in our country. We go often to visit our dead. And a whole country can't be wrong."

Hard to argue with that.

"So I found your parents' graves, and I am taking you there."

I jump up to pour more coffee.

"Besides, I want to meet your *papá*. Would he have liked me?"

"Yes, I'm sure."

"*Claro*. So my surprise is that I am taking you to see your father and tell him I love you."

Yikes. What do I do now?

"That is sweet but I don't want to go there. It's not a happy place."

"*Pues*, we go anyway. It's settled."

Two days later, on Día de Los Muertos, there are two flowers on the kitchen table. One red, one yellow. Valentín picks up the flowers. We get in the car.

We drive around the cemetery on little dirt roads. He finds the row number. We get out of the car. My stomach churns.

We walk down the row and see two rectangles of aged marble that stand side by side. I remember being here when I was twenty-two years old. There was no marble. Only deep holes in the ground. One tombstone says Harvey, one says Kathryn. My heart beats too fast. I turn to walk to the car. Valentín grabs my hand and pulls me beside him. He puts the red rose on my father's grave, the yellow, my mother's favorite color, on hers.

"*Buenas tardes*, Mr. Ferguson, I am happy to meet you. I came to tell you that I love your daughter and I am going to take care of her." He smiles.

Tears pour out of my eyes. I can't stop crying.

"¡*Apúrate!* Hurry, say hello. They are glad you are here."

"Hello," I whisper. After decades, my tears still run like a melted glacier. Valentín brushes leaves off the graves. He shines the gravestones with a cloth.

"Aren't you happy I brought you here?" he asks.

"Yes."

He beams. "Another stripe for the tiger," he says proudly.

We walk away, arm in arm. It is good to be home. I don't want to travel anymore.

CHAPTER 18

PHONE CALL

AFTER RUNNING ERRANDS all day, I return to the house, walk inside, kiss the dog, look through my mail, and notice a flashing light on my answering machine. I listen to some messages. I see on the caller ID, "USBP El PASO." I find that startling. United States Border Patrol El Paso.

I hit the button and listen to the message. "Hello, this is Maria at the U.S. Border Patrol office in El Paso, Texas. This message is for Kathryn Ferguson. Call me at this number."

I call Margo Cowan, a lawyer who works with Samaritans, to ask advice. She says call, see what they want. Next day, I call the number. Maria answers and says, "I never called your number and I never asked to speak with you."

I ask a few more questions. She says, "This is a Border Patrol procurement office. We purchase helicopters through this office. We have no reason to call you." I am confused. I hang up and replay the message. It still says the same thing. I take the small tape from the answering machine and put it in a safe place in case I need it in the future. For what, I have no idea, but I am uncomfortable with the situation.

A few weeks later, I begin to hear noises when I speak on the phone. Sometimes it is a series of clicks, sometimes a small sound like blowing air. It happens occasionally, not every call. I contact the phone company to report interference. They send a repairperson to check the lines. He says he can find no problem. The noises persist intermittently.

One day, in conversation with a lawyer, I mention the noises. She says it may be a "sweep," which is when your phone is tapped by the government. Not every call is tapped; rather, an automatic sweep occurs that records random calls.

I am not sure what to think. Why would anyone possibly want to record my calls? They are run of the mill and would be boring to an outsider.

Now it is getting personal. The spider web of no-exit wraps round. It has wrapped around my foot and is creeping up my leg. I don't like the phone call. The Border Patrol enters my private life through the phone on my desk. Perhaps in other ways, too.

Day by day, I grow more personally involved. It is not just about carrying water to thirsty people on the desert, a transparent action performed with a group of kindhearted people. It is now on my answering machine. Certainly not a transparent or kindhearted action.

I feel less carefree. I am a morning person and love each new day. I look forward to the dawn and a cup of black coffee. But now there is a tinge of something uncomfortable. It is the small foreboding I had when I started the Rita film. Each day, I think about this phone message. I can't figure it out.

Seamlessly, I get more involved. A few weeks later, I ride with Samaritans along Arivaca Road. We near the Marley Cattle Company. On the right side of the road is a big metal barn. On the other side is a fence surrounding stables, dirt roads, and the main ranch house.

Near the barn, we see four people: two women and two men, Rarámuri, wearing traditional clothing of colored skirts and white shirts. They crouch by the barn. The same crouch I remember from watching them sit and share a cigarette around a fire outside Ventura's house, from when they share a gourd of tesgüino and tell jokes. One of the women is old, like Rita.

From the other side of the road, two Latino cowboys, Marley ranch hands, run across the road in front of our car. As they trot toward the barn, one speaks into a walkie-talkie, one runs with an outstretched arm pointing a finger at the Rarámuri and shouts, "¡No se mueven. Quédense dónde están!" Don't move. Stay where you are. The Rarámuri freeze.

We watch from the car. The cowboys call Border Patrol and herd the people behind the barn, out of sight. It is the first time I have seen Rarámuri in this area. This is far north for them to come. Normally, they don't travel so far from the Barrancas. I see them in Ciudad Chihuahua and as far north as Nuevo Casas Grandes in Sonora, Mexico, a five-hour drive southeast of here.

For them to leave their land, cross the desert, and travel this great distance, they must have great needs. It is probably the ten-year drought that is moving into its thirteenth year.

The raven on my shoulder shifts. Ventura. He died before he got a chance

A border crosser's T-shirt strung between mesquite trees. Photo by Bob Kee.

to come here. I was too slow. I should have slogged through the visa system and brought him here to visit. I failed him. Now I see his people shoved behind the barn, waiting for a prison cell, then deportation.

We continue to see border crossers daily on trails and roads. A week later, I drive with Samaritans heading to the border town of Sasabe. As we crest a hill, the land rolls out in front of us, desert as far as the eye can see. Not a forlorn desert, but the Sonoran Desert, lush with yellow grasses, prickly-pear and barrel cactus, and miles of mesquite trees, simultaneously charcoaled from a wildfire and sprouting new green leaves.

The desert is as big as the ocean. We are the only vehicle, and the only other living creature is a hawk circling overhead.

In the distance is a tree stump by the side of the road. As we near, it moves. It is a person. We slow down. A man sits on the ground slumped over, his arms wrapped around his knees. A dark ball cap covers most of his face; he wears a dark shirt, dusty pants, and beat-up shoes. As we approach, he lifts his head, smiles, jumps up, and grabs his backpack, ready to hop into the car.

His round face makes him seen younger than his twenty-six years. He grins and looks happy to see us. He says his name is Martín and he wants to go back to Mexico. He is alone, thirsty, and wants to go home.

We sit and drink water together. As he drinks, he informs us that he crossed the border with eight others. They walked in hundred-degree heat for three days and were almost out of water. The pollero told the group that they were walking to Phoenix, a hard thirteen-day walk from the U.S.-Mexico border, a death march in fact since a person cannot carry enough water to cover that distance. But the pollero said it was only another day or two.

On a hot day with heavy exertion, the human body loses fifteen liters of water. It is necessary to carry that amount per day. Fifteen liters weighs over thirty-two pounds—for just one day of walking. Imagine how much it weighs for four days of walking, the amount of time to get from the border to Tucson, with luck.

Since Martín had worked in California two years earlier, he was savvy about the desert and the game of crossing. Headed to a job in Los Angeles, he decided not to continue, worried that the group would perish.

He explains that they had already walked more days than expected. The first day of the trip, a short woman who weighed 270 pounds joined them in Sasabe, Sonora. She paid to cross. But the pollero said she wasn't in good enough condition to walk the distance because she was overweight. He didn't want her to come.

The others, simpatico to the desire of the woman to join her son in the United States, wanted her to travel with them. So she did. After the first three hours of walking, she was far behind, stumbling and breathing heavily.

As everyone became aware that she would not be able to continue, they said they needed to escort the woman back to the border. So the entire group returned to the border and began the journey again without her, adding a day of walking.

This consideration for an individual's well-being will change in the future. As years roll on and thousands of migrants cross, the "guide" business will go viral and drug cartels will seize control. The cartel polleros, who are paid by the head, will drop any pretense of caring about migrants. Even now, if a person can't keep up, the pollero pushes the group forward and leaves the straggler behind. These are the bodies we continue to find.

Although Martín is scared to be alone, he tells us that he decided to separate from the group. As they walked away, he thought they would die.

Martín says he is from Guadalajara. I say that I am going to a wedding in Guadalajara next month. An outgoing, cheerful man, he says please come visit his family. He asks for paper and pencil. We dig around in our backpacks and come up with a box of Band-Aids. He writes down his contact information.

I copy Martín's phone number from the Band-Aid box and carry it with me to Guadalajara a few weeks later. I arrive at the hotel two days before the wedding, so I call him. The following day, I go to the lobby to meet him. I barely recognize the shiny man in a green vaquero shirt. Standing next to him is his shy wife, who cradles a one-year-old daughter in her arms. Holding Martín's hand is his four-year-old son with an ironed white shirt and moussed, spiked glistening black hair.

We walk out of the hotel to a borrowed blue Nissan, a little dented here and there but with enough room for all of us. The engine doesn't turn over the first or second time, but on the third try, we are off to see the city.

After driving twenty minutes, we arrive at an open-air restaurant with tiled floors and cowhide leather chairs and strings of blue lights hanging on the walls. Martín orders birria for the table, and fresh-squeezed orange juice. At first we are shy with each other and I don't know what to talk about. I have to get into my mode of no English. After the food arrives, the talking becomes easier with *mmm*s and *aah*s at the delicious meal. I later learn that in order to pay for this meal, and the gasoline for driving around Guadalajara today, he had to work a week mixing cement.

He tells me that after spending two days at Tucson Border Patrol detention in a cell so packed with men standing shoulder to shoulder that he had to sleep standing up, he was deposited in the night across the border into Agua Prieta, not Sasabe, the port of entry near which he passed. He had never been in Agua Prieta and knew no one.

He didn't have enough money for a bus ticket, so he wired for money from his father. He had to hang around Agua Prieta a few days to wait for the money. He said he just sat on a curb and watched people, on guard to make sure no one would try to harm or kidnap him. He sat near a school because he felt safer if he surrounded himself with people. He didn't speak with anyone for days.

After lunch, we go to Lake Chapala and wander around with the ducks. We walk through stalls with vendors selling Frida Kahlo T-shirts, hammocks, and CDs of popular bands. Families eat ice cream together as small children yell and play. We have a quiet afternoon.

Then they take me to their house. After a half hour of driving six-lane streets packed with honking cars, music blasting from the side of the road, vendors selling everything, and people everywhere, we enter a colonia of dirt streets and cinder-block houses. We park and walk up to an unfinished house made of gray blocks with a tin roof. We enter a small room with one couch and one chair. A few feet away are the stove and a table.

There are two other rooms. One room has a bed where Martín and his family sleep. The other room has a small bed but other than that is empty. He tells me this room is for me and will be for me the rest of my life. I don't understand.

He explains that since I helped him on the desert, he wants to help me somehow. I am embarrassed. First of all, it wasn't me; I was with Samaritans, and all we did was give him water. It was so nothing.

He said, "You were nice to me." I begin to realize that behind his cheerfulness that day on the desert, he was scared and defeated sitting by himself. I guess a little water and conversation momentarily eased the fear.

Suddenly the front door bursts open, and a sixty-year-old woman in a flower-print dress runs in, calling out. I think there must be an emergency. She sees me and starts pouring out rapid-fire Spanish. I catch a few words. She runs to me and shakes my hand. A puppy follows into the house. The woman yells, and pandemonium follows as the dog zips around with Martín's son in the chase. The dog slides under the couch, happy for so much attention, and is finally shooed out with a broom. "Qué bárbaro!" says the woman.

"Cálmate, mamá, cálmate." Martín introduces me to his mother. She grabs my hand and says, "Gracias a Dios, gracias." She tells me her son was alone on the desert in *el Norte*, he could have died, what would she have done, how could they continue their life without him? He is her baby boy and it is too soon for God to take him. Tears come to her eyes.

Martín doesn't say anything. His mother now has the run of the house. We sit down and she tells me the story of their lives. Martín's wife makes coffee.

CHAPTER 19

DETAINED

IT'S WAY TOO early for that sound. That blasted alarm. Thank god Valentín is at his house, not here. He hates to wake up early. 4:30 a.m. I get out of bed to prepare for a Samaritan trip to the desert. I am back in Tucson and back to my daily life, but still tired from the trip to Guadalajara.

Thwak! Ow. I bump into the dresser with my knee. It hurts.

Crash!—I knock something over. It breaks on the tile floor. I fumble for the light switch in predawn darkness.

Damn. It's my photo of Hiram as he reaches up to his horse, his back to me, his fingers spread wide on the horse's warm neck. I like that photo. Oh well. I don't need glass in the frame.

As I sweep up the glass, I wonder how Hiram is. I remember another dawn at Casita Blanca, my little house in Norogachic. Across the Arroyo Grande, the sun peeked over the mesa. The morning stepped across the riverbed and climbed the hill to my balcony. I threw on my Levis and stumbled outside to watch the sunrise. I boiled water for coffee with a little camping gizmo. Out over the arroyo, there were no humans in sight, although I knew that inside all the houses, Rarámuri and mestizo women were also boiling water for coffee. It's a sunup to sundown life.

It took a while for the water to boil, but finally I sat outside on the white adobe balcony wall sipping the black brew.

Across the way, I saw Hiram walking the hill from his house. He always walked this trail to Gabriel's house. His cowboy hat sat a little back on the head, the hat the color of peach in this early light. His moustache was trimmed, his shirt fresh. He looked good, like the Mexican movie star Luis Aguilar. Neat and clean like he had been up for hours. I marvel at how Sierra people and houses look ironed and kempt, even before breakfast.

"Buenos días," he called.

"Café?" I called back.

He climbed up the little hill to my porch. He was going to Gabriel's house to help him haul a big barrel of water onto the roof so water could flow down a hose to make a shower inside the house.

I started to make him coffee but remembered I had only one cup. I freshened it and stepped outside.

We sat on the balcony wall and shared the cup. Down the hill at Gabriel's house, chickens foraged, and sleepy Susana, Gabriel's eight-year-old daughter and my hairdresser, walked toward the outhouse. I figured she would be joining us up on the porch as soon as she cleared the cobwebs from her eyes. She always wanted to snoop around my "otherness."

"Qué fresca es el aire," Hiram said. How cool the air is.

"Yes, so cool," I said. "Have you had breakfast?"

"Pues, sí," he said. Of course. His wife took good care of him.

Then the conversation faded. There was no need to talk. The chickens were enough noise, the rising sun enough excitement. We sipped from the cup and watched the arroyo wake up. A burro passed. A bird flew. We were simply people on a porch.

But I don't have time for coffee this morning. I finish sweeping the glass and toss it into the trash. I throw on my clothes, grab my backpack, and run out to the truck.

I drive to meet Robin Redondo and her twelve-year-old son, Liam Etheridge. We pack up the Samaritans' Isuzu Rodeo with food, water, medical supplies, backpacks, blankets, and warm clothing. We head south on I-19 for an hour's drive to a trail at the border, where we will search for people in distress.

After we spend a few minutes locating the trail, Liam calls out, "Here's one!" He points to a footprint.

"Pretty fresh," I say. "Could be from early this morning."

"Here's another one," he yells as he charges forward. "And look, there are some broken branches on the bush!"

"Are you some kind of scout, or something?" I ask. Looks like he's done his tracking homework.

Liam has a school assignment to help someone and write an essay about the experience, so he rides with us to search for people. Happy as a squirrel nestled between gear in the backseat, he says, "I've been so excited about this all night. When Mom said we had to get up before dawn, it felt like we were going to Australia or something."

As far as I can tell, he is a member of the crow family. He is uncannily observant, pokes around into everything, fits into the natural world here in southern Arizona like skin on a snake, and he keeps us laughing. And he is gung ho to do some good.

After hiking in the Batamonte Hills for a few hours, we drive west of the town of Arivaca. We pull off the road and park near a grove of mesquite trees to eat lunch. The Mexican border is twelve miles south.

Looks like it is going to be a quiet day. We haven't seen anyone for a couple of weeks, although we see footprints. The last time I saw someone was in a narrow canyon, just a mile north of the Mexican line. As we hiked, we saw three men run past us, headed back into Mexico. Border Patrol agents with assault weapons longer than my leg chased them. One of the men running for his life wore a thin Mexican laborer's shirt. He was about forty-five years old, short and chubby, and he limped, kind of like he had a clubfoot. He was the last man of the three, stumbling, and he panicked. Weapons aimed, the agents were in hot pursuit.

While Robin, Liam, and I sit in the car and make plans for the afternoon, a big shiny gray Ford 4x4 pickup pulls up behind us and parks. It sits about fifteen feet back. We don't pay much attention to it.

After a while, Robin says, "Wonder what they are up to," and looks out the passenger side mirror.

"I was wondering, too," I say, looking in my rearview mirror.

Three men in the cab of the truck watch us.

"So where do we go next?" asks Liam.

"I don't know. Do you want to go over to the Baboquivari area?"

We look in the mirrors again. All three of the men in the truck are hunched forward, elbows on the dashboard.

"They keep looking at us," I say. Liam turns around to watch them.

"Don't stare, Liam," Robin says. "Maybe they're just ranchers."

"OK, do you want to go south near the De La Osa road?"

"Sounds good, but I don't want those guys to follow us."

"I'm trying to be mellow but they are creeping me out," says Liam.

"Maybe they're hunters," says Robin.

"Maybe they're special agents like *Men in Black*," says Liam.

After about ten minutes, we get out of the car and walk to the rear of our Rodeo. The men in the truck don't move.

We open the tailgate to get water bottles and rearrange supplies. They keep watching.

"Honestly. This is annoying. Let's just go over and see what they want," I say to Robin.

She and I walk toward the driver's door. As we approach, three big men in street clothes jump out of the truck and the tall driver charges toward us. Robin is Scandinavian blonde, tall and lanky like a fashion model. But the driver is taller and looms over us.

"Can we help you?" I ask.

"Can we help you?" says the driver, in a mimicking, high-pitched voice that sounds like he just inhaled helium.

"Who are you?" I ask.

"Who are you?" trills the helium voice.

By now I am sure they must be Minutemen with the ridiculous behavior. Or maybe they are undercover Border Patrol.

"Are you law enforcement?"

"Yes!" squeaks Helium Voice, and he smiles. Then he abruptly walks away to the other side of Arivaca Road into the trees. We won't see him again for an hour.

Two men stand in front of their truck. One has short dark hair, wears a lumberjack shirt and Levis; the other has a shiny shaved head and wears a vest over a sweatshirt. As the lumberjack shirt man moves, I see a gun under his clothing. But that is not too alarming. Almost everyone we encounter around southern Arizona wears a gun. This is rattlesnake country.

"*Are* you with the government?" I ask Lumberjack.

"Yes," he says gruffly.

"Who are you with?"

"Department of Interior."

Robin and I look at each other. In the years we have been with Samaritans, we have never heard anyone say that. It is a weird answer. Always, people say "Fish and Wildlife" or "Sheriff's Department." They announce their connection to agencies specific to the location.

Feeling uncomfortable with his answer, I say, "Can I see your identification?"

Dark and irritated, Lumberjack pulls out a wallet, flips it open and closes it immediately. All I see is plastic. He snaps it shut quickly so I can't read anything that is written.

"OK, let's go," Robin says, and we all start to walk to the Rodeo.

Lumberjack calls out, "Whose car is that?"

"Samaritans."

"Why are you driving it?"

"We're with an organization, and it's the vehicle we use." I point to the red Samaritan sign on the car door.

He seems perplexed. As we walk, he shouts angrily and waves his arms. "Stop! I need to see everyone's identification."

Liam is on the other side of the car, monkeying with stuff, watching to see what his mom and I do. He tells me later that the men didn't seem like cops.

Lumberjack stands beside me. I reach into my purse and pull out my wallet, open it and show him my driver's license. He says, "Give it to me." I don't trust him. I have no idea who he is so I don't want to hand it to him. I just hold it up for him to read.

"Why are you questioning us?" Robin asks.

He doesn't answer.

He walks away. Robin says, "Liam, get in the car."

I get a pen and paper out of my purse and walk to their pick-up. There is no plate on the front, so I walk around the back. Since I didn't see his ID, I want to write down his license plate number. Just in case.

The cab door is open. He stands outside the truck, facing the seat on the passenger side. He fiddles with a fishing tackle box full of something on the seat. As I get closer, I see that the box is full of metal handcuffs, drill bits, and screws.

He stands at a right angle to me, suddenly spins, and strikes me hard across the collarbone, then snaps his fist up against my jawbone. I fall back a few feet.

Shocked, I say, "You hit me . . . you can't just hit people." In an instant, he grabs my arms, jerks them behind my back, turns me around, puts handcuffs on my wrists, and says, "You're under arrest." I can't believe it. I say, "What for?" He says, "For not giving me your license." He pauses, and then says, "For interfering with law enforcement."

He says, "Are you carrying a weapon?"

"Of course not."

"I'm going to frisk you." He grabs my shoulders and jerks me around to face him.

He quickly squats down in front of me. I see his dirty hair on top of his head.

He places one hand on each of my shoes and touches my feet.

As soon as I feel that touch, the ground shifts. Balance is a curious thing. You never think about it until it is not there.

There are many kinds of touch. A touch of friendship. A touch by accident. A touch of play. A touch of intimacy. A touch of control.

Before this moment, I knew the place of each thing. The earth was solid. The mesquite tree was rooted. The rock sat. I heard the bird call.

In this moment, something reaches out from the underbelly and tilts me. My legs are jelly. In this moment, his refusal to look at my eyes warns me. I see only the oversize bulk of this man. I smell only him. I hear nothing. I am far away like when you dream that you are awake while you sleep. I can't right my legs or my thinking. I retreat into my airless cave.

I cannot take my eyes from the top of his head and I think if I look out from the cave, forward toward the trees, I will fall. *Shhhhh.* I think too much. It is so quiet. *Shhhhh.* I think too much. Stay inside the cave.

I am never surprised at the force and fierceness of a desert storm. I am surprised at the force of this quiet, crawling unpredictability.

My arms are braided behind my back. I am handcuffed. There is a goon crouched in front of me.

I hear his voice say again, "I am going to frisk you." He pushes my legs apart. Then he forces them apart again, wider. I almost fall forward on top of him.

At first his movements are furtive, like a rodent. He plants his hands on my feet. He stretches his neck, pats my shoes, and pats my socks. He pats my calves. His hands stop and hold. His warm palms cup my calves. He lifts his torso and stretches his neck on the other side, like he has all the time in the world, like he is getting ready to settle in to a task. But he doesn't look at my eyes.

Then he moves his hands slowly, up behind my knees the way an insect crawls under your clothes and you try to hit it before it strikes. Even through denim, I feel warmth from his palms. He slows his hands as they spread up the inside of my thighs. They don't pat. They rub.

Then the hands move to my hamstrings, alternating as one goes high, the other drops, like milking a cow, slowly up and down. I can't breathe. He takes his time. He is in no hurry.

Then he moves his hands from the hamstring back to the inner thigh. Even slower. Rubbing. In circles. As his hands get higher, I say, "Don't." He pauses and inches his fingers upward. I don't breathe.

From far away, I hear "I am calling now." Robin. I didn't know where she went. I lost track of her. I look over toward her voice. Slowly, like waking from a spell, I climb out of the cave. I wrench my mind to the moment. The cool Scandinavian. She stands near with a cell phone. She calmly punches numbers into the cell. "I am calling our lawyer," she announces.

At the sound of her voice, the man looks over. He jerks his hands off me. He is angry. It is as if he forgot that other people were there.

Shaved Head walks from behind the truck and yells, "You just had to keep going, didn't you?"

I think he is talking to me. I think there is no end to this insanity. Then he jerks his arm forward, and I realize he is ordering Lumberjack to walk with him. Shaved Head storms to the back of their truck where they whisper angrily.

I realize no one ever read me my rights. Does that really happen? I have no idea what my rights are except what I see in the movies. Where is a good script when you need it?

Robin tells me, "There is no connection. I can't get service."

"If you can't reach Margo, call one of our friends. The numbers are in my purse on the seat of the Rodeo."

Robin walks to get my purse, brings it back to me, pulls out the phone numbers, gets our car keys out of my Levis' pocket since I can't use my hands, and tries the phone again. No one seems to mind that we are walking around. The two men whisper behind the truck.

Still there is no cell service. Robin and I agree she should go to Arivaca to get a landline. I ask her to keep my purse with her so these men don't steal anything from it.

Twenty minutes later, Lumberjack returns to us with a calmer demeanor. I ask where they are taking me. He says Federal Corrections. Robin asks where that is. She is writing. He says he doesn't know.

Robin and Liam walk to the car. Liam says, "What's going to happen?" She says, "Kathryn has been arrested and we are going to find a phone."

As they start to drive away, a concerned Liam looks at me out the window and says, "Mom, you're never supposed to leave a member of the pack behind!"

I remember Maya, my dog. As the Rodeo starts down Arivaca Road, I run after them, hands cuffed behind, and I call out. Robin stops. "Please feed Maya. The house key is on my keychain. I don't know how long this will take."

Again, no one shouts at us to stop. The men don't seem to mind that we are running in the road, dealing with purses, keys, phones, and dogs.

Robin drives away.

I am alone in the desert with three thugs. I need to pay hard attention.

Then the loneliness hits. It is unexpected and I don't know why I feel it. It is bigger than my fear. Just an immense sense of being alone. It is not even my own private loneliness. It is the kind you feel as if everyone's loneliness has just been given to you to hold for a few minutes, an accumulated loneliness of all humans and animals. The loneliness of a boy kicking a can down the alley, the loneliness of a leopard in a cage, of an old man who spent a life in prison and never knew youth, a dog whose owner left him at the pound, of a tethered Turkish circus bear with a ring in his nose, the loneliness of the girl on the bridge, the boy coming home from war, the child walking from mesquite to mesquite looking for his dead mother.

And then the shout. One of the men shouts across the road, looking for his buddy. It is as if the Puppet Master snaps his finger—abruptly the embalming loneliness leaves and the heart jumps. Adrenaline is my friend. I am scared, but not pit-of-the-stomach scared, not an immobilizing scared. Blood surges through my body. I walk around. I keep moving. I try to stretch my arms. But it is just an isometric movement of muscles. The handcuffs hurt and my arms are immobile because my shoulder blades are pinched together and the bound wrists don't permit movement.

In the Sierra, I never really felt afraid. In all the years that I came and went from the canyons, I didn't feel like this. And I often traveled alone. Here I am now in my own country. I speak English, I understand what these men say, and I have no idea what is happening or who they are, or why they have treated us like criminals.

Soon after Robin leaves, another vehicle, a jeep, drives up, red and blue lights flashing. A man gets out of the jeep wearing a beige uniform and a vest that says POLICE. Shaved Head instructs the new man to come over to guard me. I assume they have called him.

He says to me, "Do you have any weapons on you?"

"I just told the other man 'no.'" Not again. I'm trying to figure out if this man is as nuts as the others.

Lumberjack makes calls on a phone from the policeman's jeep. He says to someone, "She was sneaking up behind me. I was afraid for my life." He orders someone to take me to the federal facility, but it seems that no one is available. Jurisdiction problems.

I ask the man with the POLICE vest what agency he is with. He says, "U.S. Fish and Wildlife." I say, "Fish and Wildlife! Gosh, I used to like you guys!" He doesn't say anything.

I ask his name. "Sam," he says.

"How long have you been with Fish and Wildlife?"

"Two years. Before that with Customs."

"Which job do you like better?"

"This one." He is not very talkative.

"I bet it's because you like being outdoors."

"That's right. I like it out here."

"So do I. Fish and Wildlife. I guess you don't deal with the fish part too often, being in the desert and all."

He smiles and says no. Then he asks if I would like to be in the shade. I say yes, so I am allowed to sit on the door stoop of Lumberjack's truck.

"Can I have some water?" I ask. None of the men have water. No water? That's like going fishing without a pole. We are in the middle of a desert and no one carries water.

A half hour later, as I sit on the edge of the truck door, I hear voices from the road.

"What's going on here?" someone asks.

Shaved Head says, "We're just checking things out, making sure everything is OK around here."

"Oh, that's good," says a man's voice. I stand up and walk around the truck.

I see a man and woman in their sixties, straddling bicycles in the middle of the road.

I say, "A little more than that is going on." I explain that the men have detained me, and I want someone to know I am here.

The man looks frightened as he sees my wrists handcuffed behind me and says, "Let's go," as he turns his bike. The woman says, "Oh dear. Our name is Smith and we live up on that second hill if you need us," as she points to their house a half mile away.

After they leave, I am nervous but again no one seems to care what I do. Shaved Head starts looking for Helium Voice. He walks across the road, ducks under a barbed-wire fence into dense mesquite trees. Shortly the two men return.

After many phone calls, Lumberjack comes over and says that he wants me to be comfortable and changes the handcuffs so now I am cuffed in front of my body. It is a relief. I see my wrists for the first time. They are purple and puffy, like small eggplants. My arms ache in a way I have not experienced. I've never had my arms bound behind my back. I bet they haven't either.

I later learn that Robin reached Margo, and Margo called the Arizona U.S. attorney, requesting that he release me, explaining that I will appear in court.

Someone tells Helium Voice to give me an electrolyte drink. He comes over to me, his face handsome like a movie star. He smiles with perfect teeth, pulls his arm back and jabs me hard in the abdomen with the bottle. My torso jackknifes forward. I am bent double. I am so embarrassed. That is what I feel most. Embarrassment. I have no control over my body. I guess that is what they want.

I feel like the Sierra Madre cow that Hiram butchered, the one with a .22 bullet lodged in its brain. I feel there is a bullet lodged in the center of my emotions. I ricochet from humiliation to anger to feeling small as a microbe to indignation to recognizing the thugs as small in the heart. Helium Voice pushes the bottle between my cuffed hands. He walks away.

I can't open the bottle. I try to open it between my legs, and finally put it to my mouth to open with my teeth. But I don't feel like drinking.

After what seems like forever, but is a few hours, I see Lumberjack get off the phone. All four men walk over to me. They undo the handcuffs. We stand around the hood of a truck.

Lumberjack says, "I've talked with the U.S. attorney. I am going to give you a citation and release you. You still get to see that judge you're dying to see."

He removes the handcuffs. I can smell him as he steps close.

He says, "Sign this." The paper is written on a U.S. Fish and Wildlife form. He has written, "Creat Nusanse."

When we finish the form, I say, "Can you all give me your identification?" Helium Voice says, "I'll never give you anything." And smiles again.

Lumberjack gives me his card. It says Bureau of Land Management, his name, and "Special Agent." Maybe Liam was right.

It seems we are finished because they all walk away. I am four miles from the nearest town, on a desert road, ninety miles from Tucson. I say, "How do I get back to Tucson?" No one says anything. They look at each other.

Sam says he can give me a ride to Arivaca. I get in the Fish and Wildlife jeep with him and Shaved Head.

I sit in the passenger seat next to a gun. The tip of the gun rests on the floor next to my feet. The handle slants up, well past my shoulder. It has five or six bullets; the top of each bullet is the size of a quarter, and the bullets are five or six inches long. An assault weapon. Was this for me? Why did the others call him here in the first place?

As I get out of the jeep in Arivaca, Shaved Head gives me his card. His name is printed on it, along with "U.S. Fish and Wildlife."

I go into the Arivaca Mercantile and realize I don't have my purse. I can't buy a soda and I don't have money to call anyone. I walk up and down the aisles for a few minutes. I don't know how to explain to strangers what just happened. But if I keep walking up and down the aisles, the clerks will think I am weird. I don't know where else to go.

I have been in the store dozens of times but I don't know the owner well. I decide to ask for help. She is kind, sets me in a chair, tells me to explain my story to her husband while she makes hot tea. I don't have any phone numbers so they help me make calls. Eventually I get hold of Robin and Liam, who are almost to Tucson; they turn around to come get me at the Mercantile.

As instructed by Margo, we take photos of my swollen purple-and-black wrists and write down everything we can remember about the experience. She says do this before you have that tequila.

When I am at home the next night, I start to feel afraid. At the same time, I feel like being private. I don't want to call Valentín. It's not the kind of fear that will be helped by having someone hold your hand. It is a fear that has to be figured out.

In a way, I am more afraid than when I was handcuffed in the desert; those men were aberrations, and now they have access to my personal information like my address and phone number. Surely they would not come to my house.

I become observant during the day, watching for unfamiliar cars around the neighborhood, occasionally wondering if I am being followed. For a few nights, I keep all the lights on in the house until the sun comes up. But when I hear noises, I turn off all the lights inside so no one can see me from the outside, and I walk through a dark house investigating sounds.

One night I hear something. I stand in the dark and listen for the noise to repeat itself. I have an inventory of sounds; I know the noises my house makes. There is a *thump thump* that comes when a car runs over a metal drain in the street. There is the *click-whoosh* of the refrigerator. There is the *pop pop* of roof timber.

But what do I hear now? Is it a feral cat outside the kitchen door? Or a neighborhood dog that sneaked out a gate? I listen. I hear my heart beat. The wind. Maybe it is the wind. I look out the dark window, no moon, and the tree leaves are still. I stand for a long while. No sounds follow. I guess I am imagining. I convince myself that outside my kitchen door is evil-free territory.

It is just at one of these moments that I look out the window. It is 3 a.m. Across the street I see a light on in an apartment. The neighbor who lives there keeps his lights on all night, every night, year after year. When we pass in the daylight, he shifts and dodges and doesn't look me in the eye and doesn't say hello. Am I becoming like this unusual neighbor? Am I getting weird? The answer is yes. I make a note to change.

I have an appointment with Margo at her office. Margo does things in a big way. She drives a big yellow truck, has big dogs, has a big calendar with big legal matters and big commitments to all her clients who keep her working round the clock seven days a week, and she still has time for pro bono; she invites friends and family to make a thousand tamales every Christmas, closes off a whole street to throw a birthday party for her partner, Lupe Castillo, that includes mariachis and two other bands, and she brings a *carrito*—a big hot dog stand—to the party and cooks Sonoran hot dogs at midnight, all for a big fiesta that rocks from afternoon until 3 a.m. And she wins her legal cases in a big way.

But when you are in her office, she makes herself small so that *you* are the one who fills the room. She quietly listens while you talk and talk. She asks a few small questions and you tell her everything. Should you feel like crying, she chuckles and says, "That's no big deal, sister, we'll take care of it."

So Margo guides me through the first steps of what is to be a federal case. Then I am passed to Bill Walker, an excellent attorney who defended sixteen volunteers from the Sanctuary Movement, including ministers, priests, and nuns, during the 1980s conflict in El Salvador.

A few weeks after the desert incident, I appear in federal court with Bill for an arraignment. I dread going because I assume I will see one or two of the men from the desert. But only their government lawyer is present.

After the proceedings with a judge, I am to go downstairs with a uniformed woman to have a photo taken.

"Is this normal?" I ask Bill. "Why do I need to do this?" It is procedure, I am told. Yikes. This doesn't seem like fun. I've lived my life pretty much under the radar, and having a government photo taken changes that.

And I have a busy morning ahead. I hope this doesn't take long. I came here to be arraigned, then I need to go to the bank, and then have lunch with another filmmaker an hour from now.

The woman takes me to the basement of the Federal Courthouse building. We walk down a long empty hallway painted institutional gray, past locked doors. She unlocks a door and we step into another hallway that has been set up as a processing station. It is noisy in the hall. People talk. I hear sounds of metal on metal.

At this station, there are a few tables and computers that are handled by two twenty-somethings in uniform. The woman who brings me here hands them papers from the courtroom.

As my guide leaves, a young man with black hair sits behind a table. He shouts, "Stand with your feet on those two lines!" I do. I wonder why he is shouting. I am five feet from him.

A young woman, mid-twenties with tied-dyed dreadlocks, has her back to me as she types something into a computer on a shelf. He hands her the papers.

She still has her back to me and mumbles. I don't say anything. He yells at me, "Answer her!" I say I can't hear her.

"Don't talk back!" he yells. This is not going well. She mumbles something else. I don't say anything. She turns to me impatiently and says, "Look. Into. The. Camera." I do.

"You moved!" yells the man.

"Sorry, I didn't realize . . ."

"Shut up. Didn't I say don't talk back? Get your feet on the lines!" he shouts. He seems to have only one level to his voice.

Looking at the computer, her back still toward me, she says, "Spell your name for me. I can't find you in the system."

"I'm not in the system. I don't have a record."

"Don't talk back to her!" He shouts.

"Do you have an alias?"

An alias? What am I? "No."

"Give me all your names."

I say my full name.

"No, nothing. How many times you been married?"

"Once. My married name was Cundiff."

"How do spell that? Cunt-off? Don't think that's going to be in here." She and her companion laugh like there's no tomorrow.

This goes on and on. Suddenly another young man walks up. He is in a hurry. "We got a number 27," he says.

"What do we do with her?"

"Take her to 6."

Suddenly they both get up. The first man tells me to walk down the hall. The second man says, "She can't have her purse in there."

The first man takes my purse.

"Where are you putting it?" I ask.

"No questions."

"What is your name and where are you putting my purse?"

"My name is Gonzalo." They all double over with laughter like he is George Lopez. The second man grabs my purse.

Gonzalo ushers me into a six-by-six room with a small wire window and one chair. He closes the heavy door and I hear it lock. I try the door. It won't open. I just stand there. And sit there. And walk there. And stand. And sit. And walk. I can't tell if I am being suffocated by the cell, or by my anger.

I hear someone shouting orders, "Turn right, line up, no talking." Then I hear the same words in Spanish. I hear chains, and people shuffling. I learn later they are men and women in the hallway who will eventually be moved into a courtroom. The people are chained at the wrists, and then wrists are chained at the waist, then the chain runs to shackles on the ankles.

There are seventy to a hundred of these men and women who crossed the desert days earlier and still wear the same clothes. Soon, they will appear before a federal judge; all will be told that they have entered the United States illegally. They can be sentenced to prison for six months to two years. If they reenter the United States without documents, they may face prison terms of two to twenty years for illegal entry.

This is called Operation Streamline, and it plays out every day at the Tucson Federal Courthouse. It costs over $1 billion in taxpayer money per year. It has no effect. People who are deported one day turn around and reenter the next day, through the desert. The courtroom has two distinct smells. One is perfumed lawyers; one is sweat from the desert.

After what seems forever but is probably an hour, Gonzalo opens the door to take me out. I go back to the processing area, where we finish the comedy routine of photographing; they hand me my purse and take me to the door where I entered, and I walk into the long hallway.

I am angry. I walk to a lobby, where there is a big sign that says "Office of the U.S. Marshals. Justice. Integrity. Service." It is a wall of black-tinted glass that rises from waist level to the ceiling. There is a counter and a door. I knock on the door. No answer. I knock on the black sliding glass window. No response. I call out. No response. I want to complain. I wander around the cavernous courthouse floor. There is no human being walking the halls.

The federal courthouse reminds me of the movie *The Conformist* by Italian director Bernardo Bertolucci, shot in huge governmental interiors of the 1930s ruling elite that dwarf the common person who tries to navigate the hallways.

I walk several halls outside the courtrooms and don't meet a soul. I finally go to the main floor where people have to pass through the checkpoint and I ask a guard if there is someone in charge that I can talk to. "I don't know, ma'am, I just work in this spot," he says.

I ask a woman with a briefcase if she is a lawyer. She says she is. I say that I was in the basement and treated badly. As I speak, I feel she doesn't believe me. And just the fact that I was in the basement makes me an unreliable

190

person. And I think this is probably no big deal, everyone is probably treated this way.

I say never mind and I go outside and sit in my truck for a long time.

A year later, after several postponements by the government, they drop the charges.

But the spider's thread of involvement wraps thicker. I wonder if this *ultra* law-enforcement style along the border is an aberration, or a new design and here to stay.

CHAPTER 20

THREE TIMES A CHARM

AFTER DEALING WITH the government, I return to the desert, again on a search. No matter what happens in my personal life or in the basement of the federal courthouse or in government border policy, families continue to cross. It is the biggest migration in Mexico-U.S. history.

Unlike the stale courthouse basement, the desert is open and fresh, a relief. I drive the twenty-three-mile road from the interstate to Arivaca, a road favored by bicyclists and motorcycle riders for its sloping curves and great views of the lush Sonoran Desert. At the same time, it is a road that migrants must dart across to continue the journey north.

While I am in Arivaca, I get a call from a nurse, Lisa, who is out on another search trip. We hear that there is a young man in distress. We agree to meet near Virginia's Rancherita outdoor restaurant and go together to find the man.

We drive the low-hill country. We find him. He sits off Batamonte Road in a wash.

He is tall, thin, and dusty. Eight days in the desert. Carlos from El Salvador. Nineteen years old, he tells us. He looks sixteen.

At first glance, he seems healthy. He greets us cautiously and warmly. But as Lisa asks him medical questions, like when is the last time you drank water, when is the last time you urinated, he can't remember. She pinches the skin on his forearm. It stands erect like a tent, indicating there is little liquid in his body. His eyes are clouded. He is unsteady. His words are not fully formed.

"Here, let's get you out of the sun," she says. She pulls out a blanket from the car and walks to a tree that shades like a sieve. Not enough shade for a scorpion. As she puts the blanket on the ground, Carlos takes it from her to smooth it out and arranges it for us to sit on. We are women and he is taking care of us. We are his guests in the three-foot circle of safety he has staked out in this wide desert.

"No, Carlos, this blanket is for you. *Siéntate. Sit.*"

He tells us that hours ago he left Marisol, a thirty-four-year-old woman from Ecuador, and a seventy-four-year-old man from Honduras under a tree. Eight days in the desert, not a drop of water the last two days.

They got lost together after the Border Patrol dusted them, a procedure in which a Border Patrol helicopter flies low to the ground, intentionally causing rocks, sticks, and plants to shoot up into the faces of migrants, slicing eyes and skin, causing them to cover their faces and run. Dusting separates children from parents as they run helter-skelter from flying debris. Then a ground crew of agents moves in to capture people. Some get away; many are injured.

He says he is pretty sure that Marisol, the woman he left behind, is dying. So he came to find someone to help her. This is not good news. We decide to get him to a hospital first, and then look for the other two people. He had wandered hours to reach this road.

We explain that if the Border Patrol arrives, they will take him. He panics. He can't return to El Salvador, he says. He has family in the United States, and in El Salvador he is on a hit list of the Mara Salvatrucha. The Maras are a violent transnational gang that conscripts members. If you don't join them at their request, they will murder you and put out the eyes of family members.

We crouch low as Carlos sits so that we can give him water and food and assess his physical condition.

The Border Patrol will not permit water to be given to people they detain because, as agents and Border Patrol lawyers tell us, "If you give a migrant water and he chokes on it, he can sue the United States government." We hear this regulation stated during many interactions with the Border Patrol in the field. To date, not one thirsty migrant has sued the United States for choking on water. But you can never be too careful.

Contrary to Border Patrol public-relations stories sent daily to the Associated Press about how the organization rescues people, Border Patrol agents inform us, personally, that they are not in the rescue business. They don't carry water except for an occasional jug for themselves. Their

BORSTAR rescue unit was originally created to help agents who are down in the field, not to rescue migrants. There is video showing agents emptying water from gallon jugs left on migrant trails. They slash and destroy our water jugs. We had more than three hundred written incident reports of destroyed water containers in a two-month period, some of the damage done by agents.

As Lisa tends to Carlos's health, I sit on the ground while I punch numbers into my cell to call one of our lawyers. I want to know if it is possible to get asylum for Carlos and what the process will be when we encounter the Border Patrol.

As the lawyer talks to me, I see Carlos lie down. He is not well. And he is concerned that we are not going to look for his companions. He is fading. He looks like he needs *suero*, rehydration fluid. Carlos finally says we should call for medical assistance.

We call 911. A voice asks what is the emergency. We tell her that we have a man who is ill and we need emergency medical help. She says she will get someone to respond and that they will call us back.

We wait a half hour. No one calls. Samaritan protocol in emergency situations is to call for help, and if no one responds, call 911 again and tell them who we are, that we have a sick passenger whom we are evacuating to a hospital, and that they should send an emergency vehicle to stop us on the highway and take the man more quickly to the hospital.

It is not as simple as putting a migrant in the car and driving. Transporting normally carries a five-year prison sentence. But our lawyer informs us that anyone can transport someone to the hospital, because that transportation is not in furtherance of illegal presence. So taking someone to the hospital who is ill or injured is not a crime no matter who does it.

We don't want to leave a very sick man alone on the desert in 110-degree heat. Who would do that?

"No, if he is an illegal alien, you can't drive him anywhere," says the 911 voice.

"We are with a man who needs medical attention," says Lisa.

So we get him comfortable in the car and start driving. After fifteen minutes on this remote desert road, an Elephant Head Paramedic truck with flashing lights roars toward us in a cloud of dust.

Things move fast. The chief paramedic is a woman who has been doing this for thirty years. With efficiency, she and her coworker take his vital signs, in Spanish speak kindly to him, and administer aid.

Ten minutes later, more flashing lights on the dirt road, and four Border Patrol vehicles pull up around us.

A thirty-year-old agent jumps out of the vehicle and storms toward us.

"We'll take him," he says. "You are breaking the law. You can't give them anything, that's aiding and abetting," he says as his big, solid body advances toward us.

Ignoring his anger, Lisa says that she is a nurse and knows that Carlos needs to go to a hospital. She explains his symptoms. She says his kidneys are in bad condition, and he has a fever.

"They are all like that," says the agent. "We didn't ask them to come here. So we don't owe them anything. You need to leave, or we can take you in," he warns.

"We are not leaving until we see that he gets medical care," she says.

"Stand over there," he shouts.

An older agent pulls him aside and they talk. The older one walks over and speaks calmly, saying that he appreciates what we do, but they will take the "illegal" now.

Meanwhile, a third agent handcuffs Carlos and pats him down. He takes the backpack, belt, shoelaces, bottled water that we gave him, and personal belongings, all of which Carlos will not see again.

The paramedics talk to a couple of men, then drive away.

As Lisa speaks with an agent, I reach a lawyer on the cell phone. He explains that Carlos needs to say in his own words that he wants asylum. Carlos tells an agent. I ask the agent if we can have it in writing. No, he says. I glance at four of the eight other agents to see if they can assist. They are engaged in casual conversation, not interested in us.

Lisa writes down Carlos's full name, date of birth, and where he was born—all things that will be needed to find him in a hospital.

They put Carlos in the back of a BP vehicle and close the doors. I am agonized. He is completely gone. But he is only behind a door. It is like when the dead are on the other side of the curtain. They are gone forever by sleight of hand. An inexplicable and permanent separation.

Lisa tells an agent about the man and the woman who may be dying; can he go look for them? Thirty minutes later, armed with a verbal description of "to the left, over those hills, under a tree," we drive agents to the area described by Carlos. They say they have good equipment and will search for Marisol and her companion.

We drive off to do our own search but don't see any place similar to what Carlos described. Each hill and arroyo starts to look like the one before. No Marisol, no man.

Eventually, and with sadness, we call it a day. I drive Lisa back to her car at Virginia's Rancherita. I will learn that the following day, when Lisa tries to locate Carlos in a Tucson or Nogales hospital, she finds him. When she goes to visit, he is gone. The Border Patrol came to get him. Lisa calls the station to inquire after him. The agent finds no record of Carlos. They say they have never heard of him.

After I drop Lisa off at Virginia's, I head out onto Arivaca Road, still about an hour and a half from Tucson. I am tired. I am drained and just want to go home and sit under the swamp cooler.

On the side of the road, I pass two Border Patrol vehicles and a G4S Wackenhut bus. Wackenhut, a private security company, has a government contract to park buses in various desert locations. Throughout the day, the buses will be filled with migrants detained by Border Patrol agents in the desert. When the bus is full, they are driven to detention centers in Tucson.

I jump. There are eight migrants straddled against the side of the bus, legs wide apart, arms raised, palms flat against the bus. Border Patrol agents shout orders at them. I panic. I can't believe what I see. I would recognize his back anywhere.

It is the arm reaching up the horse's neck, the arm in the photo, the arm in a checkered cowboy shirt, but today the palm presses the metal siding of the bus. The arm is not in cowboy clothes; instead, the arm is covered in black migrant clothing. The cowboy hat has been replaced by the black ball cap migrants wear. Dark clothes, or camouflage, clothing that blends migrants into the desert. It is the photo taped to my wall years ago when we edited *The Unholy Tarahumara*. It is Hiram, his arm reaching upward. It is the photo on my dresser that I knocked over in the dark. Even without his cowboy hat, I would know him.

After I pass the bus, I turn the car around without thinking about consequences. They have my friend.

I drive up to the scene. There are four agents. On their hips they wear mace, a gun, a baton, a knife, a Taser. Two of them pat down the migrants. One yells orders.

My hands sweat. What am I going to do? Grab him and run, and let them shoot us? Watch helplessly as they put him on the bus? Ask to talk to him? With no plan in mind, I jump out of the car, and trip on a rock. I regain my balance and move toward the bus. The agents, two migrants, and Hiram turn their heads to look at me.

The dark eyes and movie-star moustache. He stares at me. No telltale sign of recognition. No muscles move in his face. His eyes look tired. I can't take my eyes off him, hoping he will signal me with some sign of recognition.

But they are not his eyes. Not his moustache. No dimples at the corner of the mouth. It is not him. Is it an imposter? I stop. I look. It is not Hiram. I keep staring. I look at each man. Hiram is not there. He was never there.

What is wrong with me? How can I be so wrong? I don't say anything. I turn around and walk back to the car.

From the outside, it is a nonevent. A woman gets out of a car, turns around, gets back in and drives away. On the inside, I am exploding and out of control. I am exhausted.

Sad and angry that there are so many people wandering my desert, I can't pull a calming or kind thought into my mind. I need to stop all this and take a long rest. I drive to Tucson. I walk to my bedroom dresser and pick up the photo. Hiram is still in the photo, still reaching up to the horse with his back to me, still in Norogachic. Surely he is safe. I am crazy.

Two days later I get a call from Jason De León. He teaches anthropology at the University of Michigan. Each summer, he brings students to Arivaca to work on his production, the Undocumented Migration Project, a study of undocumented migration in the Sonoran Desert, Mexico, and Central America that uses ethnography, archaeology, and forensic science.

Jason, the Black Lion. He usually wears his black hair cropped, or sometimes full like a big lion's mane that circles his head. His unreadable feline eyes rest above a very readable wide smile and brown round cheeks, the complex face reflecting his Mexipino (Mexican and Filipino) heritage.

He is a rigorous scholar who is just as rigorous at tossing back a cold one at La Gitana Cantina. After a long day of hiking in summer heat, discovering piles of personal items left behind by migrants, cataloguing artifacts, and training anthropology students, he can be found on the corner stool at the carved wooden mesquite bar. Well liked by Arivaca locals, he finds himself telling friends about his day's trials, and he listens long and well when they explain their day.

Should you drive around the desert with him, he will hook up his iPod and perhaps play country violinist Amanda Shires or maybe hip-hop, which works well with bumps on dirt roads.

In Ann Arbor, I visited a class he teaches, Anthropology of Rock and Roll. As he talked about the visuals projected on the screen of a rock musician smashing a guitar, I looked around the packed room. Not one student was sleeping or texting. Jason held their full attention. His class syllabus reads, "This course examines key anthropological topics such as culture, identity formation, [and] globalization" and offers a warning in bold letters that the class "deals with serious social issues . . . including racism and violence." Which brings us back to the desert.

"We found the woman," he says.

"Where?"

"In the area we discussed, off Batamonte."

"The Border Patrol said they searched there. They didn't find them."

"We were just following a trail. She was there but we didn't find the man. And we didn't see the Border Patrol. No one was out there. Come with us. Tomorrow we're going to hike and build a shrine."

So the next day, we drive until the dirt road ends. Then we bushwhack. My calves are killing me as we climb yet another steep hill, up and down for three miles in stunningly grand but desolate country. Only hills and valleys and wide sky as far as you can see.

I am with Bob Kee, Jason, and twelve students who carry water, bags of cement, a tin cross, and pieces of wood with which they will create a shrine.

Some of them hike ahead. By the time I reach them, I see a tree at the top of the hill. Beneath it, a trail snakes down to an arroyo. Halfway down the trail, I see a *zarape*, a blanket. It lies next to a dark oily spot. The brightly colored blanket cheers me until it sinks in.

"This is where we found her," says Jason. "She didn't make it to the tree. She was probably climbing up there to get shade." They had found the zarape in the arroyo but carried it uphill to mark the location of death.

I look down. Then I realize that the dark oily spot is the size of a torso and that this is where her insides came out. The entrails had been cleaned up

Photo by Paul Ingram, art creation by Stephen Romaniello.

before I arrived. But the orchid scorch is still there. She had fallen face for-ward onto the trail and died, her knee prints engraved in this spot next to my feet.

For a while, we walk the trail further north until it disappears. Marisol had attached her last effort, all the willpower that was left, to her final steps; attached everything to a trail that dead-ends. No one uses this trail; she didn't have a chance. She was walking to nowhere.

I feel empty. A kind young man is returned to death-by-gang in El Salva-dor. A woman dies on a disappearing trail. Unseen altars dot the desert. My vaquero Hiram is caught but was never there.

No ravens sit on my shoulders. That was a foolish thought, the belief of someone who has enough time on her hands to invent and imagine. I banish the ravens.

Way up there, circling high, they peer down at the desert of my soul. Since I do not believe in them anymore, they keep their distance. My bony shoulders no longer invite them. My spook-filled cave no longer has room for them. Since I do not believe in them anymore, they retreat to nameless-ness.

This is a whole-bottle-of-tequila lonely moment. A wide-open descent to the epicenter of my inadequacy. I stand in a wasteland of invisible shrines, bones that walk the night, and chained ankles at an Operation Streamline monkey trial where, if these people survive these terrible conditions out here, they are taken to federal court and presented to a judge in shackles and shame. I burn inside.

I go home and sit down to read a book after dinner. I see her in the corner. In her black dress and black shawl and black hair. We don't speak. I go to get a glass of water. She follows me to the kitchen. I get in the truck to go to the store. She sits in the cab beside me. I return home and get into bed. She stands over the bed. All night. Marisol's mother. She doesn't tell me who she is, but I know.

Courage, fear, greed, hope, violence, and endurance are stirred into the cauldron called Border. Power of the sorceress, where are you now?

Help me.

Return to me, my bruja soul, with strands of garlic to repel evil, snake venom to clear angry words, fennel to open eyes, cloves to open ears, ground rose petals to open hearts *para contrar embrujo*, to counter this hex. And sweep this desert clean with sage to welcome lost souls. Where have you gone, my power?

CHAPTER 21

CROSSING

THE MORNING COMES. I cover my deep personal unrest with my morning ritual. I wake at dawn, make the coffee, peek at the sleeping dogs, and sit down to write.

My life is in the arts. And because of that, I often feel joy. I believe in celebrating *something* each day, even if it is just black coffee in a yellow cup.

And it means tons of annoying passion. I find everything to be pretty incredible. I rarely sleep and when I do, I wake up happy most days of my life. The end of the day may be a different matter, but mornings are good.

I am immersed in color, music, movement, words, ideas, and images, and I am grateful to discover films like *Beasts of the Southern Wild* and *The Three Burials of Melquíades Estrada* and writers like Sandra Cisneros and Cormac McCarthy, and history about Sor Juana Inés de la Cruz, and I can't get enough laughter from comedians like Bill Murray and George Lopez.

So I am not particularly political. Until now. The hours are long on the desert and the deaths don't stop. This morning I can't find my happiness.

Nowadays, no matter what I am doing—while I dance, write, film, daydream, or eat lunch—a low hum, an *mmmmm*, crawls beneath. It is like a constant tapping on the shoulder, but when I turn to look, no one is there.

I have thought and thought about it and have come to the conclusion that it is alarm and a slow-burning unfamiliar fear. A fear that never existed in my life before. It wasn't there when I traveled alone in the Sierra. It wasn't there before I joined Samaritans. It wasn't there before I met Valentín. It wasn't there when I rode horses with Hiram in the Barranca del Cobre. But it popped out front and center when I saw an imagined Hiram by the bus with the Border Patrol.

It is the incident of being roughed up in the desert. It is the radical change in our border community in the past twenty years.

My fear and unease grow from five things—senseless deaths on the desert, U.S. agents shooting and killing young unarmed men with impunity, the permanent separation of families with predawn deportation sweeps, and the silent flood of U.S. agencies forcing their flavor of "protection" worldwide. And, fifth, is the ease with which we morally drop the curtain on people who are not from our neighborhood, not from our country, not from our genealogical tree.

Then there is the wall. Scott Nicol, an artist who teaches at South Texas College, seven miles north of the border, pried cost information from the grasp of U.S. Customs and Border Protection. With the Freedom of Information Act, he learned that portions of the U.S.-Mexico border wall, say with a length of 1.6 miles, cost $7,929,957. Or another section, of 2.42 miles, costs $29,515,617. There are pages of these numbers. The worst part is that these are just base costs, not factoring in land condemned and taken by the government, or millions more for "oversights." Take a read. It is more fun than the evening news.

Historically, everything has passed through the Arizona desert. There were illegal activities such as moonshining during prohibition, or cattle finding themselves nudged over to the wrong side of the fence, or Chinese being smuggled in from Mexico to build U.S. railroads. There were always government agents at the border.

But now law enforcement behaves in the extreme. Agents are assigned to the area, do a job, and leave. They are part of a no-accountability culture. Robin, Liam, and I were caught up in this milieu and were suspect. We don't know if these agents are programmed to believe that seemingly innocent people are dangerous, or if they are psychos with badges.

In the past few years, there have been six known cross-border shootings, meaning that U.S. agents have shot across the border into Mexico to kill a Mexican. None of these agents have been found culpable or lost their jobs. And at least twenty people, including a U.S. citizen, have been shot in the face or back and killed by Border Patrol agents. And only a handful of people seem to notice.

It is all pretty dystopian, and I can't read dystopian books because they are too close to reality. I think of dystopian as a place of intrigue, where people are frightened and the eye of the camera is everywhere. Kind of like where I live.

And it becomes personal. I am afraid Valentín will be deported even though we have taken all the correct steps. It is the fear that he will permanently be separated from his kids and the American part of his family, and that I will have to leave my country, my family, and my friends in order to live with him in his country. Forever. Or that he returns to Mexico and I never see him again.

I wake up in the middle of the night thinking how we would live in Mexico. How would we earn a living? Where would we live? In his mother's three-room house with five others? Retiring to Mexico has a nice bohemian appeal if you have a monthly income check arriving in your mailbox. Some of us don't have that.

Another fear is when I don't hear from Valentín for six hours. Six hours is our agreed-upon limit of no communication. In less than six hours, to start calling him is cloying. After that, it is a worry.

We have a plan that if he disappears, I will start a list of phone calls. That, in itself, is frightening, when your life depends on a list of numbers. They are only marks on a page. Little black marks that hold the same allure as sorcery. If you use the numbers properly, doors will open and your prince will be returned. If not, darkness will fall upon your spot of earth. Wrap ten yellow lemons in black silk and bury them in front of your door. Protect yourself.

Recently, I had a run of bad luck. I sprained my ankle, the plumbing burst under the floor, and my car broke down on the interstate.

"Someone put a spell on you," Valentín tells me.

"Do you really believe in spells?" I ask.

"Yes, once my sister broke her thumb, lost her job, and was on a diet but couldn't lose weight. We found out later that someone had put a spell on her, and the result was supposed to be that her diet would fail and she would get fat and blow up."

"Do you really think that?" I ask, laughing.

"Yes. I believe in God, and I believe there is Evil. And that people can make harmful spells." He smiles.

This from a man who repairs and solders motherboards, reads the *New York Times*, and speaks two languages fluently.

So I think, what spells do I believe in? What *brujería*, what abracadabra is in my culture? For all the science involved, technology has the long fingers of witchcraft. It weaves spells of misinformation, instantaneously and world-wide on the Internet. Think about the whammy of public opinion and social judgment: powerful, inaccurate, but always entertaining.

I am becoming fearful that the Mole People rule the world. The Mole People are those of us who sit in our dark rooms under the glow of a computer screen as we strike "like" or "dislike" in answer to complex and multilayered moral concerns, usually about subjects we know nothing about. We sit hunched over the keyboard with our narrow eyesight and even narrower foresight. We cheerfully drop a fingernail on a computer key, like the guillotine drops on the neck. No accountability. We the Mole People. Modern-day Cimmerians in the land of fog and darkness, breeding at the edge of the world.

The day arrives for Valentín to renew his Mexican driver's license. It's crucial to have a foreign driver's license in the United States. If you can't show a license with your visa, it's deportation time. To renew requires that he go to Mexico and return, that he cross back into the United States at a port of entry. This is a terrifying moment, as its success always depends on the agent at the border and his mood. Maybe Valentín won't be able to cross back in.

A bit of a procrastinator, he says, "Tomorrow we have to go renew the license. It expires in two days." Groan. OK, I drop everything and we get ready to go. Neither of us says how much we dread this.

This is my first trip into Mexico with Valentín. He says he wants to see Mexico through my eyes. So I try to eliminate the dark cloud hanging over us and just enjoy the trip.

We arrive in his hometown and drive up to a stuccoed house on top of a hill. Kids play in front; dogs announce our arrival. A Christmas tree fills much of the space of one big room, which also includes a modern kitchen. The tree drips with elegant gold, copper, and red decorations made by his sister.

The house is spotless. I mean spotless. White kitchen-floor tile shines; windows look as if there is no glass in them, they are so bright. Note to self: clean the house upon return to Tucson.

When we enter the family home, Valentín's mom is making tamales. As she sees Valentín, she drops everything to run to her son. Big hugs all around. A sister opens the door, and she and her two kids enter chattering. Then another sister arrives, and another, then a couple of brothers.

In addition to the one large front room, there are two bedrooms and a bathroom. All space is filled with family of ten brothers and sisters and their families. It is the wonder of the cell phone. In a mere fifteen minutes, the entire family hears that Valentín has arrived, and everyone hurries to be with him.

It is the gauntlet. When a family member or friend arrives, each person is to be kissed. Like going down a greeting line, kiss, kiss, kiss. This is a small eternity in a large family. When you leave, you must kiss each person again and say good-bye. Even if you have been together only seven minutes.

Once in Tucson, a group of twelve of us had a carne asada, eating and drinking until late into the night. When it came time for me to go home to sleep, I said good-bye to Valentín's sister, the hostess, and quietly left. I felt that it would be rude to interrupt everyone just because I was leaving. Well, I guess that was the topic of conversation for the rest of the evening. *Cluck cluck cluck.* So now I kiss everyone hello and good-bye until my lips ache.

Soon after the kisses, Valentín and I go to a government building. We have two hours before it closes and two hours until his license expires. That's what I like. A man who prepares in advance. But as it often goes in Mexico, my worry about being too late for his renewal is for naught. He fills out some forms, takes a new photo, we sit to wait, and in ten minutes a secretary hands him a new license.

We return to his mom's house. While food is cooking, we decide to run to the store to get beer. Another observation about Mexico is that all errands require twelve people. Before I totally understand what is happening, twelve people pile into two vehicles to ride one mile to buy cerveza.

It is a cheerful mile. One nephew tells me about the Hulk, a sister is talking about her new fabulous husband, and before you know it, we all pile out at the OXXO to get beer. Purchase accomplished, we climb back into the cars, return home, and eat hot *cocido*, tamales, beans, rice, and *calabacitas*, everything smothered in tiny fresh green limes and chiltepines.

The night is cold. We sleep under three blankets in Valentín's mom's room. Three to a bed, his mom and I flank Valentín. Out of kindness, the rest of the family sleeps in the other room.

At Valentín's home, after a sad breakfast of good-byes, it is time to leave. Today we will make the border crossing. No one says anything about it. It is always like this when they are about to cross the border. They all have papers and they all worry.

Valentín's mom rides with us so she can catch a bus to another town. We pass through red-bark trees and dry arroyos. It is a crisp, sunny day.

We have to stop at a Mexican checkpoint. They ask where we are going. They want to see papers for the car since we have U.S. plates. We show registration. The car belongs to Valentín's sister, who is a U.S. citizen.

The government agent says that Valentín has no authority to drive the car because he is not a U.S. citizen and the car is registered in the United States. They want to know if it is stolen.

The agent says we have to have a certified paper from his sister giving us the authority to drive the car in Mexico. A couple of men lean on their *cuernos de chivos*, which translates as goats' horns but which means AK-47s. One of them goes inside and types away at his desk to check us out.

As we wait, another agent asks Valentín what he does for a living. "Computers," he says. "Oh, that's what I did before I took this job," the agent says. They talk computers, agreeing on which ones are best, and the agent finally says, "OK, you can leave but next time get papers from your sister." Common ground paves the way.

We arrive in a town with a church surrounded by a plaza with trees and vendors selling tickets to heaven. You can buy a plastic Virgin of Guadalupe that has an electric cord. When you plug it in, the Virgin merrily lights up with red, green, and orange flickering lights of Christmas. The rays that surround her are spines from the maguey, the cactus plant. At the tip of each spine is a tiny flashing light.

I buy one of these Virgins immediately as an insurance policy. We need all the help we can get. You can also buy rosaries, earrings with crosses, wooden saints, and scarves with the Virgin or Jesus, or Jesús Malverde, a drug lord adored by the poor.

We're on a mission. We have arrived at this church not by mistake, but because Valentín made an agreement that if he behaves according to what Saint Francis wants, the saint will help him in other matters throughout the year. So Valentín has come to talk with him before we head to the border. It is always best to do these things in person.

We get into a line of the faithful. I am not Catholic, so I sit on a bench inside the small chapel, four feet from where a big, dark-haired, bearded man in a Jesuit robe lies on a table, hands folded over his stomach. He is made of wood and plaster.

I sit and watch the line of people file past the saint, touch his robe, and kiss him. They say that if you can lift his head, you are sin free. If the head is so heavy you can't pick it up, you need to cut down on all that sinning.

I watch each person. Some walk past the saint, kiss, and say prayers. Many of the older women wear black. Most have the fallen faces of sadness. Burden and worry float through the chapel.

An old man sits beside me on the bench and puts his head down in his hands. Outside, the day is clear, inside cloudy. His sadness takes up a lot of room on the bench.

We go outside, walk around the plaza, and eat some churros. We kill time.

The border crossing looms ahead. We don't mention it. We walk to the bus station and find that Valentín's mother's bus leaves in twenty minutes. He also needs to send a business package on the bus, so we hurriedly drive to find a postal service building.

After asking several people directions and receiving conflicting instructions, we arrive. Valentín runs inside to get proper legal papers for sending the box. It is easier for the box to travel than it is for Valentín to travel. We sit in the car. I look at my watch. Fourteen minutes until his mother's bus leaves.

After getting the transport papers, Valentín rushes back to us. We drive as fast as the crazy Mexican traffic allows. We park at the bus station. Valentín sets the box, paper, and scissors on the asphalt. We cut a cardboard box and stuff newspapers inside. We realize we don't have enough wrapping tape. Her bus leaves in eight minutes. Valentín says, "I'll be right back." He runs across the street looking for tape.

We are so nervous, running like chickens with our heads cut off. And it is not about mailing a package. It is the border. Just keep moving, I tell myself.

Before we can blink, Valentín is back, waving a package of tape. He wraps up the box just in time to throw it on the bus, kiss his mom good-bye, and wave as the bus pulls onto the road.

We get in the car and drive. We stop at a taquería on the side of the road. We have chicken grilled over a fire, corn tortillas, salsa, grilled onions, and *horchata,* a rice drink. We don't mention that it is only two hours before we arrive at the border in Nogales.

As we approach the outskirts of Nogales, we barely speak. Valentín, normally a relaxed driver, grips the steering wheel. Traffic is heavy and he has to be alert. I start to feel sick in my stomach. I tell him that I have diarrhea. He says, no you don't.

After a half hour of driving, we are a few blocks from the DeConcini Port of Entry. Soon we will enter a lane where you can't turn around as you approach the gate.

I say I feel awful; we need to find a bathroom before we cross. I have to throw up. He says, "No, you are just nervous, and there is no bathroom nearby." "But maybe it's the food we ate," I protest. "No," he says.

Traffic is terrible. We see the gates ahead.

The plan is that Valentín will walk across at a checkpoint because we don't want to have problems with the fact that his sister owns the vehicle. I will drive the car across. We need to coordinate.

Valentín takes out his cell phone and removes the batteries to put into a different cell phone because it gets better reception.

"But I don't know the number for that phone," I say.

"Well, write it down, dammit," he says.

"I don't have any paper."

"Just hurry up," he says.

"Why?" I say. "There is no hurry. We act like we are being followed. We should have changed the batteries early this morning."

He drops the phone. We search the floor for the rolling battery. We find it.

"OK, I'll call you when I get across," he says.

"What if the call doesn't go through?" I say.

"¡Maldito sea! (Dammit!) It will!"

"So I'll wait for you at McDonald's on the other side?"

"No, don't you remember? I'm taking the shuttle to Tucson."

"Oh, I forgot." We have to pass another checkpoint on the interstate and will still have the car-ownership issue. So instead of driving together, he will continue to Tucson on the shuttle.

"OK, apúrate," he says.

"Hurry? I am going to be in this line for two hours before I even reach the gate," I say. "See how the traffic has slowed down?" I am sick to my stomach. I look at the traffic.

I turn back to tell him good-bye. He is gone. Where is he? Over there, almost to the railroad tracks. I get out of the car and call, "Valentín!" He doesn't look back. Oh my god. This is not like in *Doctor Zhivago*, with a final embrace silhouetted against the sky and a long kiss good-bye.

Instead, he is just gone. What if they detain him? How will I know? What will I do then? Should I just wait on the other side if I don't hear from him? Or drive to Tucson as planned?

One thing at a time. Just get in the car and drive, I tell myself. After much honking and yelling, I am back in the traffic. In a few minutes, I am in the lane to cross, waiting.

Vendors walk by the car selling little maps of the United States with removable rubber states on a board. They sell caramel and cotton candy. Men in wheelchairs sell carvings. It is cold inside the car. The vendors must be very cold outside.

I breathe and sit. We inch forward, and after one hour, I am near the Customs and Border Protection booth. Valentín should have called by now. This is way too long. He should have walked through the gate by now.

I sit and think about the people who are walking around me, what kind of lives they have, coming every day to sell candy to people who don't want any.

I remember this same spot at the border when I was young. My family and I crossed just to go grocery shopping. We especially liked Abuelita chocolate powder for hot cocoa drinks and the tall bottles of vanilla for cooking. And of course, Café Combate coffee beans and tortillas. And my father loved the quiet, skinny burros where we had our pictures taken. He always wanted to feed them and got no objection from the owners. And our patio table was adorned with Mexican oilcloth painted with circus colors.

As a girl, I dreamed of a life where we spoke Spanish and English and lived on a hacienda, like in a Mexican calendar photo of a girl with braided hair carrying a bucket of water. I wanted to grow up to be a goatherd and carry a bucket of water, too. Across from my family home was a desert. In the sand, I outlined rooms of my imaginary house with rocks, and wiped away stickers from the dirt floor with mesquite-tree branches. Then I practiced walking barefoot through the desert in order to make my feet tough, knowing that in the future, I would own many goats, walk with them through the desert, and be free.

My calendar world is long gone.

At that time, the border crossing itself was just a little box with a man standing next to it. Usually the men were old. And maybe there was an awning, I can't remember. But my father never showed ID. We just stopped, and drove on. Both directions. And there was no fence, let alone a million-dollar-a-mile wall.

Now it looks like a 1950s architectural nightmare. Neutral colors, concrete, tall tubes of fencing, asphalt, rectangular sections of wire, wire, and more wire. I feel like a chicken in a cage, bound for slaughter. No way out. And cameras above, below, and in between. They can probably hear everything we say. Maybe they hear what I am thinking.

Once, at midnight, I stood at Checkpoint Charlie in Berlin, when the Berlin Wall was there. I stood on a platform as I looked across into No Man's Land, a strip of earth with buried land mines. All was lit by Klieg lights from the East Berlin side. This place is just as ugly. Now I sit here, a frightened woman, more frightened at my own border than all the time I traveled in the Sierra.

The cell phone rings. I grab for it. I drop it. I pick it up.

"Estoy en el otro lado. Estoy caminando al shuttle." I'm on the other side. I'm walking to the shuttle.

"Oh my god. OK. See you in Tucson."

I get to the booth. Uh-oh, is the Customs and Border Protection (CBP) agent going to ask me whose car this is? Will I have to call Valentín's sister, will she have to drive to Nogales to verify? Will they believe her?

He starts his questions. Where are you coming from? How long were you there? I need to see identification. He has a stick with a mirror to search under my car.

He looks inside the trunk. "What is that?" he asks. "An apple," I answer, wondering where he has lived all his life not to recognize an apple. "You can't take that with you," he says. "OK," I say. He takes it. I get back in the car. He motions me through. Then, just like that, I am in the United States.

CHAPTER 22

MOAT

"I DO," I say.

"Acepto," he says.

Whoops and hollers, cheers and applause. So we are married. *Flash, pop pop*. Photos and more photos. Of us, of the families, of musicians, of the sunset, of candlelit tables, of paella, of margarita glasses. A lovely day.

The next day, we dig in to make it all work. We sell Valentín's car to pay for the lawyer and filing fees, in order to begin his legalization process. The U.S. government is only now beginning to process the legalization status of people who applied for citizenship eighteen years ago. Since we are married and Valentín has a visa, we are a little further along in the application line.

With guidance from attorney Margo, we fill out form after form of government requirements. It takes us months to gather all the papers that are required. It is not possible to navigate the U.S. immigration system without a lawyer.

After a couple of months of compiling documents, one evening we drive to the post office to mail the papers.

"Here, you write it. My hand is shaking," I say, as we fill out the Certified Mail trackable envelope. "Make sure you write the address inside the little box. And they said no abbreviations."

"Don't tell me what to do," he snaps.

Every step is terrifying. We are at each other's throats over addressing an envelope. We can't afford to make any mistakes, or, months later, they may return the papers unread, or may not return them at all. We hand the package to the postal clerk. He gives us the receipt, which we carefully guard. Every piece of paper is crucial.

We walk outside, take a deep breath, and hug each other.

In a week, Valentín receives a notice that says he can get a Social Security card. We are surprised at this. Even though he is not yet legal and has no green card, the U.S. government says that he can get the coveted Social Security number. We go to an office, file more papers. A week later he receives the card. Now he can work. But we have received no word whether his application for a United States Lawful Permanent Resident card has been accepted.

The dreaded interview looms. If we don't pass this interview with an immigration agent, Valentín must leave the country. We wear our best conservative clothes and sit in the immigration waiting room with five other couples.

The man next to us announces to the room in a too-loud voice, "I am marrying her for a green card." *Ha ha ha.* The woman next to him is quiet. "No, I really love her." *Ha ha ha.* She looks down. "Her mother never believed we would get married, ha ha," he says. "No governments can keep us apart." *Ha ha ha.*

My heart is pounding, and this boisterous man makes me nervous. I am sure there are cameras in this room. We had to pass through a metal detector at the front door when we entered.

A door opens. A man calls our names. We follow him to his office. He is Latino. "And what did you say your name is?" he asks me again. I tell him my name a second time.

He asks the usual questions, where were you born, date of birth. Then he asks where we were married. I hand him a shoebox full of photos. Margo suggested photos. They like to know the marriage is for real, she says.

He pours all 200 wedding photos onto his desktop. He pokes through them. He says, "Nice flowers. And who is this?" Then he literally picks up and looks at 180 of the photos, one at a time, and asks questions. Who is this person, and how do you know him? I am feeling pretty comfortable because, days before, I practiced the double last names of all the members of Valentín's vast family.

Then he asks if we are involved with drugs or know anyone who is. He looks straight at Valentín and asks again. He never releases the eyes. Valentín answers no.

He asks if Valentín is gay. Valentín says no. Then the agent asks again about drugs. We again say, no we are not involved. Being gay or a mafioso killer, equal in the eyes of the law.

"And how did it happen that you got married?" he asks. I don't understand the question.

"How did that come about?"

"Well, we dated, then we got married," I answer.

"How did it happen?" he asks.

I explain that we met listening to music, and then we dated for two years.

"But how did it happen?"

I have no idea what he wants to know. Valentín takes a stab at it but fails. We don't want to say too much or too little about anything.

"How did it happen?" he asks again.

How exasperating.

He says to me, "Did you ask him to marry you?"

I say, "Of course not."

He pushes the photos around. I sense we failed the question but have no idea what to do about it.

He shifts in his chair. We shift in our chairs. He turns over a paper. He puts the photos back in the box. He doesn't look at us. He lifts a group of papers and taps them into a neat rectangle. He looks at Valentín one last time. He pulls a paper from another pile and passes it to Valentín.

"Sign it," he says.

He explains that we should receive the green card in the mail in a few weeks. After one of the longest hours of my life, the interview is over. We don't say a word to each other until we reach the car. My hands sweat. Valentín's dark face is pale.

We drive to Taco Giro. It is 10 a.m. We order two margaritas for me. The waitress brings them both at once. They come with a pink parasol. I still have the parasol on my dresser.

We continue to live our daily lives pretty much as before but with a green card, albeit a temporary one. This one is good for one year. Valentín still drives carefully, and he still cannot go with Samaritans or me to the desert. Even with a green card, he can be deported by the Border Patrol, and they are on all the roads near the border.

It is a year later. We receive a letter from Immigration. Valentín's temporary green card expires in thirty days. We must reapply, get fingerprinted, and get photographed again. And pay more money. They say we have not proved that ours is a financially stable marriage or a real relationship. This time we must add letters from members of the community verifying that this is a marriage of love. We enlist friends to write letters saying how much we love each other. It is embarrassing.

We are told that immigration officials may arrive at our house at 6 a.m. on an arbitrary morning to look in our bed to see if we are sleeping in the same bed, and not just sharing a house.

My heart sinks. A stranger can really come look in my private bed?

So we imagine how it might happen. Valentín says that since I wake at dawn, I will probably be up, drinking coffee. I will hear a knock at the door at 6 a.m. I will open it and there will be two Latino/a officials in polite blue clothes. The woman will wear tiny and appropriate earrings. The man will have a clipboard. They will ask to go directly to the bedroom.

I will lead them into the room where Valentín still sleeps.

As he awakens, the woman will say to her associate, "Why is his hair hard?"

He will say, "I don't know. And I don't see a sombrero in the room."

They will look at the clipboard to verify that they are at the correct address. They arrive expecting to see a Mexican with a big hat sitting under a saguaro. Instead they find an urban metrosexual man with hair standing up, stiff from last night's gel, and Versace cologne on the sheets. Fake Prada sunglasses on the nightstand.

But then Valentín will get out of bed, give them a cup of his famous coffee, and introduce them to the dogs. When they see how much the dogs jump and love him, they will know for sure that he lives at this house, and they will shake his hand and leave.

We do everything they tell us. Immigration agents say we will be contacted soon. So we wait. Each of us privately spends part of the day trying to figure out what we will do if we have to start putting our belongings into moving boxes. But we never, never, speak about this to each other.

What would we leave behind? What would we take with us to start a new life in a forever-new place? Choosing what to take is easy. Choosing what to let go is different. Our dogs? If we don't know where we will live, we don't know where they would live. Please, I can't get rid of the dogs.

Three things could happen. One, he receives a permanent green card in the mail. Two, he has to appear for another frightening interview. Three, he will be notified that he has to leave the country in seventy-two hours.

We are in the kitchen. I pour another cup of coffee and hand him the cream.

"How did it go today?"

"It was fast. I got to the Tufesa station in plenty of time to put the packages on the bus. They will get to Los Mochis on schedule."

"Was everything OK when you crossed?"

"Until the checkpoint at I-19. I had to stay there a long time."

"What happened?" The interstate checkpoint is one of our major worries, that and the DeConcini Port of Entry.

Valentín tells me that he stopped at the interstate checkpoint. A German shepherd dog walked around the car with the Border Patrol agent. Another agent at the driver's window said, "Move the vehicle to secondary inspection and stay in the car."

Valentín hesitated, not sure that he had heard correctly.

"I said drive over there and park," the agent said with less patience. Valentín drove to the lane. Another agent said, "Give me the keys to your car and get out of the vehicle."

"Why?" asked Valentín.

"The dog smells drugs."

Valentín got out. Another agent came to the car. They opened both front doors. An agent tried to open the glove compartment. Since the latch was broken, Valentín had glued it shut because the door keeps falling down. The agent ripped it open. Seeing nothing of interest, he ran his hand under the belly of the dashboard, searching. Again finding nothing of interest, he yanked on wires. Soon, black wires and connectors dangled the length of the dashboard.

Agents continued the process under the hood and in the trunk. Valentín watched.

He takes extra jobs to make his monthly payments on the car. It shines like marble. The windows sparkle, and after he washes the car, he wipes it down, rubbing circles with the perfect soft cloth. The interior is spotless. And he adds just a bit of fragrance so when others ride in his car, they will be happy. He watched as the agents bulldozed through the vehicle.

And nothing more happened. They gave him back his keys. You can go, they said. Have a nice day, they said. Just like that. Wires dangled.

I pour more coffee, watching him. When we go together into Mexico to ship his computers to clients, we never have this problem. I am white. A citizen. Border Patrol just waves us through.

He says, "They were nice. They treated me OK. No problems."

I roll my eyes. Nice? We continue our day.

Again, we do as we are told by the government. We must build yet another packet to send to Immigration. I spell-check all words. We must verify to the government that we are vital beings, good for the State. In fact, I am not sure what they want, just like with the interview with the Immigration officer. I am pulling answers out of a hat, hoping this is the magic description of a husband and wife.

They want to know who we are, where we are from, and how much love and what kind of financial relationship we have. But it is like with Rita. When she was discovered in Kansas, she could not prove her identity. According to the authorities, she came with no point of origin or identifiable language. Like Rita and others who enter the United States, Valentín, and I—already a citizen—must make a case for our viability. We must verify who we are as human beings and the place and time that produced us, hoping that it fits within the corral of what the United States currently deems valuable.

This is difficult when you don't know to whom you are speaking. I keep trying to conjure up the immigration agent who reads our papers. Is it a person of kindness, generosity, and humor? Or is it a person who hates his or her job and doesn't care who is accepted into the United States and who isn't? Or is it a person who sees no human in the equation and eliminates people rule by rule, line by typewritten line?

We make sure each paper is in proper order, that the blue sheet is on top of the yellow paper, and so on. I feel that I am a prison secretary coordinating papers for an execution that is soon to take place, ignoring the outcome as I pile paper on paper.

I must suspend all feelings while I place one family photo on top of another, identification cards, birth certificates, lives of vibrant family members reduced to a description of height and weight, Valentín's beloved father's life condensed to a Mexican death certificate.

We present our loved ones as silhouettes. The depth and passion of my sister is merely a contact address. We must identify a brother of Valentín's, whose hard sweat and twelve-hour-a-day labor to support his family on the other side of the border is reduced to a name and DOB. With this personal

Street where the Border Patrol fired from Arizona into Nogales, Sonora, shooting sixteen-year-old José Antonio Elena Rodríguez ten times in the back. Photo by Barry Gosling.

information, will the government dig into the private lives of our relatives? This packet is now almost two inches tall. We mail it to Immigration.

Thirty days pass and Valentín's green card expires. We do not hear from Immigration. We receive no letters, no new card, no information. We are afraid to call an office and ask if they got the packet, and ask why we didn't get the green card, because we are afraid he will be deported.

That night, lying in bed, eyes on the ceiling, he says, "Why do they hate us so much?"

"Who?" I ask, already knowing.

"Anglos. The migra."

"You already know. The old white guard is scared that they are losing their power. They believe that people like you are lesser beings. They are afraid you are going to take over America."

"We are."

"You were lucky; you had a visa and didn't sneak across the border with your mom. They would have deported you to Tijuana and her to Juárez."

Silence.

He is stiff. He lies there, unreachable. I push his shoulder. He doesn't respond. No one can enter his kingdom. Anger separates us like a moat.

His beautiful smile doesn't happen. His shiny eyes don't shine. I want to hold him but he pushes me away. He doesn't voice his river of anger and I don't try to bridge that raging water. We lie side by side, not moving.

"I am going back to Mexico to live," he suddenly says. I panic.

"That's ridiculous. You are almost finished. We have gone step by step. We're almost there. Besides, what will you do in Mexico—you'll have to start over."

"Even if I become a citizen here, I don't belong here. And I don't know Mexico anymore. I have no place."

Then comes the D word. He asks, "Should we get a divorce?" I can't breathe. I don't know what to say. I don't move. I want this to pass.

I ask him if he wants a piece of chocolate cake. He stares at the ceiling.

We live the cliché.

The cliché of men with guns who are trained to hate. The cliché of carefully constructed politics that creates fear of foreigners. You know these things—they are in all the action blockbusters at the movie theaters. They are a script well learned.

We live the cliché of a looming wall. The cliché of deaths in the desert. And we live the cliché of private prison systems that depend on incarcerating all our dear Valentíns, who translate as gold for their financial gain.

Phantoms at the border, the haunting of the arroyos, and the haunting of our national conscience that will never be permitted to rest.

This flood drenches us. We can't fix these things.

Our marriage erodes.

CHAPTER 23

AND NOW . . .

THE LIZARDS HAVE returned. The ones with a black ring around the neck, and the fat ones with green bellies. I thought the neighbor's cat had killed them. I guess they were just hibernating. I sit under the tree with my coffee and watch my friends do their push-ups.

As far as I know, there is always a place that calls the heart. For me, it is the Sierra Madre and its sister, the Sonoran Desert that lies at its feet. I am called to the Sierra for its wildness, the desert for its silence.

Wicked on the outside but generous on the inside, this conjoined piece of earth nourishes us. When we die, it pulls us into its heart as it grinds our bones into the very substance that it is made of. If we are lucky, we will end up as arroyo sand that pours from Sierra canyons, to the desert and out to the ocean, oblivious to borders that we cross.

When I was young, my only border was the thought "Can I do this?" Like my first trips to Mexico. At first, I was nervous to travel into a foreign country by myself. Ultimately, it was a lark. I threw things into my car and drove south and thought, "Where will I go?" Then I headed to the next town on the map. And when I ran out of money or tired of traveling, I could turn around and go home. I could always walk away.

After time passed, I met my good friend Ventura, and Hiram the ideal vaquero, and I couldn't get enough of their company, seven years making a documentary. But still, I could walk away. After that, I met mysterious Rita, a woman who walked from her Sierra home to Kansas, where she didn't know the language. Entranced, I made a film about her. But I could abandon it if I wanted.

Then, hearing about the terror on the Arizona desert, I joined Samaritans. For years, I searched trails, gave water to thirsty travelers, worked with people I respected, and made new friends. Still, I could leave.

I could walk away from the Sierra, from filmmaking, from Samaritans, but now, years after my first childhood trips into Mexico with my family, I can't leave. I am married to a man who has brought me to a gaping intimacy that can't be walked away from. He brings his Sierra to our life and he is part of all I lived in the Sierra.

He wears a baseball cap instead of Hiram's cowboy hat. He grinds fiery chiltepines into his food instead of blowing it around the room Rarámuri style to ward off evil spirits. He is as dark as the brooding Sierra death owl and light as a phantom. When he sings, he balances on the high note of "Ave Maria," sung like a tightrope walker's prayer. I can sit by him without talking. He is my toss-back-a-shot-twirl-me-around-till-the-sun-comes-up dance partner. He is my misunderstanding. He is my canyon cliff I can't cross. He is my rage that I throw against the wall. He is my language barrier and cut-off tongue.

I am married to this man, and to all that he brings with him. I am married to the border, to the Border Patrol. I am married to fear, to crossings, green cards, passports, to the Swap Meet where he works and to the CBP as they destroy vendor stalls and rub silk blouses on their genitals. I am married to interrogations, the bomb of deportation, and government agents looking in my bed.

I hear the door open. I look over. Valentín steps into the garden, walks toward me, and sits down as the lizards scatter. He opens the laptop. We look for places to live in Cuernavaca, a colonial city in southern Mexico, or maybe in Magdalena to be near his family in the north. Somewhere not too expensive. Our bags are packed.

I will miss my desert, but it has changed. When I was a young woman, the desert was my friend and secret place. I loved the horny toads, the white-tailed deer. The desert was pink sunsets and margaritas. As a child, I wanted to be a desert goatherd, like the barefoot girl with braids, and have a life of freedom. Now my desert is the dark oily spot of a young woman's entrails in a land of surveillance.

In the Sierra, I walked hunting trails. I walked with the Rarámuri and the vaqueros. I hunted for a movie; they hunted for food.

Now I walk the trails of southern Arizona, where those good people are hunted on my home soil. Hunted by the Border Patrol, by lasers, vigilantes, *bajaderos*, ranchers, humanitarians, journalists, and people who want to travel a migrant safari so they can glimpse a migrant in the wild.

I was roughed up in the desert and had my Kafkaesque moment in the basement of the federal courthouse. But what happened to me was trivial. I wasn't killed. No one in my immediate family died. My husband is not yet one of the two million people who have been deported from the United States, although his friends and relatives are.

My sixteen-year-old Mexican son did not die on a Mexican street, just south of the Nogales border, shot ten times in the back across the international fence by the U.S. Border Patrol. My U.S.-born son was not mistaken for a Mexican and killed, shot in the back by agents in Douglas, Arizona. My Honduran son was not shot and left to die in the Baboquivari Mountains. I am not their mother. I do not know their grief.

Tía, Aunt, my nephew will say to me, we are sons and daughters of the dust. Created not of earth but of need, we stepped forward on our journey. Across the wide land we moved. The shoes walked side by side like friends. Day after day, we forged a path between cactus and arroyo. Walking to a life of peace. Full of hope. Song on the tongue.

Then came the river of blood. It started quietly, unseen, a trickle across the sand. We heard rumor, then saw it in the distance. As it grew, we looked over our shoulders and saw it pour toward us. We became afraid and ran. The scarlet river roared over our feet, over our knees, over our hearts, drowning mothers and fathers and sisters and brothers. Blood on the tongue. Red bones floated to the river's edge. Red bones dried under a killing sun.

And Tía, if you look, you will see orange dust rise along the horizon as far as the eye can see.

And if you tilt your head and squint your eyes, through the red dust you will see the shoes and the guns and the running running running down the trails, across the land into the coming world, and you will hear strange languages and you will see lines of people appear from all corners of earth, running, running, and you will hear the guns and bombs and fires, and if you look, Tía, through the dust you will see a wall of blood crash onto faces and there will be only the sound of guns, and soon the roaring river will lap at the edge of a shore littered with bullets. Red bones will float to the edge. Red bones will bake in the sun.

And Tía, look across the land, out to the world's rim, as I shout to all—friend and foe, sister and stranger—let us know the pain, let us hear the dark sounds. Then let us call upon unclaimed spirits to fly along the side of hope. Red raven. Eye of newt. Lip of lizard.

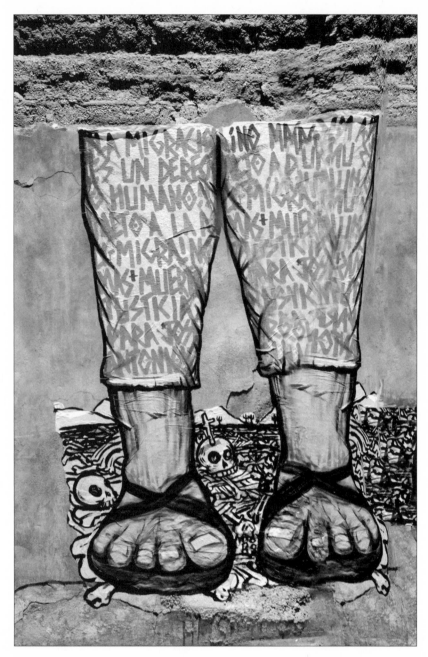

Artwork on a wall in Nogales, Sonora. Photo by Barry Gosling.

For we all are the web of the spider, the overlay of paths. Ally and enemy, we are the intersection. The same lacework of blood runs through us. The same skeleton props us upright.

The cosmos is not small, and it is full of sorcery we can't know. On our own globe, we are a parade of mountebanks. We are imposters with suitcases full of languages, luggage full of traditions, pockets of need, dragging our wagons of weapons and violence—all traveling under the same tent. The world renews its shape minute by minute, shifting political affairs like sacks tossed from a juggler's hand. So let us throw up our flags of truce, light the fires, stir kinship into the cauldron, and break bread together. The only hope for the new order.

End

IN MEMORIAM: SANTIAGO JIM BARNABY

July 22, 1946–January 26, 2014

THE NEWS IS ringing across the United States and Mexico by phone, e-mail, text, and tambor. Santiago left the planet.

Fire took him.

A fall did not take him. He could not die from a fall off a thousand-foot cliff because he could hike those cliffs in his sleep.

Water did not take him; he boated the wild rivers.

Ice did not take him; for fun, he hiked the Montana mountains and slept in holes carved into winter ice.

Sun did not take him. He left the planet. Fire took him.

They sent the big guns for Santiago—Xiuhtecuhtli, Aztec Fire God from the fathers of the Rarámuri.

Fire found him in Montana.

Knowing that Santiago was sad because he could not return to the Sierra, Fire hid inside the cast-iron stove until he was asleep, then took him home to the canyons.

Look, Santiago is there by the flames, dancing with Peyote.

ACKNOWLEDGMENTS

LIKE A FILM, a book cannot exist without the efforts of many people. Thank you to Clark Whitehorn, the University of New Mexico Press's editor-in-chief, for his humor, wisdom, expertise, and enthusiasm. And thanks to the University of New Mexico Press staff. It is a pleasure to work with such an artistic and focused group. Thanks also to the copyeditor, Norman Ware, for his canny ability with language and his thoughtful comments.

I am grateful to those who advised, especially to the creative poet Leesa Jacobson, who patiently slogged through the first edition of the manuscript and gave endless encouragement. A million thanks to historian Lupe Castillo, whose calm reading, keen eye, and unsurpassed border knowledge set the book in order.

Y gracias a mi esposo, Baldemar, for enriching my life and teaching me how to live in two cultures. And thanks for teaching me how to cook. Ándale. Of course, I must thank my sister, Annalee Gault, who has put up with me for a lifetime. And thanks to my family, both my husband's family and mine, who are scattered around the United States and Mexico.

Thank you to Raúl Al-qaraz Ochoa and the Southside Worker Center, an energetic and innovative organization.

And to the people of the Barranca del Cobre, especially Norogachic and Choguita, Chihuahua, thank you for a time of laughter and learning. And to Rosario and Miguel Giner and their generous family, who opened homes and hearts for me in Kansas and Chihuahua.

Boundless thanks to the thousands of people working along the Mexico-U.S. border, who give all and ask for nothing in return, working for peace in the middle of madness.

I give an enduring thanks to Sandy Lanham for her unparalleled courage as a pilot, who flies where most would never dare, and for her life of generosity.

For years of filmmaking support, thank you to Giulio Scalinger and Claudia Jespersen, Tucson's Screening Room movie theater, and the Arizona International Film Festival.

While at the Hedgebrook Writers in Residence Program on Whidbey Island, Washington, I was able to find solitude in which to finish the book, and to meet women writers from around the world. Thanks for that once-in-a-lifetime opportunity to live in a Hedgebrook cottage.

And for bridging borders through the arts, gracias al Consulado Mexicano de Tucson for the international exchange of artists.

Thank you, Stephen Romaniello, painter, sculpture, and graphic artist, for attending to visual details.